Unimodal and Multimodal Induction of Linguistic Structures (UM-IoS 2022)

Abu Dhabi, United Arab Emirates
7 December 2022

ISBN: 978-1-7138-9151-2

Printed from e-media with permission by:

Curran Associates, Inc.
57 Morehouse Lane
Red Hook, NY 12571

Association for Computational Linguistics
209 N. Eighth Street
Stroudsburg, Pennsylvania 18360

Phone: 1-570-476-8006
Fax: 1-570-476-0860

acl@aclweb.org

Additional copies of this publication are available from:

Curran Associates, Inc.
57 Morehouse Lane
Red Hook, NY 12571 USA
Phone: 845-758-0400
Fax: 845-758-2633
Email: curran@proceedings.com
Web: www.proceedings.com

UM-IoS 2022

Unimodal and Multimodal Induction of Linguistic Structures

Proceedings of the Workshop

December 7, 2022

Organizing Committee

Organizers

Wenjuan Han, Beijing Jiaotong University
Zilong Zheng, Beijing Institute for General Artificial Intelligence
Zhouhan Lin, Shanghai Jiao Tong University
Lifeng Jin, Tencent AI Lab
Yikang Shen, Mila, Universite de Montreal
Yoon Kim, Massachusetts Institute of Technology
Kewei Tu, ShanghaiTech University

Program Committee

Reviewers

Wenjuan Han

Lifeng Jin, Zijian Jin

Yoon Kim

Zhouhan Lin

Jiaxin Shen, Yikang Shen

Shawn Tan, Kewei Tu

Bailin Wang

Songlin Yang

Liwen Zhang, Zilong Zheng

Keynote Talk: Learning Grounded Task Structures from Language and Vision

Joyce Chai
University of Michigan

Abstract: See https://induction-of-structure.github.io/emnlp2022/ for more details.

Bio: Joyce Chai is a Professor in the Department of Electrical Engineering and Computer Science at the University of Michigan. Prior to joining UM in 2019, she was a Professor of Computer Science and Engineering at Michigan State University. She also spent a couple years at the IBM T. J. Watson Research Center as a research staff member before joining MSU in 2003. Her research interests include natural language processing, situated dialogue, human-robot communication, and artificial intelligence. Her recent work explores the intersection of language, vision, and robotics, particularly focusing on grounded language processing to facilitate situated communication with robots and other artificial agents. She has served on the executive board of North America Chapter of Association for Computational Linguistics (NAACL), as a Program Co-chair for multiple conferences - most recently the 2020 Annual Meeting of Association for Computational Linguistics (ACL), and as an associate editor for several journals including Computational Linguistics, Journal of Artificial Intelligence Research (JAIR), and ACM Transaction on Interactive Intelligent Systems (TiiS). She is a recipient of the National Science Foundation Career Award (2004), the William Beal Distinguished Scholar Award from MSU (2018), and a number of paper awards including the Best Long Paper Award from ACL (2010) and an Outstanding Paper Award from EMNLP (2021). She holds a Ph.D. in Computer Science from Duke University.

Keynote Talk: Evaluating a statistical learning hypothesis for human grammar acquisition

William Schuler
The Ohio State University

Abstract: See https://induction-of-structure.github.io/emnlp2022/ for more details.

Bio: William Schuler is a Professor at Department of Linguistics of the Ohio State University. His interests are in building and evaluating computational models of cognitive processes involved in parsing and interpreting speech and text. He is the director of Computational Cognitive Modeling Lab and Center for Cognitive Sciences.

Keynote Talk: Scaling Up Probabilistic Grammar Induction with Tensor Decomposition

Kewei Tu
ShanghaiTech University

Abstract: See https://induction-of-structure.github.io/emnlp2022/ for more details.

Bio: Kewei Tu received BS and MS degrees in Computer Science and Technology from Shanghai Jiaotong University, China in 2002 and 2005 respectively and received a PhD degree in Computer Science from Iowa State University, USA in 2012. During 2012-2014, he worked as a postdoctoral researcher at Departments of Statistics and Computer Science of the University of California, Los Angeles, USA. Since 2014, he has been an assistant professor and then an associate professor with the School of Information Science and Technology at ShanghaiTech University, Shanghai, China. He has around 80 publications in major conferences and journals including ACL, EMNLP, NAACL, AAAI, IJCAI, NeurIPS and ICCV. He served as a PC member at many NLP and AI conferences, as an area chair at several conferences such as EMNLP and AAAI, and as an action editor of ACL Rolling Review.

Keynote Talk: Towards a More General AI: From Big Data to Big Task from the Perspective of Multimodal Joint Parsing

Song-Chun Zhu
University of California, Los Angeles; Beijing Institute for General Artificial Intelligence; Peking University

Abstract: See https://induction-of-structure.github.io/emnlp2022/ for more details.

Bio: Song-Chun Zhu received Ph.D. degree from Harvard University in 1996, and is Chair Professor jointly with Tsinghua University and Peking University, director of Institute for Artificial Intelligence, Peking University. He worked at Brown, Stanford, Ohio State, and UCLA before returning to China in 2020 to launch a non-profit organization – Beijing Institute for General Artificial Intelligence. He has published over 300 papers in computer vision, statistical modeling and learning, cognition, Language, robotics, and AI. He received the Marr Prize in 2003, the Aggarwal prize from the Intl Association of Pattern Recognition in 2008, the Helmholtz Test-of-Time prize in 2013, twice Marr Prize honorary nominations in 1999 and 2007, a Sloan Fellowship, the US NSF Career Award, and ONR Young Investigator Award in 2001. He is a Fellow of IEEE since 2011. He serves as General co-Chair for CVPR 2012 and CVPR 2019.

Keynote Talk: Learning a Grammar Inducer from Videos

Songyang Zhang
University of Rochester

Abstract: See https://induction-of-structure.github.io/emnlp2022/ for more details.

Bio: Songyang Zhang has joined OpenMMLab, Shanghai AI Laboratory. He leads a team working on foundation model, includes the research and open-source platform. His team develops and maintains the OpenMMLab projects MMClassification and MMSelfSup. He obtained his Ph.D. in Computer Science at the University of Chinese Academy of Science, in the joint program at PLUS Lab, ShanghaiTech University, supervised Prof. Xuming He in 2022. He got his B.Sc. degree in 2017, and worked at MC^2 Lab, Beihang University, under the supervision of Prof. Mai Xu. He also worked as the research intern in TuSimple, Tencent Youtu Lab, and Megvii Research.

Keynote Talk: Constraint Mining and Constrained Decoding in NLP

Kai-Wei Chang
University of California, Los Angeles

Abstract: See https://induction-of-structure.github.io/emnlp2022/ for more details.

Bio: Kai-Wei Chang is an associate Professor at UCLA-CS. His research interests include computational approaches to natural language processing; tractable machine learning methods for complex and big data and FATE (Fairness, Accountability, Transparency, and Ethics) in AI.

Table of Contents

Program

Wednesday, December 7, 2022

09:00 - 09:10	*Opening Remark*
09:10 - 09:50	*Keynote 1*
09:50 - 10:30	*Keynote 2*
10:30 - 11:00	*Coffee Break*
11:00 - 11:40	*Keynote 3*
11:40 - 12:20	*Keynote 4*
12:20 - 14:00	*Lunch Break*
14:00 - 14:40	*Keynote 5*
14:40 - 15:20	*Keynote 6*
15:20 - 16:00	*Coffee Break*
16:00 - 17:00	*Poster session*

A Multi-Modal Knowledge Graph for Classical Chinese Poetry
Ting Bai, Ruihua Song, Ji-Rong Wen, Bin Wu, Yuxin Zhang and Yuqing Li

Search to Pass Messages for Temporal Knowledge Graph Completion
Xuelong Li, Quanming Yao, Haotong Du and Zhen Wang

DIGAT: Modeling News Recommendation with Dual-Graph Interaction
Kam-Fai Wong, Xingshan Zeng, Hongru Wang, Jian Li and Zhiming Mao

Subword Segmental Language Modelling for Nguni Languages
Jan Buys and Francois Meyer

Chaining Simultaneous Thoughts for Numerical Reasoning
Minlie Huang, Fei Huang and Zhihong Shao

Seeded Hierarchical Clustering for Expert-Crafted Taxonomies
Kathleen McKeown, Heng Ji, Emily Allaway, Amith Ananthram and Anish Saha

17:00 - 17:30 *Oral Presentation I*

Structural Contrastive Representation Learning for Zero-shot Multi-label Text Classification
Anshumali Shrivastava, Tharun Medini, Zhaozhuo Xu and Tianyi Zhang

SMARTAVE: Structured Multimodal Transformer for Product Attribute Value Extraction
Hao Ma, Madian Khabsa, Zenglin Xu, Sinong Wang, Bo Dai, Jitin Krishnan, Jingang Wang, Li Yang and Qifan Wang

17:30 - 17:45 *Mini Break*

17:45 - 18:50 *Oral Presentation II*

Named Entity Recognition as Structured Span Prediction
Urchade Zaratiana, Nadi Tomeh, Pierre Holat and Thierry Charnois

Global Span Selection for Named Entity Recognition
Urchade Zaratiana, Niama Elkhbir, Pierre Holat, Nadi Tomeh and Thierry Charnois

A Subspace-Based Analysis of Structured and Unstructured Representations in Image-Text Retrieval
Erica K. Shimomoto, Edison Marrese-Taylor, Hiroya Takamura, Ichiro Kobayashi and Yusuke Miyao

StrAE: Autoencoding for Pre-Trained Embeddings using Explicit Structure
Mattia Opper, Victor Prokhorov and Narayanaswamy Siddharth

Probing Script Knowledge from Pre-Trained Models
Zijia Jin, Xingyu Zhang, Mo Yu and Lifu Huang

Wednesday, December 7, 2022 (continued)

18:50 - 19:00 *Ending Remark*

Named Entity Recognition as Structured Span Prediction

Urchade Zaratiana[*†], **Nadi Tomeh**[†], **Pierre Holat**[*†], **Thierry Charnois**[†]
[*] FI Group, [†] LIPN, CNRS UMR 7030, France
{urchade.zaratiana,pierre.holah}@fi-group.com
{charnois,tomeh}@lipn.fr

Abstract

Named Entity Recognition (NER) is an important task in Natural Language Processing with applications in many domains. While the dominant paradigm of NER is sequence labelling, span-based approaches have become very popular in recent times but are less well understood. In this work, we study different aspects of span-based NER, namely the span representation, learning strategy, and decoding algorithms to avoid span overlap. We also propose an exact algorithm that efficiently finds the set of non-overlapping spans that maximizes a global score, given a list of candidate spans. We performed our study on three benchmark NER datasets from different domains. We make our code publicly available at `https://github.com/urchade/span-structured-prediction`.

1 Introduction

Named Entity Recognition (NER) is an important task in natural language processing whose goal is to identify and extract salient entities such as persons, organizations and locations from texts. NER systems are typically designed as sequence labelling: token-level prediction utilizing the BIO scheme. While traditional approaches use hand-crafted features along with classical Machine Learning algorithms such as SVMs or decision trees (Carreras et al., 2002; Li et al., 2004), deep learning models learn features directly from the data using for example bi-directional LSTMs (Huang et al., 2015; Lample et al., 2016; Akbik et al., 2018) or more recently pre-trained language models such as BERT (Devlin et al., 2019; Yu et al., 2020).

Recently, span-based NER has gained in popularity. Unlike sequence tagging which operates at the token level, span-based NER operates directly at the span level. The main idea is to enumerate all possible contiguous sequence of tokens of an input text and predict their identity (Lee et al., 2017). One of the major advantages of the span-based NER is that it can learn a rich representation of the span instead of only learning the representation of each token. In addition, a recent study by Fu et al. (2021) reveals that span-based NERs are better in a context with more OOV words and Li et al. (2021) showed that span-based NERs are much better than sequence labelling in settings with unlabelled entities (missing entities due to annotation errors).

However, unlike sequence labelling, *unconstrained* span-based approaches tend to produce overlapping entities, which is undesirable for flat, non-overlapping NER tasks. To avoid overlap in span-based NER, two main approaches have been adopted in the literature. The first is the Semi-Markov conditional random field (Sarawagi and Cohen, 2005) that trains a globally normalized model and then uses a Viterbi algorithm to produce the optimal segmentation without span overlap, we call this approach *Semi-CRF*. The second algorithm is the one employed by Li et al. (2021) for locally normalized span-based NER; it first eliminates all non-entity spans and deals with the overlap conflict by keeping the span with the highest prediction probability while eliminating the others. In this work, we call this approach *greedy decoding*.

In this paper, we analyze and compare two formulations of span-based NER. The first is a *segmentation* model of the Semi-CRF; the second is the two-step pipeline of span filtering and decoding. In addition to greedy decoding, we propose an exact algorithm based on Maximum Weighted Independent Set (MWIS) (Hsiao et al., 1992; Pal and Bhattacharjee, 1996) on internal graphs. We build such graphs to encode the overlapping structure between spans. This formulation of the NER task is novel up to our knowledge. For completeness, we include in the comparison a token-based sequence labeling model with a linear-chain CRF.

In order to understand the effect of span representation, we explore different alternatives includ-

Proceedings of the Workshop on Unimodal and Multimodal Induction of Linguistic Structures (UM-IoS), pages 1 - 10
December 7, 2022 ©2022 Association for Computational Linguistics

ing max-pooling, convolution and endpoints (representing span by its extreme tokens) and show that endpoints are effective across models and datasets.

Our contributions can be summarized as follow:

- We propose an exact decoding algorithm to eliminate span overlap on locally trained models that overcomes the myopic bias of the greedy approach (Li et al., 2021). We present a detailed comparison with global models.
- We investigate different span representations for span-based NER when using pretrained Transformer models. Our experiment provide a confirmation that the endpoint representation, the currently dominant representation strategy is the most robust.
- We conduct few-shot performance analysis for different modelling. We found that classical sequence labeling models provide strong result for datasets with few entity types, while span-based approaches are better for larger type sets.

Our code for models and experiments is publicly available.[1]

2 Span Representation

Given an input sequence $x = [x_1, \ldots, x_n]$, a span (i, j) is the contiguous segment of tokens $[x_i, \ldots, x_j]$. The goal of representation is to compute an embedding vector for each span of an input text which can be used for downstream prediction tasks. We denote $\boldsymbol{h}_i \in \mathbb{R}^{d_h}$ the representation of the word at the position i and $\boldsymbol{s}_{ij} \in \mathbb{R}^{d_s}$ the representation of the span (i, j) with the width $k = j - i + 1$; here $d_h, d_s \in \mathbb{N}^+$ are respectively the embedding sizes for word and span representations. The token representations are computed using a BERT-based model (Devlin et al., 2019). However, since BERT-based tokenization divides the input words into subwords, we take the first subword to represent the whole word, which has proven to be very competitive for several token classification tasks (Beltagy et al., 2019). In the following, we present different approaches for representing the spans.

Endpoints This representation consists in representing a span using the representation of the tokens of its right and left extremities, in addition to a span width feature. Specifically, the representation of the span (i, j), $\boldsymbol{s}_{ij}$ is computed as:

$$\boldsymbol{s}_{ij} := [\boldsymbol{h}_i; \boldsymbol{h}_j; \boldsymbol{w}_k] \tag{1}$$

where $\boldsymbol{w}_k$ is a learned vector of width k and $[;]$ denotes the concatenation operation. Endpoints have been widely used in previous works for span prediction tasks such as NER and coreference resolution (Lee et al., 2017; Luan et al., 2019; Zhong and Chen, 2021).

Span representation	Num params.
Endpoints	$(2d_h + d_k)C$
Maxpool	$d_h C$
Convolution	$\frac{1}{2}d_h^2 K(K+1) + d_h C$
Convolution (shared)	$d_h^2 K + d_h C$
FirstToken	$d_h^2 K + d_h C$

Table 1: Number of parameters for different representation, without including the word representation layer which is the same for any approach. d_h, K and C are respectively the word embedding size, the maximum span width and the number of classes. Blue terms are parameters for computing span representations and Red terms denote number of parameters for the final layer.

Max-pooling Since spans consist of a contiguous segment of tokens, pooling operations are a fairly natural way to compute their representations. In this context, we use an element-wise max-pooling operation to all tokens inside the span. Formally,

$$\boldsymbol{s}_{ij} := \texttt{MAX}([\boldsymbol{h}_i; \boldsymbol{h}_{i+1}; \ldots; \boldsymbol{h}_j]) \tag{2}$$

where MAX is the element-wise max pooling operation. Max-pooling has been previously used by Eberts and Ulges (2020) for joint entity and relation extraction.

Convolution Instead of simply applying the pooling operation, we explored aggregating tokens using learned filters via convolution. Specifically, representations of all spans of size k are computed simultaneously using a 1D convolution of kernel size k. To keep the number of parameters linear with respect to the maximum span width, we share the convolution weights across the different span widths.

$$\boldsymbol{s}_{ij} := \texttt{Conv1D}_k([\boldsymbol{h}_i; \boldsymbol{h}_{i+1}; \ldots; \boldsymbol{h}_j]) \tag{3}$$

Lei et al. (2021) used this convolutional approach to represent spans for keyphrase extraction.

[1] Anonymized for review.

FirstToken For this representation, we only use the start token along with span width information:

$$\boldsymbol{s}_{ij} := \boldsymbol{W}^{(k)}\boldsymbol{h}_i \quad (4)$$

where $\boldsymbol{W}^{(k)} \in \mathbb{R}^{d_h \times d_h}$ is the weight matrix associated with width k. Note that the computation of the representation of all spans for this approach can be done in parallel and in a single line of code using einsum operation (Rogozhnikov, 2022). This representation was inspired by the synthetic attention from Tay et al. (2021), where the authors predict attention scores without pairwise interaction.

Number of parameters The number of parameters required for each span representation is shown in Table 1.

3 Span scores

We model the task of NER as assigning to each span (i, j) a label from a set of C different types that correspond to named-entity types and special `null` type, indicating that the span does not correspond to an entity. Label assignment is constrained so that no pair of overlapping spans have entity types (both different from `null`).

We present two models to solve this structured prediction problem: a locally normalized approach with a zero-order scoring function which does not take into consideration the interactions between label assignment (§4); and a globally normalized approach with first-order scoring function which considers dependencies between pairs of consecutive spans (§5).

Both formulations employ the following span scoring function. Given a span representation $\boldsymbol{s}_{ij}$, the logits $\phi(i, j) \in \mathbb{R}^C$ for the C different labels are computed using a non-linear activation function followed by an affine transformation:

$$\phi(i, j) = \boldsymbol{W}\texttt{ReLU}(\boldsymbol{s}_{ij}) + \mathrm{f} \quad (5)$$

where $\boldsymbol{W} \in \mathbb{R}^{d_s \times C}$ is the final weight matrix, $\mathrm{f} \in \mathbb{R}^C$ is the bias vector, and `ReLU` is the activation function. We denote by $\phi(i, j, l) \in \mathbb{R}$ the (unnormalized) score of the label l for the span (i, j).

4 Locally Normalized Models

Under this approach, we perform span labeling in two steps, span classification followed by a decoding step.

4.1 Span Classification

Each span (i, j) is assigned its highest scoring label $\hat{l}_{ij} = \arg\max_l \phi(i, j, l)$, and we denote $\hat{k}_{ij}$ the corresponding highest score. The set of spans classified as entities may contains overlapping spans, a decoding step is therefore required to select a subset with no overlaps.

We learn the parameters[2] of this classifier under a locally normalized setup. The training's objective is to maximize the likelihood for every span label (up to a maximum lenght K) from the training data. The loss function is as follows:

$$\mathcal{L} = -\sum_{(i,j,l)\in\mathcal{T}} \log \frac{\exp\{\phi(i, j, l)\}}{\sum_{l'} \exp\{\phi(i, j, l')\}} \quad (6)$$

which is the well-known cross-entropy loss.

4.2 Greedy Decoding

Let $S = \{(i, j) : \hat{l}_{ij} \neq \texttt{null}\}$ be the set of spans classified as entities. The goal of decoding is to find the subset of S that maximizes a global score function:

$$\begin{aligned} E^* &= \arg\max_{E\subseteq S} \sum_{(i,j)\in E} \hat{k}_{ij} \quad (7) \\ &\text{s.t. } \forall e, e' \in E : \texttt{!overlap}(e, e') \\ &\quad \forall u \notin E, \exists e \in E : \texttt{overlap}(e, u) \end{aligned}$$

where $\texttt{overlap}(e, e')$ is True if the spans e and e' overlap but are not equal. The first constraint in Eq. 7 ensures that the set E is *independent*, i.e. it doesn't contains overlapping spans; the second constraint ensures that it is *maximal*, i.e. adding any other span breaks the no-overlap constraint.

Greedy decoding constructs an approximation to E^* by iteratively adding the highest-scoring entity not overlapping with any previously selected entity. This algorithm is efficient and has a complexity of $O(n \log n)$ with $n = |S|$.

4.3 Exact Decoding with MWIS

We define an *overlapping graph* as the graph G whose nodes are the elements of S and contains an edge between each pair of overlapping spans. Its adjacency matrix is defined as:

$$\boldsymbol{A}[e, e'] = \begin{cases} 1, & \text{if } \texttt{overlap}(e, e') \\ 0, & \text{otherwise} \end{cases} \quad (8)$$

[2]The parameters include all weight matrices from span representation and scoring functions. We omit the parameters from the notation for simplicity.

We associate a weight to each node as provided by its label score $\phi(i, j, \hat{l}_{ij})$.

An exact solution to Eq. 7 is given by the Maximum Weight Independent Set (MWIS) of the overlapping graph. For general graphs, computing the MWIS is NP-Hard but since our graph can be seen as an *interval graph* (spans can be considered as intervals over their start and end positions), MWIS has a complexity of $O(n \log n)$ or $O(n)$ if the spans are sorted by their endpoint (Hsiao et al., 1992).

4.4 Exhaustive Search Decoding

For efficient decoding, the scoring function in Eq. 7 decomposes as a sum over graph nodes. More complex scoring functions do not necessarily admit efficient decoding. Finding an optimal set under the mean scoring function for instance, that is $\frac{1}{|E|} \sum_{(i,j) \in E} \hat{k}_{ij}$, requires enumerating all possible candidates subsets of S, which is NP-Hard (Johnson et al., 1988; Raman et al., 2007) but feasible for reasonably small interval graphs. In this paper, we experiment with this scoring functions but leave more complex ones for future work.

5 Globally normalized model

Under this approach, NER is modeled using a semi-Markov segmentation CRF introduced by Sarawagi and Cohen (2005). The input sentence x is segmented into a labeled sequence of spans y. Each segmentation is scored as:[3]

$$\Omega(\boldsymbol{y}) = \sum_{y_k = (i,j,l)} \phi(i, j, l) + \boldsymbol{T}_{l',l} \qquad (9)$$

with $y_k = (i, j, l)$ being the labeled span at position k. Unlike the scoring function in Eq. 7, the score here contains the transition scores from label l' at position $k-1$ to label l, in the *learnable* matrix $\boldsymbol{T}$.

Training The parameters of the model are learned to maximize the conditional probability of the gold segmentation in the training data. The probability of a segmentation is computed by globally normalizing the score: $P(\boldsymbol{y}|\boldsymbol{x}) = \exp\{\Omega(\boldsymbol{y}) - Z\}$, where Z is the log partition function $\log \sum_{\boldsymbol{y} \in \mathcal{Y}(\boldsymbol{x})} \exp\{\Omega(\boldsymbol{y})\}$, which sums over all possible segmentation $\mathcal{Y}(\boldsymbol{x})$. This normalization term can be computed in polynomial time using dynamic programming.

[3]We drop the dependence on the input x for simplicity.

Decoding algorithm	Time complexity
CRF	$O(L\|Y\|^2)$
Semi-CRF	$O(LK\|Y\|^2)$
Greedy decoding	$O(n \log n)$
MWIS	$O(n \log n)$
Exhaustive Search (EXT)	$O(3^{n/3})$

Table 2: This table reports the complexity of the different decoding algorithms. L is the input length, K the maximum segment width, $|Y|$ the number of classes and n the number of spans after filtering non-entities, which is approximately equal to $0.15 \times L$ empirically.

Following (Sarawagi and Cohen, 2005), we assume that segments have strictly positive lengths, adjacent segments touch and we assume that non-entity spans have unit length. For instance, a segmentation of the sentence "Michael Jordan eats an apple ." would be *Y=[(0, 1, PER), (2, 2, O), (3, 3, O), (4, 4, O), (5, 5, O)]*.

Decoding Selecting the most probable segmentation $\hat{\boldsymbol{y}} = \arg\max_{\boldsymbol{y} \in \mathcal{Y}(\boldsymbol{x})} \Omega(\boldsymbol{y})$ is efficiently performed using the segmental variant of the Viterbi algorithm (Sarawagi and Cohen, 2005).

6 Experimental Setup

6.1 Datasets

We evaluated our model on three benchmark datasets for Named Entity Recognition: Conll-2003 (Tjong Kim Sang and De Meulder, 2003), OntoNotes 5.0 (Weischedel et al., 2013) and TDM (Hou et al., 2021). Conll-2003 is a dataset from the news domain that was designed for extracting entities such as Person, Location and Organisation. OntoNotes 5.0 is a large corpus comprising various genres of text including newswire, broadcast news and telephone conversation. It contains in total 18 different entity types such as Person, Organization, Location, Product or Date. TDM is a NER dataset that was recently published and it was designed for extracting Tasks, Datasets, and Metrics entities from Natural Language Processing papers.

Dataset	**Entity types**	**Train / Dev / Test**
Conll-2003	4	14987 / 3466 / 3684
OntoNotes 5.0	18	48788 / 7477 / 5013
TDM	3	1000 / 500 / 500

Table 3: Dataset statistics

Model	Span Representation											
	Convolution			*Endpoints*			*Maxpool*			*FirstToken*		
	P	R	F	P	R	F	P	R	F	P	R	F
Conll-2003												
Local	91.40	89.86	90.62	91.07	90.48	90.77	90.52	90.52	90.52	90.34	89.25	89.79
+ Greedy	91.97	89.74	90.84	91.5	90.1	90.79	91.26	90.1	90.67	90.64	89.08	89.85
+ MWIS	91.97	89.76	**90.85**	91.5	90.11	90.8	91.22	90.09	90.65	90.64	89.08	89.85
+ EXT	91.97	89.75	**90.85**	91.54	90.11	**90.82**	91.33	90.11	**90.71**	90.66	89.09	**89.86**
Semi-CRF	89.45	88.99	89.22	89.64	89.23	89.43	89.48	88.82	89.15	89.5	89.17	89.33
OntoNotes 5.0												
Local	88.59	88.99	88.79	88.06	89.55	88.8	88.42	89.34	88.88	88.18	88.73	88.45
+ Greedy	89.3	88.62	**88.96**	88.93	89.0	88.96	89.38	88.83	89.11	88.8	88.22	88.51
+ MWIS	89.26	88.61	88.93	88.9	88.98	88.94	89.38	88.87	**89.13**	88.81	88.26	**88.53**
+ EXT	89.31	88.61	88.95	88.95	89.01	**88.98**	89.37	88.79	89.08	88.80	88.20	88.50
Semi-CRF	87.35	87.76	87.55	87.36	88.26	87.81	87.04	87.99	87.51	87.11	87.86	87.48
TDM												
Local	73.05	69.38	71.15	67.75	69.88	68.78	70.86	70.69	70.73	68.54	65.06	66.74
+ Greedy	75.86	68.28	**71.84**	75.12	67.82	71.26	73.24	69.43	71.26	69.82	64.40	66.99
+ MWIS	75.46	68.07	71.55	75.25	68.12	**71.48**	73.31	69.53	**71.34**	69.89	64.50	67.07
+ EXT	75.72	68.07	71.67	74.63	66.97	70.57	73.24	69.43	71.26	69.82	64.40	66.99
Semi-CRF	68.34	72.55	70.35	69.38	72.85	71.05	70.32	69.89	70.09	69.98	70.64	**70.31**

Table 4: This table reports the main results of our study. It shows the performance along different settings including the datasets, the training, decoding and span representations. We report the average across three seeds. **Bold** numbers indicate the best model/decoding for a fixed representation and underlined numbers indicate the best representation for a fixed model/decoding.

Dataset	P	R	F
Conll-2003	91.24	90.68	90.96
OntoNotes 5.0	87.80	88.92	88.36
TDM	69.77	73.65	71.66

Table 5: Performance for the baseline sequence labelling approach, a BERT-CRF tagger averaged over three seeds.

6.2 Evaluation metrics

Our evaluation is based on the exact match between predicted and gold entities. We report the micro-averaged precision (P), recall (R) and the F1-score (F) on the test set for models selected on the dev set.

6.3 Implementation Details

Backbones For span encoding, we used RoBERTa-base (Liu et al., 2019) for models trained on Conll-2003 and OntoNotes 5.0 because they come from general domains and we employed SciBERT (Beltagy et al., 2019) for models trained on TDM, which is a scientific NER data set.

Baseline model We compare the span-based approaches to a sequence labelling BERT-CRF (Beltagy et al., 2019), which we trained on our datasets.

Hyperparameters All models were trained using a single V100 GPU. We trained for up to 25 epochs using Adam (Kingma and Ba, 2017) as the optimizer with a learning rate of 1e-5. We opted for a batch size of 10 and used early stopping with a patience of 5 (on the F1-score) and keep the best model on the validation set for testing.

Libraries We implement our model with pytorch (Paszke et al., 2019). The pre-trained transformer models were loaded from the HuggingFace's Transformers (Wolf et al., 2020). We employed AllenNLP (Gardner et al., 2018) for data preprocessing and the seqeval library (Nakayama, 2018) for evaluating the baseline sequence labelling model. Our Semi-CRF implementation is based on pytorch-struct (Rush, 2020).

7 Results

7.1 Span Representation

In the following, we analyze the performance of the span representations on both the local model and the Semi-CRF model, as shown in the table 4.

Local models On local models, we find that *Convolution*, *Endpoints* and *Maxpool* all got competitive results while *FirstToken* representation obtains

Dataset	Model	#Examples						
		100	250	500	1000	2500	5000	All
Conll-2003	CRF	68.92	**77.49**	**82.05**	**85.38**	**88.50**	**89.40**	**90.96**
	Local	63.09	70.95	77.21	82.46	85.51	87.62	90.77
	+ Greedy	66.44	73.02	78.70	83.39	86.2	88.05	90.79
	+ MWIS	66.54	73.1	78.70	83.47	86.23	88.01	90.80
	+ EXT	65.54	72.53	78.49	83.35	86.10	88.00	90.82
	Semi-CRF	**69.21**	73.91	79.26	82.6	86.03	87.26	89.43
OntoNotes 5.0	CRF	61.0	69.59	74.17	77.18	78.86	81.08	88.36
	Local	60.23	68.13	73.33	76.69	81.32	82.49	88.80
	+ Greedy	62.60	70.20	74.95	77.46	**82.13**	83.09	88.96
	+ MWIS	**63.03**	**70.28**	**74.97**	**77.52**	82.08	**83.10**	88.94
	+ EXT	61.95	69.88	74.69	77.37	82.06	83.07	**88.98**
	Semi-CRF	63.02	69.46	72.79	77.03	80.33	81.97	87.81
TDM	CRF	**63.39**	**68.39**	**69.76**				**71.66**
	Local	54.87	63.1	67.08				68.78
	+ Greedy	55.94	65.28	67.64				71.26
	+ MWIS	57.04	65.22	67.60				71.48
	+ EXT	55.06	64.38	67.43				70.57
	Semi-CRF	60.49	65.06	66.52				71.05

Table 6: Few-shot performance. We report the average F1-score across three different seeds in all datasets and different training set sizes.

a result one notch below the others. On both the conll and TDM datasets, *Convolution* performed the best, yet the endpoints performed only slightly worse. However, on OntoNotes, the *Maxpool* representation outperforms all other approaches, while the *Endpoints* and *Convolution* got very similar performance. Out of all the datasets, *FirstToken* had the lowest score.

Global models On Semi-CRF models, the *Endpoints* representation consistently achieves the best results across datasets. We also notice that the *FirstToken* representation has better result than *Maxpool* and *Convolution* on two datasets, Conll-2003 and TDM in this setting.

The *Endpoints* representation is the most reliable overall, since it achieves robust performance regardless of the context in which it is used. However, for optimal performance and given a sufficient amount of compute resources, the span representation should be best tuned on a held-out set.

7.2 Comparison of Decoding for Local Models

Table 4 shows the performance results of the different decoding algorithms under different settings. For the local models, we can see that the application of decoding always improves the performance of the F1 score, by increasing the precision and by decreasing the recall score. However, there is no significant difference between the greedy decoding and the global decoding since the models are already well trained and thus, the overlap filtering does not make much difference in terms of quantitative results. We will provide more insight on decoding in the subsections 7.3 and 7.5.

7.3 Few-Shot Performance

We conducted a study to compare the performance of each model in a few-shot scenario. The evaluation was performed on the test set of each dataset using from 100 to the full training dataset. For this study, we used the Endpoints representation for spans because it is widely used and has shown good performance across different training and decoding schemes. The results of our few-shot evaluation are presented in Table 6.

Semi-CRF is better than the local spans-based approach when overlap filtering is not performed but the local approach performs better than Semi-CRF when the number of data become larger. Furthermore, while the difference between Greedy decoding and MWIS decoding is narrow in the high data regime, we can see that MWIS outperforms Greedy decoding in the low and very low data regime. Furthermore, we notice that the in-

	Conll			OntoNotes			TDM		
	P	R	F	P	R	F	P	R	F
Local	91.07	90.48	90.77	88.06	89.55	88.80	67.75	69.88	68.78
+ decoding	0.47	-0.37	+0.05	+0.89	-0.54	+0.18	+7.5	-1.76	+2.7
Neg. Sample	90.69	90.54	90.61	86.81	90.23	88.49	66.83	73.66	**70.01**
+ decoding	+0.84	-0.43	+0.21	+1.58	-0.98	+0.33	+7.7	-2.12	+2.97
Down-weighting	90.88	90.10	90.49	87.70	90.24	**88.95**	57.79	78.63	66.52
+ decoding	+0.48	-0.27	+0.1	+1.24	-0.72	+0.28	+13.77	-3.92	+6.57
Thresholding	90.80	90.96	**90.88**	87.49	88.81	88.14	63.99	74.56	68.85
+ decoding	+0.90	-0.41	+0.25	+1.00	-0.61	+0.21	+6.78	-2.70	+2.32

Table 7: Result for the local model when changing the training/loss. The best results before decoding are in **bold** and the best results after decoding are underlined. For this experiment, we use MWIS as decoding. We report the average over three seeds.

crease in performance by decoding is higher when a local model is training on a few datasets while the difference becomes less significant when the number of training data is large.

We find that the baseline sequence labelling, BERT-CRF approach is indeed competitive. It most of the time obtains a better performance on Conll-2003 and TDM datasets across any dataset sizes. However, the span-based approach is better on the OntoNotes 5.0 dataset. This can be explained by the fact that OntoNotes 5.0 contains 18 entity types and, therefore, the labelling approach would require 37 labels since it uses a BIO scheme, which makes the task much more difficult.

7.4 Analysis of Local Modeling

We previously found that decoding had little effect on our local model performance, especially for high resource datasets. We believe this is due to the fact that we were training with all negative samples (non-entity spans). As a result, the model was overconfident regarding non-entity spans (and not confident enough to predict entity spans) due to this unbalanced training. To resolve this issue, we propose three alternative training procedures to make the classifier leave more room for the decoder.

Negative sampling This approach randomly drops a percentage of the non-entity spans during training, but keeps all positive samples (entity spans). By training with fewer non-entity spans, we expect the model to be less confident and thus predict more entities. This negative sampling has been previously used by Li et al. (2021) to avoid training NER models with unlabeled (or missing) entities.

Down-weighing This method is similar to negative sampling, but instead of randomly eliminating negative samples, this approach retains all negative samples and down-weights their loss contribution while keeping loss for entity spans intact.

Thresholding This approach separates the span classifier into two models: a filtering model to classify whether a span is an entity or not, and a second an entity classification model to classify the entity type. During training, both models are trained end-to-end by multi-task learning with equally weighted losses. For prediction, span filtering is first performed and then the result is passed to the entity classification layer. By default, a span is passed into the entity classification layer if its probability of being an entity is greater than 0.5; however, we here adjust this threshold on the dev set and select the one with best F1 score.

The result from this analysis is show in the table 7. The results of this analysis show that, overall, the use of regularization techniques leads to a significant improvement in decoding accuracy for most datasets. As the most striking example, we can see that on the TDM dataset, the down-weighting approach which initially had a precision score of 57.79 was able to increase this score by 13.77 thanks to decoding improvements. Furthermore, it appears that the best approach according to these empirical results is the downw-eighting approach. Under this method, the decoder was most "successful" on both OntoNotes and TDM datasets, meaning it brought the largest improvements relatively to the performance of the local classifier before decoding.

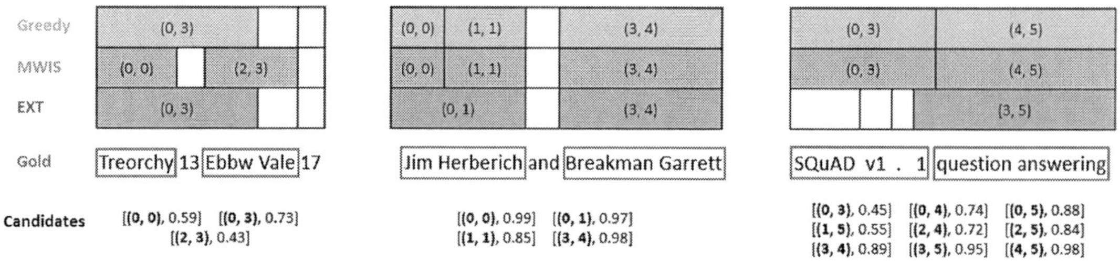

Figure 1: Shows how overlapping conflicts are handled by the different decoding algorithm on local span-based NER models. We only include overlaps involving at least three entities, because otherwise all decoding produce the same result.

7.5 Qualitative Comparison of Decoding

We performed a qualitative analysis to compare the three decoding approaches for local models. This study is presented in Figure 1, which shows the input text (truncated), the raw prediction with overlap, and the results after applying greedy decoding and the global decoding (MWIS and EXT). We only include overlaps involving more than two spans, because when two spans overlap, all algorithms take the span with the highest score.

We can see that the greedy approach always retrieves the most probable entity since it iteratively selects the best spans that do not overlap with previously selected spans. However, this algorithm tends to suffer from a myopic bias. Second, the MWIS approach, which maximizes the sum of span scores, tends to select as many spans as possible, which means that it favours shorter spans over longer ones. Also, MWIS decoding has a slightly higher recall score most of the time than other decoding algorithms. Finally, EXT decoding, which selects the set of spans that maximizes the average score, tends to select the smallest number of spans, but the selected spans generally have a high score. In general, this decoding tends to favour precision over recall score.

8 Related Works

Different approaches for NER NER is an important task in Natural Language Processing and is used in many downstream information extraction applications. Usually, NER tasks are designed as sequence labelling (Chiu and Nichols, 2016; Huang et al., 2015; Ma and Hovy, 2016; Lample et al., 2016; Strubell et al., 2017; Rei, 2017; Akbik et al., 2018) where the goal is to predict BIO tags. Recently, different approaches have been proposed to perform NER tasks that go beyond traditional sequence labelling. One approach that has been widely adopted is the span-based approach (Liu et al., 2016; Luan et al., 2018, 2019; Fu et al., 2021; Li et al., 2021; Zaratiana et al., 2022; Corro, 2022) where the prediction is done in the span level instead of entity level. Li et al. (2020) has also approached NER as a question answering task in which named entities are extracted by retrieving answer spans. In addition, recent work such as (Cui et al., 2021) considers NER as template filling by fine-tuning a BART (Lewis et al., 2019) encoder-decoder model.

Decoding For the spans-based approach, Semi-Markov has been used previously (Sarawagi and Cohen, 2005; Liu et al., 2016; Kong et al., 2016; Sato et al., 2017), however, their use with a BERT-type model has been little explored, something we did in this paper. The work of Fu et al. (2021) and Li et al. (2021) employed a heuristic decoding to avoid overlap for span-based NER. Their algorithm iteratively chooses the maximum probability entity span that does not overlap with a previously chosen entity span. In this paper, we have proposed an exact version of this algorithm.

9 Conclusion

We investigated different span representations for NER and found that the endpoint representation is the most robust. Moreover, we have proposed a new formulation of NER using overlapping graphs for which an exact and efficient decoding algorithm exists. We used the formulation to eliminate span overlap on locally trained models. Finally, we conducted few-shot performance analysis for different modelling approaches and found that classical sequence labeling models provide strong results for datasets with few entity types, while span-based approaches are better for larger type sets.

Acknowledgments

This work is partially supported by a public grant overseen by the French National Research Agency (ANR) as part of the program Investissements d'Avenir (ANR-10-LABX-0083). This work was granted access to the HPC/AI resources of [CINES/IDRIS/TGCC] under the allocation 20XX-AD011013096 made by GENCI.

References

Alan Akbik, Duncan Blythe, and Roland Vollgraf. 2018. Contextual string embeddings for sequence labeling. In *Proceedings of the 27th International Conference on Computational Linguistics*, pages 1638–1649, Santa Fe, New Mexico, USA. Association for Computational Linguistics.

Iz Beltagy, Kyle Lo, and Arman Cohan. 2019. Scibert: A pretrained language model for scientific text.

Xavier Carreras, Lluís Màrquez, and Lluís Padró. 2002. Named entity extraction using AdaBoost. In *COLING-02: The 6th Conference on Natural Language Learning 2002 (CoNLL-2002)*.

Jason P.C. Chiu and Eric Nichols. 2016. Named entity recognition with bidirectional LSTM-CNNs. *Transactions of the Association for Computational Linguistics*, 4:357–370.

Caio Corro. 2022. A dynamic programming algorithm for span-based nested named-entity recognition in $o(n^2)$. *ArXiv*, *abs*/2210.04738.

Leyang Cui, Yu Wu, Jian Liu, Sen Yang, and Yue Zhang. 2021. Template-based named entity recognition using bart.

Jacob Devlin, Ming-Wei Chang, Kenton Lee, and Kristina Toutanova. 2019. BERT: Pre-training of deep bidirectional transformers for language understanding. In *Proceedings of the 2019 Conference of the North American Chapter of the Association for Computational Linguistics: Human Language Technologies, Volume 1 (Long and Short Papers)*, pages 4171–4186, Minneapolis, Minnesota. Association for Computational Linguistics.

Markus Eberts and Adrian Ulges. 2020. Span-based joint entity and relation extraction with transformer pretraining. *ArXiv*, abs/1909.07755.

Jinlan Fu, Xuanjing Huang, and Pengfei Liu. 2021. SpanNER: Named entity re-/recognition as span prediction. In *Proceedings of the 59th Annual Meeting of the Association for Computational Linguistics and the 11th International Joint Conference on Natural Language Processing (Volume 1: Long Papers)*, pages 7183–7195, Online. Association for Computational Linguistics.

Matt Gardner, Joel Grus, Mark Neumann, Oyvind Tafjord, Pradeep Dasigi, Nelson Liu, Matthew Peters, Michael Schmitz, and Luke Zettlemoyer. 2018. Allennlp: A deep semantic natural language processing platform.

Yufang Hou, Charles Jochim, Martin Gleize, Francesca Bonin, and Debasis Ganguly. 2021. TDMSci: A specialized corpus for scientific literature entity tagging of tasks datasets and metrics. In *Proceedings of the 16th Conference of the European Chapter of the Association for Computational Linguistics: Main Volume*, pages 707–714, Online. Association for Computational Linguistics.

Ju Yuan Hsiao, Chuan Yi Tang, and Ruay Shiung Chang. 1992. An efficient algorithm for finding a maximum weight 2-independent set on interval graphs. *Information Processing Letters*, 43(5):229–235.

Zhiheng Huang, Wei Xu, and Kai Yu. 2015. Bidirectional lstm-crf models for sequence tagging.

David S Johnson, Mihalis Yannakakis, and Christos H Papadimitriou. 1988. On generating all maximal independent sets. *Information Processing Letters*, 27(3):119–123.

Diederik P. Kingma and Jimmy Ba. 2017. Adam: A method for stochastic optimization.

Lingpeng Kong, Chris Dyer, and Noah A. Smith. 2016. Segmental recurrent neural networks. *CoRR*, abs/1511.06018.

Guillaume Lample, Miguel Ballesteros, Sandeep Subramanian, Kazuya Kawakami, and Chris Dyer. 2016. Neural architectures for named entity recognition. In *Proceedings of the 2016 Conference of the North American Chapter of the Association for Computational Linguistics: Human Language Technologies*, pages 260–270, San Diego, California. Association for Computational Linguistics.

Kenton Lee, Luheng He, Mike Lewis, and Luke Zettlemoyer. 2017. End-to-end neural coreference resolution. In *Proceedings of the 2017 Conference on Empirical Methods in Natural Language Processing*, pages 188–197, Copenhagen, Denmark. Association for Computational Linguistics.

Yanfei Lei, Chunming Hu, Guanghui Ma, and Richong Zhang. 2021. Keyphrase extraction with incomplete annotated training data. In *Proceedings of the Seventh Workshop on Noisy User-generated Text (W-NUT 2021)*, pages 26–34, Online. Association for Computational Linguistics.

Mike Lewis, Yinhan Liu, Naman Goyal, Marjan Ghazvininejad, Abdelrahman Mohamed, Omer Levy, Ves Stoyanov, and Luke Zettlemoyer. 2019. Bart: Denoising sequence-to-sequence pre-training for natural language generation, translation, and comprehension.

Xiaoya Li, Jingrong Feng, Yuxian Meng, Qinghong Han, Fei Wu, and Jiwei Li. 2020. A unified mrc framework for named entity recognition.

Yangming Li, lemao liu, and Shuming Shi. 2021. Empirical analysis of unlabeled entity problem in named entity recognition. In *International Conference on Learning Representations*.

Yaoyong Li, Kalina Bontcheva, and Hamish Cunningham. 2004. Svm based learning system for information extraction. In *Deterministic and Statistical Methods in Machine Learning*.

Yijia Liu, Wanxiang Che, Jiang Guo, Bing Qin, and Ting Liu. 2016. Exploring segment representations for neural segmentation models. In *Proceedings of the Twenty-Fifth International Joint Conference on Artificial Intelligence*, IJCAI'16, page 2880–2886. AAAI Press.

Yinhan Liu, Myle Ott, Naman Goyal, Jingfei Du, Mandar Joshi, Danqi Chen, Omer Levy, Mike Lewis, Luke Zettlemoyer, and Veselin Stoyanov. 2019. Roberta: A robustly optimized bert pretraining approach.

Yi Luan, Luheng He, Mari Ostendorf, and Hannaneh Hajishirzi. 2018. Multi-task identification of entities, relations, and coreference for scientific knowledge graph construction. In *Proceedings of the 2018 Conference on Empirical Methods in Natural Language Processing*, pages 3219–3232, Brussels, Belgium. Association for Computational Linguistics.

Yi Luan, Dave Wadden, Luheng He, Amy Shah, Mari Ostendorf, and Hannaneh Hajishirzi. 2019. A general framework for information extraction using dynamic span graphs.

Xuezhe Ma and Eduard Hovy. 2016. End-to-end sequence labeling via bi-directional lstm-cnns-crf.

Hiroki Nakayama. 2018. seqeval: A python framework for sequence labeling evaluation. Software available from https://github.com/chakki-works/seqeval.

Madhumangal Pal and GP Bhattacharjee. 1996. A sequential algorithm for finding a maximum weight k-independent set on interval graphs. *International Journal of Computer Mathematics*, 60(3-4):205–214.

Adam Paszke, Sam Gross, Francisco Massa, Adam Lerer, James Bradbury, Gregory Chanan, Trevor Killeen, Zeming Lin, Natalia Gimelshein, Luca Antiga, Alban Desmaison, Andreas Köpf, Edward Yang, Zach DeVito, Martin Raison, Alykhan Tejani, Sasank Chilamkurthy, Benoit Steiner, Lu Fang, Junjie Bai, and Soumith Chintala. 2019. Pytorch: An imperative style, high-performance deep learning library.

Venkatesh Raman, Saket Saurabh, and Somnath Sikdar. 2007. Efficient exact algorithms through enumerating maximal independent sets and other techniques. *Theory of Computing Systems*, 41(3):563–587.

Marek Rei. 2017. Semi-supervised multitask learning for sequence labeling. *arXiv preprint arXiv:1704.07156*.

Alex Rogozhnikov. 2022. Einops: Clear and reliable tensor manipulations with einstein-like notation. In *International Conference on Learning Representations*.

Alexander M. Rush. 2020. Torch-struct: Deep structured prediction library.

Sunita Sarawagi and William W Cohen. 2005. Semi-markov conditional random fields for information extraction. In *Advances in Neural Information Processing Systems*, volume 17. MIT Press.

Motoki Sato, Hiroyuki Shindo, Ikuya Yamada, and Yuji Matsumoto. 2017. Segment-level neural conditional random fields for named entity recognition. In *Proceedings of the Eighth International Joint Conference on Natural Language Processing (Volume 2: Short Papers)*, pages 97–102, Taipei, Taiwan. Asian Federation of Natural Language Processing.

Emma Strubell, Patrick Verga, David Belanger, and Andrew McCallum. 2017. Fast and accurate sequence labeling with iterated dilated convolutions.

Yi Tay, Dara Bahri, Donald Metzler, Da-Cheng Juan, Zhe Zhao, and Che Zheng. 2021. Synthesizer: Rethinking self-attention in transformer models. *ArXiv*, abs/2005.00743.

Erik F. Tjong Kim Sang and Fien De Meulder. 2003. Introduction to the CoNLL-2003 shared task: Language-independent named entity recognition. In *Proceedings of the Seventh Conference on Natural Language Learning at HLT-NAACL 2003*, pages 142–147.

Ralph Weischedel, Martha Palmer, Mitchell Marcus, Eduard Hovy, Sameer Pradhan, Lance Ramshaw, Nianwen Xue, Ann Taylor, Jeff Kaufman, Michelle Franchini, et al. 2013. Ontonotes release 5.0 ldc2013t19. *Linguistic Data Consortium, Philadelphia, PA*, 23.

Thomas Wolf, Lysandre Debut, Victor Sanh, Julien Chaumond, Clement Delangue, Anthony Moi, Pierric Cistac, Tim Rault, Rémi Louf, Morgan Funtowicz, Joe Davison, Sam Shleifer, Patrick von Platen, Clara Ma, Yacine Jernite, Julien Plu, Canwen Xu, Teven Le Scao, Sylvain Gugger, Mariama Drame, Quentin Lhoest, and Alexander M. Rush. 2020. Huggingface's transformers: State-of-the-art natural language processing.

Juntao Yu, Bernd Bohnet, and Massimo Poesio. 2020. Named entity recognition as dependency parsing. In *ACL*.

Urchade Zaratiana, Nadi Tomeh, Pierre Holat, and Thierry Charnois. 2022. GNNer: Reducing overlapping in span-based NER using graph neural networks. In *Proceedings of the 60th Annual Meeting of the Association for Computational Linguistics: Student Research Workshop*, pages 97–103, Dublin, Ireland. Association for Computational Linguistics.

Zexuan Zhong and Danqi Chen. 2021. A frustratingly easy approach for entity and relation extraction.

Global Span Selection for Named Entity Recognition

Urchade Zaratiana[*†], **Niama Elkhbir**[†], **Pierre Holat**[*†],
Nadi Tomeh[†], **Thierry Charnois**[†]
[*] FI Group, [†] LIPN, CNRS UMR 7030, France
{zaratiana,elkhbir,holat,tomeh,charnois}@lipn.fr

Abstract

Named Entity Recognition (NER) is an important task in Natural Language Processing with applications in many domains. In this paper, we describe a novel approach to named entity recognition, in which we output a set of spans (i.e., segmentations) by maximizing a global score. During training, we optimize our model by maximizing the probability of the gold segmentation. During inference, we use dynamic programming to select the best segmentation under a linear time complexity. We prove that our approach outperforms CRF and semi-CRF models for Named Entity Recognition. We make our code publicly available at `https://github.com/urchade/global-span-selection`.

1 Introduction

Named Entity Recognition is a crucial task in natural language processing whose purpose is to identify and classify salient entities in texts such as persons, organizations, and locations. Recognizing such entities is advantageous for applications such as relation extraction and machine translation. There are two main paradigms for NER: sequence labeling (SL) (Huang et al., 2015; Lample et al., 2016; Akbik et al., 2018) and span-based approaches (SB) (Sohrab and Miwa, 2018; Yu et al., 2020a; Li et al., 2021). SL frames NER as token-level prediction, using, for instance, the BIO (Ramshaw and Marcus, 1995) or BILOU (Ratinov and Roth, 2009) schemes, while SB considers spans (contiguous segments of tokens) as basic units instead of tokens and performs span-level classification by assigning a label to each entity and a special `null` label to non-entity spans.

SL is usually performed by representing the tokens using deep learning models, then using a Conditional Random Field (Lafferty et al., 2001) as the output layer. The best label sequence is computed using the Viterbi algorithm and learning typically maximizes the likelihood of gold sequences. In contrast, SB enumerates all candidate spans from an input text and computes their representation before feeding them into a softmax layer for classification.

One advantage of SBs is that they allow richer span representation compared to SL since span-level features are learned end to end. However, such *unstructured* SB models predict the label of each span independently. They are prone to produce overlapping entities which is forbidden in flat and nested NER. Prior works used a *greedy* decoding algorithm (Johnson, 1973; Yu et al., 2020b; Li et al., 2021) to obtain a set of non-overlapping entities. The highest-scoring entities are iteratively selected as long as they do not overlap with previously selected ones. Greedy decoding is efficient but tends to suffer from myopic bias. Choosing spans without regard to future decisions may results in suboptimal entity sets.

An alternative formulation of NER as joint segmentation and labeling with Semi-Markov CRFs has been proposed in the literature (Sarawagi and Cohen, 2005; Kong et al., 2016; Ye and Ling, 2018). This approach has two advantages: (a) it uses a globally-normalized model to compute the probability of each labeled segmentation as opposed to scoring each span independently; and (2) it guarantees no-overlap in the output entities by using a variant of the Viterbi algorithm for decoding. Nevertheless, semi-CRFs underperform in practice as we show in our experiments. We hypothesise that scoring segmentations composed of entities and non-entities is the main weakness. First, non-entity spans can be segmented in multiple ways all equally valid but only one of them is enforced by the semi-CRF, both during learning and inference. Furthermore, the majority of spans are non-entity, a considerable probability mass is wasted on uninteresting segmentations.

In this paper, we propose a new formulation for span-based NER that combines ideas from

Proceedings of the Workshop on Unimodal and Multimodal Induction of Linguistic Structures (UM-IoS), pages 11 - 17
December 7, 2022 ©2022 Association for Computational Linguistics

two-steps (filtering and decoding) approaches and globally-normalized CRF-based models. Our approach starts by filtering all non-entity spans using a span classifier and constructing an *overlapping* graph of the remaining spans. A globally-normalized model is then used to compute the probability of each *maximal independent set (MIS)* within the graph. Each such set corresponds to a selection of non-overlapping entities. Learning and inference can be performed efficiently using dynamic programming as we explain in §2.2. Furthermore, we train the span classifier and the global entity selection model jointly using a multi-task objective. We show that our approach outperforms both SL and Semi-CRFs on all tasks and outperform two-step (filtering and greedy decoding) models on most.

2 Two-step Span-based NER

State-of-the-art span-based approaches employ a locally-normalized, unstructured span classifier to filter non entity spans, followed by greedy decoding to select a set of non-overlapping entities (Li et al., 2021; Fu et al., 2021). We describe these two steps in this section.

2.1 Span Classification

This step consists of enumerating all the spans from the input sequence and computing their representation using pre-trained transformers such as BERT. Following previous work (Lee et al., 2017; Luan et al., 2019), the representation s_{ij} of a span (i, j) of length k is computed by concatenating the representation of its left and right endpoint tokens (h_i and h_j respectively) along with a learned span width feature f_k. A 2-layer Multilayer Perceptron with *ReLU* activation is applied to the features to get the final span representation:

$$s_{ij} = \mathsf{MLP}([h_i; h_j; f_k]) \tag{1}$$

Then, the span representation is fed into a linear layer (or an MLP) for span classification. A NER task with L entity types would have $L + 1$ labels since we allocate a `null` label for non-entity spans. The score of label y for a span (i, j) is computed as:

$$\phi(i, j, y) = w_y^T s_{ij} \tag{2}$$

where w_y is a learnable weight vector (we omit bias term for readability). These scores are further normalized using the softmax function.

The model is trained to minimize the negative log-likelihood of gold spans in the training set $\mathcal{T}$:

$$\mathcal{L}_{clf} = - \sum_{(i,j,y)\in\mathcal{T}} \log \frac{\exp\{\phi(i, j, y)\}}{\sum_{y'} \exp\{\phi(i, j, y')\}} \tag{3}$$

During inference, each span (i, j) is assigned the label $y(i, j) = \arg\max_y \phi(i, j, y)$ with score $k(i, j) = \max_y \phi(i, j, y)$. We call $\mathcal{C}$ the set of candidate entities which is the set of all spans assigned a label different from `null`. This set may contain overlapping spans which is not allowed in flat NER tasks, a decoding step is therefore required.

2.2 Maximum Weight Independent Set in Interval Graphs

An *overlap graph* over $\mathcal{C}$ is the graph G whose nodes are the elements of $\mathcal{C}$ and contains an edge between each pair of overlapping entities. This graph can also be called an *interval graph* since spans can be seen as intervals over their start and end positions. An *Independent Set (IS)* of the graph G is a set of nodes such that no two nodes in the set are joined by an edge. An independent set is said to be *maximal* if it is not properly contained in another independent set. Each node (i, j) in the graph is assigned a real number $r(i, j)$, the graph G is said to be a *weighted* graph. For each subset of nodes $\mathcal{S} \subseteq \mathcal{C}$, $\sum_{(i,j)\in\mathcal{S}} r(i, j)$ is called the weight of $\mathcal{S}$. A *Maximum Weight Independent Set (MWIS)* is an independent set such that its weight is maximum amongst all independent sets. Under this formulation, the decoding problem amounts to finding an MWIS in the graph G:

$$\hat{\mathcal{S}} = \arg\max_{\mathcal{S}\in\Psi(\mathcal{C})} \sum_{(i,j)\in\mathcal{S}} r(i, j) \tag{4}$$

where $\Psi(\mathcal{C})$, the set of all MIS of G.

Greedy Decoding Greedy decoding constructs an approximation to $\hat{\mathcal{S}}$ by iteratively adding the highest-scoring entity in C which does not overlap with any previously selected one. This algorithm has a complexity of $O(n \log n)$ with $n = |C|$.

In the next section we propose an exact alternative which uses a globally-normalized model.

Exact decoding The exact solution to Eq. (4) can be obtained by dynamic programming using an MWIS algorithm presented by Gupta et al. (1982); Hsiao et al. (1992). This algorithm has a linear time complexity $O(n)$ with n being the number of nodes in the graph which is supposed to be sorted by interval endpoints (otherwise, it can be sorted in $O(n \log n)$ time. In practice, thenumber of nodes n is much lower than the input sequence length.

2.3 A Globally-Normalized MWIS Model

One way of estimating the weights $r(i, j)$ of the graph nodes is to use the scores produced by the local classifiers: $r(i, j) = k(i, j)$. In this section we propose to learn a dedicated probabilistic model of of MIS globally-normalized and learned to maximize the probability of the gold MIS.

The probability of an MIS is computed given by:

$$P(\mathcal{S}) = \mathcal{Z}^{-1} \exp\left\{ \sum_{(i,j)\in\mathcal{S}} r(i, j) \right\} \quad (5)$$

The unnormalized score of an MIS is still simply the sum of individual span weights where each is a linear projection of the span representation:

$$r(i, j) = w^T s_{ij} \quad (6)$$

where w is a parameter vector to be learned. The normalization constant is given by:

$$\mathcal{Z} = \sum_{\mathcal{S}\in\Psi(\mathcal{C})} \exp\left\{ \sum_{(i,j)\in\mathcal{S}} r(i, j) \right\} \quad (7)$$

While $\mathcal{Z}$, the partition function, can be ignored during inference, it has to be computed for learning as we use the negative log probability of the gold MIS as a loss function. The partition function can be computed efficiently using a modification to the dynamic program of the MWIS algorithm, however, in practice, we simply enumerate all MIS, which is feasible since the number of remaining spans is low. The enumeration can be done in time $O(n^2 + \beta)$ where n is the number of spans and β the sum of the numbers of spans of all enumerated sets (Leung, 1984; Liang et al., 1991).

During training, we modify the set $\mathcal{C}$, i.e. the output of the local classifier, so that (1) it contains all the gold spans, and (2) it does not contains spans that do not overlap with the gold spans. By doing this, we ensure that gold spans form an MIS in the overlap graph over $\mathcal{C}$. Finally, we use a multitask loss function that is the sum of the local classifier loss (Eq. (3)) and the global model loss.

3 Experiments

3.1 Setup

Baselines We compare our approach to a CRF tagger, the standard span-based model and the span-based model with Semi-Markov CRF. For all the models, we used pretrained transformers for token representation.

Datasets We evaluate our model on diverse NER datasets: TDM (Hou et al., 2021), Conll-2003 (Tjong Kim Sang and De Meulder, 2003), and OntoNotes 5.0 (Weischedel et al., 2013) for English data, and ACE05 for Arabic data (Walker et al., 2006). The details about the dataset can be found in the appendix A.1.

Evaluation metrics We evaluate the models using the exact matching between the predicted and true entities. We report the Precision, Recall and F1.

Hyperparameters For Conll-2003 and Ontonotes datasets we use `bert-base-cased` (Devlin et al., 2019) to produce contextual representation, for TDM we use SciBERT (Beltagy et al., 2019) and for Arabic ACE we use `bert-base-arabertv2` (Antoun et al., 2020). We use the base size, with 12 transformer layers, for all the models. We do not use any auxiliar embeddings (eg. *character embeddings*) for simplicity. All the models are trained with *Adam* optimizer (Kingma and Ba, 2017) with a learning rate of 2e-5, a batch size of 10 and a maximal epoch of 25. We keep the best checkpoint on the validation set for testing. We trained all the models in a server with V100 GPUs.

3.2 Results

The results of our experiments are shown in Table 1. We report the results for the four datasets using CRF, Semi-CRF, Standard and Global span-based models. For both Standard and Global models, we report the results obtained by using (cf. + Global lines) or not using decoding (cf. + Greedy lines).

Main results From Table 1, we can see that holistically, our global models with global decoding achieve the best results on most of the datasets (all except on OntoNotes). Moreover, Semi-CRF has the lowest score on all data, which may explain its low adoption over the years compared to the standard CRF.

Models	Conll-2003			OntoNotes 5.0			TDM			Arabic ACE		
	P	R	F	P	R	F	P	R	F	P	R	F
CRF	92.64	91.82	92.23	87.77	89.47	88.61	69.77	73.65	71.66	82.79	84.44	83.61
Semi-CRF	91.46	90.77	91.11	87.44	88.85	88.14	69.38	72.85	71.05	82.97	84.24	83.60
Standard	93.40	91.68	92.53	89.47	90.00	89.73	67.75	69.88	68.78	83.21	83.76	83.48
+ Greedy	93.82	91.40	92.60	90.43	89.04	89.73	75.12	67.82	71.26	83.73	83.56	83.64
+ Global	93.83	91.51	92.65	90.58	89.45	**90.01**	75.25	68.12	71.48	83.72	83.55	83.63
Global	94.84	90.72	92.73	89.05	89.77	89.41	63.30	72.75	67.53	83.54	83.65	83.60
+ Greedy	95.07	90.42	92.69	89.98	88.44	89.21	74.16	68.23	71.07	83.87	82.75	83.31
+ Global	95.11	90.52	**92.76**	90.18	88.85	89.51	75.55	70.34	**72.84**	84.14	83.35	**83.74**

Table 1: **Experimental results**. We report the average over three random seeds.

Global vs. Greedy decodings For both the span-based approaches, we can see that decoding generally improves F1 score performance and Precision while decreasing Recall. We explain this behavior by the fact that when using decoding, non-confident spans are removed, so Precision increases. However, some false negatives may be also removed, hence the slight decrease in recall. Moreover, for standard models, greedy and global decoding have similar performance, while for globally trained models, global decoding always has the best performance, which shows the effectiveness of our approach. Also, we can further observe on the Conll-2003, Arabic ACE and OntoNotes 5.0 datasets that greedy decoding can even decrease the performance of the model which may be an effect of the myopic bias.

4 Related Works

Approaches for NER Traditionally, NER tasks are designed as sequence labeling (Lample et al., 2016; Akbik et al., 2018), i.e., token-level classification. Recently, many approaches have been proposed that go beyond token-level prediction. For instance, some works have approached NER as question answering (Li et al., 2020) and others use sequence-to-sequence models (Yan et al., 2021; Yang and Tu, 2022). In this work, we focused on span-based methods (Liu et al., 2016; Sohrab and Miwa, 2018; Fu et al., 2021; Zaratiana et al., 2022; Corro, 2022) where all spans are enumerated and then classified into entity types.

Decoding for NER NER is a task for which a decoding algorithm must be applied to ensure that the model outputs are well trained. For example, CRF (Lafferty et al., 2001) has been proposed for sequence labeling and Semi-CRF for the span-based approach. Due to the low performance of Semi-CRF (Sarawagi and Cohen, 2005), researchers have proposed to train a local span-based method and use greedy decoding to guarantee non-overlapping entities for decoding. In this work, we propose exact/global decoding to produce a set of non-overlapping spans that maximize the global score to avoid the myopic bias of the greedy approach.

5 Conclusion

In this work, we proposed a new approach for span-based NER. During learning, our model maximizes the probability of the best segmentation while during inference, the final spans are selected according to a global score using dynamic programming. Our model mitigates the myopic bias of the greedy decoding of the standard span-based approach and it scores best on most datasets compared to other structured models such as CRF or Semi-CRF. For future work, it would be interesting to model the interaction between the spans to compute the global score.

6 Limitations

The main limitation of our model is that it is not suitable for recognizing nested named entities since the output structure is a set of non-overlapping spaces. Moreover, our model performed worse on the OntoNotes dataset: the cause may be due to some negative interference from our multitasking loss that makes learning difficult for large type sets. We will address these mentioned weaknesses in futur works.

Acknowledgments

This work is partially supported by a public grant overseen by the French National Research Agency (ANR) as part of the program Investissements d'Avenir (ANR-10-LABX-0083). This work was granted access to the HPC/AI resources of [CINES/IDRIS/TGCC] under the allocation 20XX-AD011013096 made by GENCI.

References

Alan Akbik, Duncan Blythe, and Roland Vollgraf. 2018. Contextual string embeddings for sequence labeling. In *Proceedings of the 27th International Conference on Computational Linguistics*, pages 1638–1649, Santa Fe, New Mexico, USA. Association for Computational Linguistics.

Wissam Antoun, Fady Baly, and Hazem M. Hajj. 2020. Arabert: Transformer-based model for arabic language understanding. *ArXiv*, abs/2003.00104.

Iz Beltagy, Kyle Lo, and Arman Cohan. 2019. Scibert: A pretrained language model for scientific text.

Caio Corro. 2022. A dynamic programming algorithm for span-based nested named-entity recognition in o(n^2).*ArXiv*, *abs*/2210.04738.

Jacob Devlin, Ming-Wei Chang, Kenton Lee, and Kristina Toutanova. 2019. BERT: Pre-training of deep bidirectional transformers for language understanding. In *Proceedings of the 2019 Conference of the North American Chapter of the Association for Computational Linguistics: Human Language Technologies, Volume 1 (Long and Short Papers)*, pages 4171–4186, Minneapolis, Minnesota. Association for Computational Linguistics.

Jinlan Fu, Xuanjing Huang, and Pengfei Liu. 2021. SpanNER: Named entity re-/recognition as span prediction. In *Proceedings of the 59th Annual Meeting of the Association for Computational Linguistics and the 11th International Joint Conference on Natural Language Processing (Volume 1: Long Papers)*, pages 7183–7195, Online. Association for Computational Linguistics.

Matt Gardner, Joel Grus, Mark Neumann, Oyvind Tafjord, Pradeep Dasigi, Nelson F. Liu, Matthew Peters, Michael Schmitz, and Luke Zettlemoyer. 2018. AllenNLP: A deep semantic natural language processing platform. In *Proceedings of Workshop for NLP Open Source Software (NLP-OSS)*, pages 1–6, Melbourne, Australia. Association for Computational Linguistics.

U. I. Gupta, D. T. Lee, and Joseph Y.-T. Leung. 1982. Efficient algorithms for interval graphs and circular-arc graphs. *Networks*, 12:459–467.

Aric A. Hagberg, Daniel A. Schult, and Pieter Swart. 2008. Exploring network structure, dynamics, and function using networkx.

Yufang Hou, Charles Jochim, Martin Gleize, Francesca Bonin, and Debasis Ganguly. 2021. TDMSci: A specialized corpus for scientific literature entity tagging of tasks datasets and metrics. In *Proceedings of the 16th Conference of the European Chapter of the Association for Computational Linguistics: Main Volume*, pages 707–714, Online. Association for Computational Linguistics.

Ju Yuan Hsiao, Chuan Yi Tang, and Ruay Shiung Chang. 1992. An efficient algorithm for finding a maximum weight 2-independent set on interval graphs. *Information Processing Letters*, 43(5):229–235.

Zhiheng Huang, Wei Xu, and Kai Yu. 2015. Bidirectional lstm-crf models for sequence tagging.

David S. Johnson. 1973. Approximation algorithms for combinatorial problems. *Proceedings of the fifth annual ACM symposium on Theory of computing*.

Diederik P. Kingma and Jimmy Ba. 2017. Adam: A method for stochastic optimization.

Lingpeng Kong, Chris Dyer, and Noah A. Smith. 2016. Segmental recurrent neural networks. *CoRR*, abs/1511.06018.

John D. Lafferty, Andrew McCallum, and Fernando C. N. Pereira. 2001. Conditional random fields: Probabilistic models for segmenting and labeling sequence data. In *Proceedings of the Eighteenth International Conference on Machine Learning*, ICML '01, page 282–289, San Francisco, CA, USA. Morgan Kaufmann Publishers Inc.

Guillaume Lample, Miguel Ballesteros, Sandeep Subramanian, Kazuya Kawakami, and Chris Dyer. 2016. Neural architectures for named entity recognition. In *Proceedings of the 2016 Conference of the North American Chapter of the Association for Computational Linguistics: Human Language Technologies*, pages 260–270, San Diego, California. Association for Computational Linguistics.

Kenton Lee, Luheng He, Mike Lewis, and Luke Zettlemoyer. 2017. End-to-end neural coreference resolution. In *Proceedings of the 2017 Conference on Empirical Methods in Natural Language Processing*, pages 188–197, Copenhagen, Denmark. Association for Computational Linguistics.

Joseph Y.-T. Leung. 1984. Fast algorithms for generating all maximal independent sets of interval, circular-arc and chordal graphs. *J. Algorithms*, 5:22–35.

Xiaoya Li, Jingrong Feng, Yuxian Meng, Qinghong Han, Fei Wu, and Jiwei Li. 2020. A unified mrc framework for named entity recognition.

Yangming Li, lemao liu, and Shuming Shi. 2021. Empirical analysis of unlabeled entity problem in named entity recognition. In *International Conference on Learning Representations*.

Y.D. Liang, S.K. Dhall, and S. Lakshmivarahan. 1991. On the problem of finding all maximum weight independent sets in interval and circular-arc graphs. In *[Proceedings] 1991 Symposium on Applied Computing*, pages 465–470.

Yijia Liu, Wanxiang Che, Jiang Guo, Bing Qin, and Ting Liu. 2016. Exploring segment representations for neural segmentation models. In *IJCAI*.

Yi Luan, Dave Wadden, Luheng He, Amy Shah, Mari Ostendorf, and Hannaneh Hajishirzi. 2019. A general framework for information extraction using dynamic span graphs.

Hiroki Nakayama. 2018. seqeval: A python framework for sequence labeling evaluation. Software available from https://github.com/chakki-works/seqeval.

Adam Paszke, Sam Gross, Francisco Massa, Adam Lerer, James Bradbury, Gregory Chanan, Trevor Killeen, Zeming Lin, Natalia Gimelshein, Luca Antiga, Alban Desmaison, Andreas Kopf, Edward Yang, Zachary DeVito, Martin Raison, Alykhan Tejani, Sasank Chilamkurthy, Benoit Steiner, Lu Fang, Junjie Bai, and Soumith Chintala. 2019. Pytorch: An imperative style, high-performance deep learning library. In H. Wallach, H. Larochelle, A. Beygelzimer, F. d'Alché-Buc, E. Fox, and R. Garnett, editors, *Advances in Neural Information Processing Systems 32*, pages 8024–8035. Curran Associates, Inc.

Lance A. Ramshaw and Mitchell P. Marcus. 1995. Text chunking using transformation-based learning. *ArXiv*, cmp-lg/9505040.

Lev Ratinov and Dan Roth. 2009. Design challenges and misconceptions in named entity recognition. In *Proceedings of the Thirteenth Conference on Computational Natural Language Learning (CoNLL-2009)*, pages 147–155, Boulder, Colorado. Association for Computational Linguistics.

Alexander M. Rush. 2020. Torch-struct: Deep structured prediction library.

Sunita Sarawagi and William W Cohen. 2005. Semi-markov conditional random fields for information extraction. In *Advances in Neural Information Processing Systems*, volume 17. MIT Press.

Mohammad Golam Sohrab and Makoto Miwa. 2018. Deep exhaustive model for nested named entity recognition. In *Proceedings of the 2018 Conference on Empirical Methods in Natural Language Processing*, pages 2843–2849, Brussels, Belgium. Association for Computational Linguistics.

Erik F. Tjong Kim Sang and Fien De Meulder. 2003. Introduction to the CoNLL-2003 shared task: Language-independent named entity recognition. In *Proceedings of the Seventh Conference on Natural Language Learning at HLT-NAACL 2003*, pages 142–147.

Christopher Walker, Stephanie Strassel, Julie Medero, and Kazuaki Maeda. 2006. Ace 2005 multilingual training corpus.

Ralph Weischedel, Martha Palmer, Mitchell Marcus, Eduard Hovy, Sameer Pradhan, Lance Ramshaw, Nianwen Xue, Ann Taylor, Jeff Kaufman, Michelle Franchini, Mohammed El-Bachouti, Robert Belvin, and Ann Houston. 2013. OntoNotes Release 5.0.

Thomas Wolf, Lysandre Debut, Victor Sanh, Julien Chaumond, Clement Delangue, Anthony Moi, Pierric Cistac, Tim Rault, Rémi Louf, Morgan Funtowicz, and Jamie Brew. 2019. Huggingface's transformers: State-of-the-art natural language processing. *ArXiv*, abs/1910.03771.

Hang Yan, Tao Gui, Junqi Dai, Qipeng Guo, Zheng Zhang, and Xipeng Qiu. 2021. A unified generative framework for various ner subtasks. In *ACL*.

Songlin Yang and Kewei Tu. 2022. Bottom-up constituency parsing and nested named entity recognition with pointer networks. In *ACL*.

Zhixiu Ye and Zhen-Hua Ling. 2018. Hybrid semi-Markov CRF for neural sequence labeling. In *Proceedings of the 56th Annual Meeting of the Association for Computational Linguistics (Volume 2: Short Papers)*, pages 235–240, Melbourne, Australia. Association for Computational Linguistics.

Juntao Yu, Bernd Bohnet, and Massimo Poesio. 2020a. Named entity recognition as dependency parsing. In *ACL*.

Juntao Yu, Bernd Bohnet, and Massimo Poesio. 2020b. Named entity recognition as dependency parsing. In *Proceedings of the 58th Annual Meeting of the Association for Computational Linguistics*, pages 6470–6476, Online. Association for Computational Linguistics.

Urchade Zaratiana, Nadi Tomeh, Pierre Holat, and Thierry Charnois. 2022. GNNer: Reducing overlapping in span-based NER using graph neural networks. In *Proceedings of the 60th Annual Meeting of the Association for Computational Linguistics: Student Research Workshop*, pages 97–103, Dublin, Ireland. Association for Computational Linguistics.

A Appendix

A.1 Dataset details

Conll-2003 (Tjong Kim Sang and De Meulder, 2003) is a dataset from the news domain that was designed for extracting entities such as Person, Location and Organisation. OntoNotes 5.0 (Weischedel et al., 2013) is a large corpus comprising various genres of text, including newswire, broadcast news, and telephone conversation. It contains a total of 18 different entity types, such as Person, Organization, Location, Product or Date. TDM (Hou et al., 2021) is a NER dataset that was recently published and it was designed for extracting Tasks, Datasets, and Metrics entities from Natural Language Processing papers. Arabic ACE is the Arabic portion of the multilingual information extraction corpus, ACE 2005 (Walker et al., 2006). It includes texts from a wide range of genres, such as newswire, broadcast news, and weblogs. It contains a total of 7 entity types.

Dataset	Entity types	Train / Dev / Test
Conll-2003	4	14987 / 3466 / 3684
OntoNotes 5.0	18	48788 / 7477 / 5013
TDM	3	1000 / 500 / 500
Arabic ACE	7	2433 / 500 / 500

Table 2: Dataset statistics

A.2 Librairies

In this research, we used Pytorch (Paszke et al., 2019) to implement the models for its flexibility and ability to run on GPU machines. The pre-trained models were loaded from the HuggingFace Transformers library (Wolf et al., 2019), and some data processing was done using AllenNLP (Gardner et al., 2018). Our semi-CRF implementation is based on the pytorch-struct library (Rush, 2020). For evaluating the models, we adapted some code from the seqeval library (Nakayama, 2018). We employed Netwokx library (Hagberg et al., 2008) for graph processing in our decoding algorithm.

Visual Grounding of Inter-lingual Word-Embeddings

Wafaa Mohammed Hassan Shahmohammadi Hendrik P. A. Lensch R. Harald Baayen

University of Tübingen
wmohammed@aimsammi.org,
{hassan.shahmohammadi, hendrik.lensch, harald.baayen}@uni-tuebingen.de

Abstract

Visual grounding of Language aims at enriching textual representations of language with multiple sources of visual knowledge such as images and videos. Although visual grounding is an area of intense research, inter-lingual aspects of visual grounding have not received much attention. The present study investigates the inter-lingual visual grounding of word embeddings. We propose an implicit alignment technique between the two spaces of vision and language in which inter-lingual textual information interact in order to enrich pre-trained textual word embeddings. We focus on three languages in our experiments, namely, English, Arabic, and German. We obtained visually grounded vector representations for these languages and studied whether visual grounding on one or multiple languages improved the performance of embeddings on word similarity and categorization benchmarks. Our experiments suggest that inter-lingual knowledge improves the performance of grounded embeddings in similar languages such as German and English. However, inter-lingual grounding of German or English with Arabic led to a slight degradation in performance on word similarity benchmarks. On the other hand, we observed an opposite trend on categorization benchmarks where Arabic had the most improvement on English. In the discussion section, several reasons for those findings are laid out. We hope that our experiments provide a baseline for further research on inter-lingual visual grounding.

1 Introduction

Distributional Semantic Models (DSMs) have long been used to capture words' meaning. They estimate semantic representations from co-occurrences of words in text corpora. Even though embeddings are the dominant method for large scale data, from a psychological and cognitive point of view, distributional models suffer from the problem referred to as the *Symbol Grounding Problem* (Harnad, 1990): the meaning of a symbol (word) is entirely accounted for in terms of other symbols without any links to the outside world. In the context of natural language processing (NLP), grounding is defined as " the process of linking the symbolic representation of language (e.g., words) into the rich perceptual knowledge of the outside world " (Shahmohammadi et al., 2021). Moreover, (Huang et al., 2021) have proved that multi-modal learning outperforms uni-modal learning as it has access to a better quality latent space representation.

Many studies have addressed grounding of language in vision, typically focusing on grounding for English (Bruni et al., 2014; Shahmohammadi et al., 2022). As a consequence, inter-lingual visual grounding is still poorly understood. This study investigates whether monolingual textual embeddings benefit from the knowledge of other languages in the process of visual grounding. We extend a state-of-the-art model for monolingual visual grounding (Shahmohammadi et al., 2022) by considering different combinations of three languages, namely, English, German, and Arabic. Using various word categorization benchmarks, our experiments show that the three languages profitably exchange inter-lingual knowledge across a simple linear vector space. To the best of our knowledge, we are the first to investigate the problem of visual grounding of inter-lingual word embeddings. Overall, our contributions are as follows:

a) We propose a simple extension of a state-of-the-art visual grounding model to integrate three different languages. b) We obtain zero-shot visually grounded embeddings in three languages. c) Using various benchmarks, we reveal how visual grounding changes textual vector space across languages and show that inter-lingual knowledge transfers to downstream tasks.

Our paper is structured as follows: Section 2 briefly highlights the related works. Section 3 introduces our problem of interest. In Section 4 our pro-

Proceedings of the Workshop on Unimodal and Multimodal Induction of Linguistic Structures (UM-IoS), pages 18 - 28
December 7, 2022

posed model is elaborated. Implementation details are covered in Section 5. The results are presented in Section 6, with further discussion in section 7. In Section 8, we conclude our research, and finally, we point out the limitations and future directions of our work.

2 Related Work

There have been many studies on language grounding in vision most of which focus on monolingual visual grounding. There have been also other works on cross-modal and cross-lingual representations tailored for specific downstream applications.

Monolingual grounding: The study of Bruni et al. (2014) was one of the first studies to obtain visually grounded embeddings by simple fusion such as applying SVD on the concatenation of word and image vectors. (Kiros et al., 2018) adopted a similar fusion approach using gating mechanisms. (Silberer and Lapata, 2014) and (Hasegawa et al., 2017) encoded the two modalities as vectors of attributes and combine them using autoencoders. (Kurach et al., 2017) and (Shahmohammadi et al., 2022) adopted a simple approach where textual embeddings are directly optimized to match image representations. They propose a grounding framework that depends on the alignment of textual and visual features.

Cross-modal cross-lingual representations: In the multilingual setting, the focus has largely been on cross-modal downstream tasks. (Burns et al., 2020) proposed a scalable multilingual aligned language representation using masked cross-language modelling objective. (Ni et al., 2021) proposed a multilingual multimodal model that combines different languages and different modalities into a shared space via multitask pre-training. Similarly, (Zhou et al., 2021) introduced a machine translation augmented model for cross-modal cross-lingual learning by introducing multi-modal losses. (Mohammadshahi et al., 2019) trained a multilingual multimodal model by optimizing the alignment between languages for image-description retrieval task.

The present study is inspired by both directions explored in the literature on visual grounding and multi-lingual representations. We propose a straight forward alignment technique informing textual representations about the visual space while also making use of inter-lingual features. We generate visually grounded inter-lingual word embeddings and evaluate their performance on similarity and categorization benchmarks.

A new direction of research that has been published in parallel with this paper is the work of (Chen et al., 2022). Their model, PaLI (Pathways Language and Image model), employs scaling of joint vision and language pre-training. They make use of the largest transformers to date to train the model. They were able to achieve state-of-the-art in multiple vision and language tasks such as captioning, visual question answering, and scene-text understanding.

3 Inter-lingual Visual Grounding

Multilingual-language models hold great promise for the development of embeddings for under-resourced languages (Armengol-Estapé et al., 2021). The central idea in this line of research is that different languages bring different perspectives (e.g., cultural information and grammar) which can inform each other, resulting in a richer model that has a better understanding of words' meanings in any specific language. Moreover, since typical visual scenes are thought to produce similar information across different languages, integrating visual knowledge (e.g., images) into a multilingual model can contribute to obtaining a better quality grounded embedding space.

4 Model Architecture

Our model maps a textual description of an image into its corresponding image representation. It makes use of a linear alignment to preserve most of the textual knowledge in the word embeddings, allowing only subtle modifications by the error received from the image. It is trained using multilingual image captioning data. The model is given the task to match, for a given image, the multilingual captions to that image in such a way that language-specific features are preserved, and not overwhelmed by inter-lingual features, and image features.

Our model maps two (or three) languages to the grounded space using a shared linear alignment. For instance, figure 1 introduces the model for the combination of English and Arabic languages. Let D be the dataset consisting of triple samples of $(I, S_{en}, S_{ar}) \in D$. Here I refers to an image, S_{en} and S_{ar} denote matching captions of I in English and Arabic respectively. As shown in Figure 1, the two captions are passed through

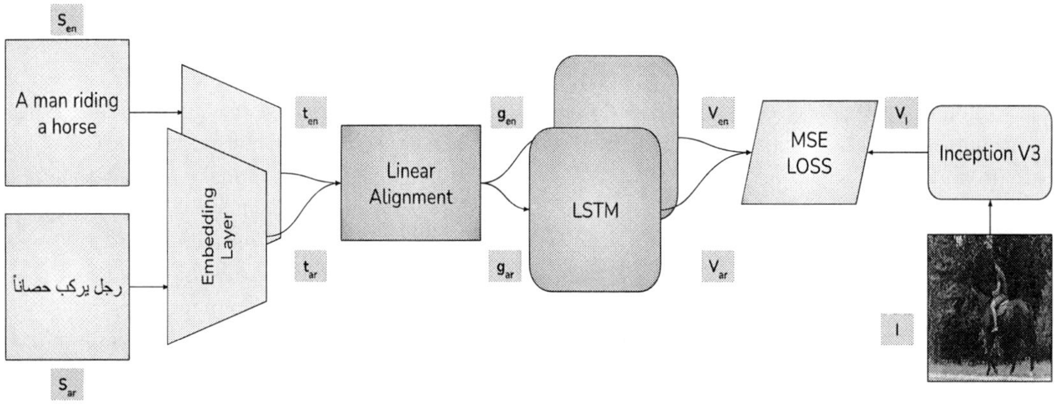

Figure 1: Model Architecture. sentences are first tokenized. Individual tokens are passed, one by one, to a pre-trained embedding layer, followed by a linear alignment that transfers the embeddings into the grounded space. Grounded vectors are encoded into a single vector by an LSTM encoder. The output of the LSTM is then optimized against the image vector generated via a pre-trained CNN model. Layers in blue are frozen during training.

a pre-trained embedding layer (GloVe) (Pennington et al., 2014) to obtain their textual representations t_{en}, t_{ar} which are then mapped to a visually grounded space through a linear transformation. We refer to this linear transformation as the alignment layer. The alignment layer is used to extract grounded embeddings after training. During training, grounded word vectors of each caption are encoded as a single vector using an LSTM layer as follows:

$$V_{en} = LSTM_{en}(g_{en}, c_0, h_0|\theta),$$
$$V_{ar} = LSTM_{ar}(g_{ar}, c_0, h_0|\theta)$$

where, g_{en}, g_{ar} denote the grounded word vectors of the English and Arabic captions respectively. c_0, h_0 and θ represent the initial cell state, initial hidden state, and the trainable parameters of the LSTM. The parameters of the linear alignment and the LSTM layer are optimized to match the sentence representations in both languages to the same image vector V_I as follows:

$$\mathcal{L}_{en}(\theta_{en}) = \frac{1}{|D|}\sum_{t=1}^{n}(V_I^t - V_{en}^t)^2,$$
$$\mathcal{L}_{ar}(\theta_{ar}) = \frac{1}{|D|}\sum_{t=1}^{n}(V_I^t - V_{ar}^t)^2,$$

where θ_{en} and θ_{ar} indicate the learning parameters for each language. The image vector V_I^* is generated using a pre-trained CNN model. The overall loss is simply the sum of the two losses: $\mathcal{L}_{all}(\Theta) = \mathcal{L}_{en}(\theta_{en}) + \mathcal{L}_{ar}(\theta_{ar})$

In this equation, Θ represents all the network's learning parameters. After training, we generate grounded word embedding using the alignment layer. A given textual word embedding $w_t \in \mathbb{R}^d$ is passed through the trained alignment, after which its grounded version is extracted from the alignment layer: $g_t \in \mathbb{R}^c$ as $g_t = w_t.M$, where M denotes the trained alignment layer.

5 Implementation details

We used the Microsoft COCO 2017 dataset (Lin et al., 2014) for our experiments. This dataset consists of 123,287 images with 5 captions each. It is split into 118k training images and 5k validation images. We experimented with three languages for the captions: English, Arabic, and German. The original dataset provided by Microsoft contains the English captions. We obtained the German captions from (Biswas et al., 2021), who translated the English COCO captions using the Fairseq neural machine translator, and the Arabic captions from (Hashim, 2020), who generated the captions using Google's advanced cloud translation API. For the Arabic version of COCO, we only had available to us translations of the captions for 82k samples, which we split into 77k samples for training and 5k samples for validation, and this is the set of images that we use for models that included Arabic. For fair comparisons, we also investigated model performance for English and German using the same 82k images. For all the experiments, we used TensorFlow as a development framework . The training environment is similar to the one used by Shahmohammadi et al. (2022). We used a batch size of 256 image-caption pairs. We trained for 20 epochs with 5 epochs as early stopping tolerance, using the NAdam optimizer (Dozat, 2016) with a learning rate of 0.001. The image vectors were obtained using pre-trained vectors from Inception-V3

(Szegedy et al., 2016), which are based on ImageNet (Deng et al., 2009). For pre-trained textual embeddings we used GloVe embeddings (Pennington et al., 2014). The vocabulary considered for training English comprised the 10k most frequent words. For German and Arabic, which have much richer inflectional systems compared to English, we took into account the 30k most frequent words. We set the dimension of grounded word embeddings to 1024 ($g_t \in \mathbb{R}^{1024}$), and matched the size of the LSTM's output to that of the image vectors (both to 2048). Both the embedding layer and the pre-trained CNN were frozen during training.

6 Results

In this section, we explain our evaluation criteria and report the results of our experiments. We use various word similarity/relatedness and word categorization benchmarks and provide both quantitative and qualitative results.

6.1 Qualitative Evaluation

Figure 2 shows the difference between the nearest neighbours of words from the three languages in the textual and grounded spaces (using the grounding setup with separate grounding of each individual language). The representations in the grounded space are semantically much more precise, and are much less dependent on simple co-occurrence statistics. Our algorithm for visual grounding thus contributes to taking a step forward in solving the symbol grounding problem. For example, the word *car* in Arabic has its nearest neighbours as *airplane* and *explosion* in the textual space, while in the grounded space, the neighbours are different declensions of the word *car*.

6.2 Word Similarity/ Relatedness Evaluation

Following (Bruni et al., 2014; Shahmohammadi et al., 2022), we evaluated our visually grounded word embeddings using similarity/relatedness benchmarks. The task is to estimate the similarity/relatedness score of a pair of words using the Spearman correlation as evaluation metric. Relatedness is a measure of the extent to which two words are associated with each other, e.g. (pen, paper). Similarity quantifies how alike two concepts are based on their location within an is-a hierarchy (e.g., car, automobile). Some benchmarks differentiate between the two while others consider them similar when scoring pairs of words.

Tables 1, 2, 3 summarize the results of visually grounded embeddings on similarity/relatedness benchmarks for English, German, and Arabic. For English, we experimented with six similarity/relatedness benchmarks: WordSim353 (Finkelstein et al., 2001), MEN (Bruni et al., 2014), RW (Luong et al., 2013), MTurk (Radinsky et al., 2011), simVerb (Gerz et al., 2016), and SimLex999 (Hill et al., 2015). For German, evaluations are based on the Multilingual versions of WrdSim353 and simLex999 (Leviant and Reichart, 2015). For Arabic, similarity was evaluated using four benchmarks: Almarsoomi (Almarsoomi et al., 2013), MC30 (Hassan and Mihalcea, 2009), Saif40 (Saif et al., 2014), and WordSim (Hassan and Mihalcea, 2009).

Across the three languages, visual grounding yields embeddings that perform substantially better than embeddings that are based on text only. It is noteworthy that the grounded embeddings achieved superior results on all the similarity benchmarks, for all three languages.

For both English and German, adding German and English respectively as a second language to the model leads to a further improvement in performance on the benchmark tasks. Adding Arabic as a second language along with English or German, however, led to a reduction in accuracy. The experiments evaluating Arabic word embeddings revealed that fusing in English or German did not improve performance on the Arabic benchmarks. Furthermore, experiments implementing visual grounding for three languages jointly did not provide further accuracy.

The same findings can also be observed even when varying the size of the training and validation data. For example, for the same set of 82k images, adding German embeddings to English embeddings led to an improvement on benchmark tasks, whereas adding Arabic embeddings did not. In the discussion section, we provide a detailed discussion of why Arabic embeddings do not provide further precision for English or German grounded embeddings.

6.3 Word Categorization Evaluation

We also evaluated our embeddings on six categorization benchmarks: Battig (Battig and Montague, 1969), AP (Almuhareb and Poesio, 2005), BLESS (Baroni and Lenci, 2011), and three tasks published at (ESSLLI, 2009), (ESSLLI-a, 2009), which focuses on grouping concrete nouns into semantic

	WSim	MEN	RW	MTurk	SimVerb	SimLex	Mean
Textual	73.8	80.5	45.5	71.5	28.3	40.8	56.7
Grounded EN	77.7	**84.8**	51.9	73.3	**38.02**	**52.2**	62.9
Grounded EN (82k)	76.03	84.5	50.3	72.7	34.9	48.6	61.2
Grounded EN + DE	**79.2**	**84.8**	**52.3**	74.1	36.6	51.03	**63**
Grounded EN + DE (82k)	75.3	84.3	50.8	**74.2**	34.5	49.1	61.4
Grounded EN + AR	76.9	84.7	50.3	73.1	34.3	48.3	61.3
Grounded EN + DE + AR	76.7	84.3	51.1	73.9	33.3	48.04	61.2

Table 1: Performance of textual and grounded English embeddings on similarity/relatedness benchmarks. Results include different combinations of the three languages, English (EN), German (DE), and Arabic (AR). Inter-lingual grounding in English and German outperforms both the textual and monolingual grounded embeddings.

	WSim	SimLex	Mean
Textual	46.6	30.9	38.8
Grounded DE	56.2	36.9	46.6
Grounded DE (82k)	56.3	35.8	46.1
Grounded DE + EN	**57.02**	**37.2**	**47.1**
Grounded DE + AR	55.5	33.2	44.3
Grounded DE + EN (82k)	56.6	35.1	45.9
Grounded DE + EN + AR	54.1	33.2	43.7

Table 2: Performance of textual and grounded German embeddings on similarity/relatedness benchmarks. Results include different combinations of German embeddings with two other languages: English (EN), and Arabic (AR). Grounding in both German and English outperforms all other monolingual groundings.

	WSim	Almarsoomi	MC30	Saif40	Mean
Textual	30.7	65.9	49.9	71.8	54.6
Grounded AR	**41.9**	72.8	**59.2**	80.6	**63.6**
Grounded AR + EN	39.7	72.8	56.9	**83.2**	63.2
Grounded AR + DE	36.9	**75.2**	52.6	77.05	60.4
Grounded AR + EN + DE	39.6	73.9	56.2	75.5	61.3

Table 3: Performance of textual and grounded Arabic embeddings on similarity/relatedness benchmarks. Results include different combinations of Arabic embeddings with two other languages: English (EN), and German (DE).

	Battig	AP	BLESS	ESSLLI-a	ESSLLI-b	ESSLLI-c	Mean
Textual	45.4	60.4	**87.5**	75.0	75.0	62.2	67.6
Grounded EN	47.03	60.7	80.5	75.0	75.0	**64.4**	67.1
Grounded EN + DE	48.6	62.4	87	**84.1**	77.5	60.0	**69.9**
Grounded EN + FA	47.1	64.4	85.5	81.8	**80.0**	**64.4**	**70.5**
Grounded EN + AR	**49.8**	**64.9**	79.5	**84.1**	75.0	**64.4**	69.6
Grounded EN + DE + AR	47.5	64.7	85.5	75.0	75.0	62.2	68.3
Grounded EN + DE (82k)	47.1	65.9	81.5	84.1	77.5	55.6	68.6

Table 4: Performance of textual and grounded English embeddings on Categorization benchmarks. Results include different combinations of the three languages, English (EN), German (DE), Arabic (AR), and Persian (FA).

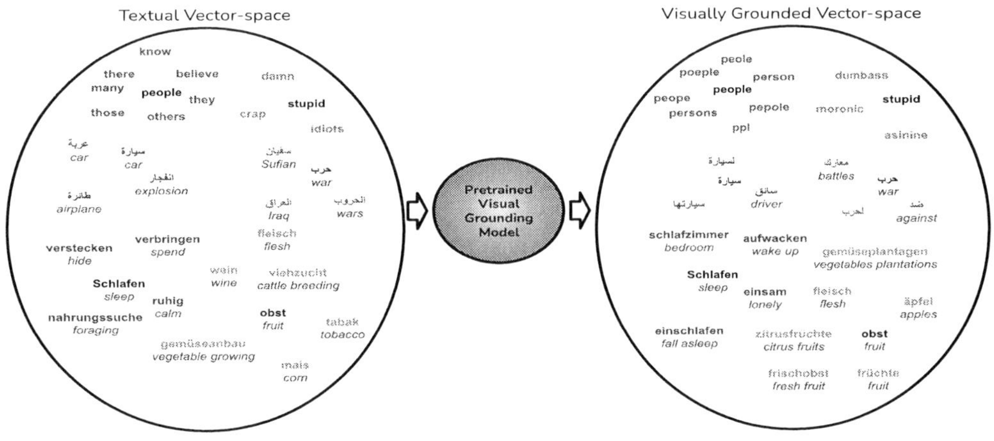

Figure 2: Comparisons of the textual and grounded vector spaces for English, German, and Arabic. For each query word (in black), out of the 10 nearest neighbours, the neighbours unique to each space are displayed. Visual grounding better captures a word's meaning and reduces the dependency on just co-occurrence statistics.

categories; (ESSLLI-b, 2009), which tests computational models for their ability to discriminate between abstract and concrete nouns; and (ESSLLI-c, 2009), which groups verbs into semantic categories.

The concept-categorization task requires clustering a set of nouns expressing basic-level concepts into gold standard categories. To evaluate on this task, clustering is performed using a k-means clustering algorithm (Likas et al., 2003). Performance is evaluated using a purity score between the truth and predicted cluster labels. Results are presented in Table 4. Monolingual grounding did not result in improvements on this benchmark; grounded English embeddings revealed worse performance on BLESS compared to the textual embeddings. However, adding a second language solved this problem. Incorporation of both German and Arabic embeddings resulted in improved performance of the English embeddings on all benchmarks. However, combining the three languages did not give rise to further improvements. Interestingly, for the smaller dataset size (82k images), Arabic had a better performance than German, a result that contrasts with those obtained for the similarity benchmarks.

More Languages: We further extended our experiments by using the Persian language. For this aim, we translated the COCO captions using google translate API[1] and made use of a pre-trained GloVe word embeddings model[2] train on OSCAR (Abadji et al., 2022). Similar to other languages grounding textual Persian embeddings significantly boosted the result (Spearman's correlation) by more than 10% (from 36.7 to 47) on the SemEval2017 benchmark (Camacho-Collados et al., 2017). Due to time constraints, we only trained the grounded embeddings from English + Persian and evaluated them on the word categorization benchmarks. As shown in Table 4, Adding Persian (denoted as FA) results in the best mean performance.

To further analyze the interaction of visual grounding with multiple languages, we made use of the BLESS (Baroni and Lenci, 2011) dataset. This dataset consists of tuples of the format *(concept-relation-relatum)*. For example, *lizard-attri-striped*: the concept *lizard* is linked to the relatum *striped* via the *attribute* relation. BLESS focuses on a set of basic concrete nouns and explicit semantic relations. Additionally, it contains a number of random relatum words that are not semantically related to any of the concepts. The tasks that come with this dataset it to detect which words are related to a given concept, as well as determining the type of relation involved. The dataset comprises 200 concepts grouped into 17 classes.

BLESS includes 5 types of relations, in-addition to the random relations: **COORD**: the relatum is a noun that is a co-hyponym (coordinate) of the concept: *dishwasher-coord-oven*. **HYPER**: the relatum is a noun that is a hypernym of the concept: dishwasher-hyper-appliance. **MERO** : the relatum is a noun referring to a

[1] https://libraries.io/pypi/googletrans

[2] https://github.com/taesiri/PersianWordVectors

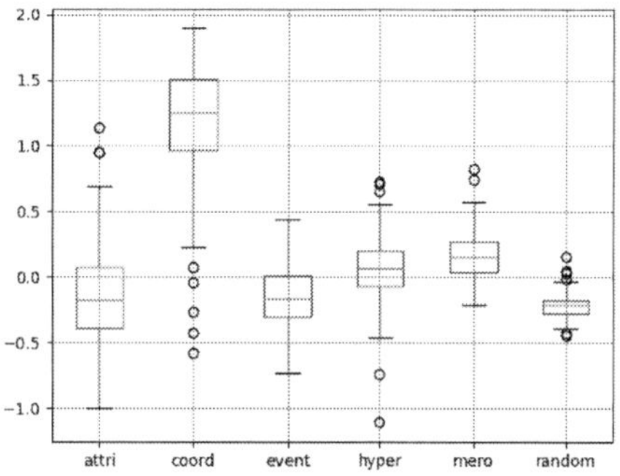

(a) Textual English embeddings

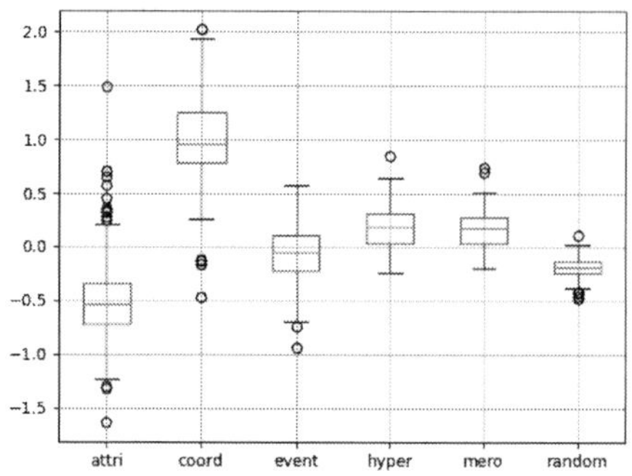

(b) Grounded English embeddings

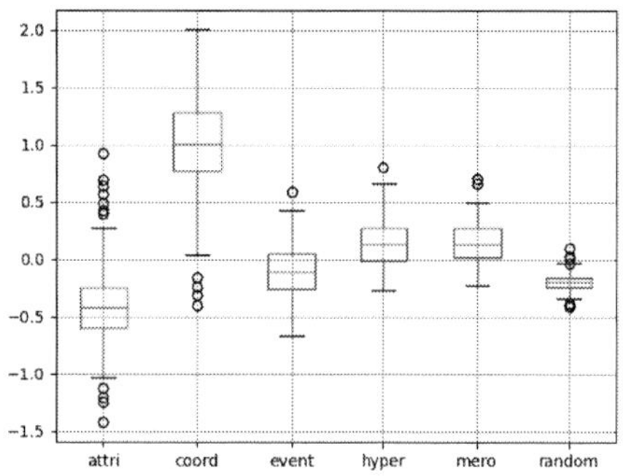

(c) Grounded English + German embeddings

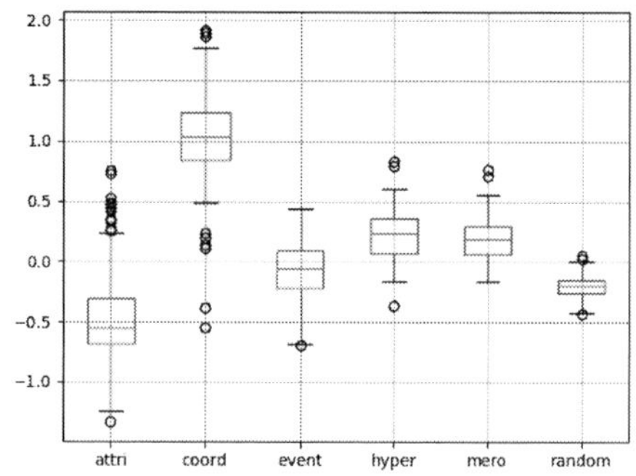

(d) Grounded English + Arabic embeddings

Figure 3: BLESS (Baroni and Lenci, 2011) Analyses of textual and grounded English embeddings with the combination of other languages. Visual grounding clearly reduces the variance on *attri* and *coord* categories resulting in more refined clusters and higher word categorization scores.

part/component/organ/member of the concept, or something that the concept contains or is made of: *dishwasher-mero-button*. **ATTRI** : the relatum is an adjective expressing an attribute of the concept: *dishwasher-attri-full*. **EVENT** : the relatum is a verb referring to an action/activity/happening/event the concept is involved in or is performed by/with the concept: *dishwasher-event-use*.

Using our embeddings, we calculated the mean cosine similarity score of each concept to all its relata across all relations. For each of the 200 BLESS concepts, we obtain six cosine similarity scores, one per relation: $C_{ir} = \frac{1}{n}\sum_{j=1}^{n} cos(C_i, Rel_{rj})$ where C_{ir} denotes the mean cosine score of concept i for relation r and n indicates the number of words per relation. The scores are then normalized across each concept as: $C_{ir} = \frac{C_{ir}-\mu_i}{\sigma_i}$, where μ_i and σ_i denote the mean and the standard deviation of the scores of C_i across all relations. Figure 3 presents the distribution of scores per relation across the 200 concepts. While the coarse structures of all the embeddings are relatively similar with respect to the scores (cosine similarity) across relations, the figures reveal interesting properties. For instance, the distributions in both *attri* and *coord* are more compact when visual grounding is applied. That is, the model is more certain about the similarity between the words and hence creates a more refined cluster of words. Another interesting point is the increased mean in the *hyper* category, especially for Arabic, in line with the results reported in Table 4.

Moreover, visual grounding lowers the mean score on *coord* category across all languages; this is probably because of the visually different word pairs in *coord* category. For example, (*turtle*, *alligator*) and (*toaster*, *stove*) are not visually similar. Therefore, their word vectors diverge as the result of grounding. These findings are in line with previous findings that visual grounding prioritizes similarity over relatedness (Shahmohammadi et al., 2021). Surprising at first sight is that the mean score of *attri* category is lower in all grounding setups. This, however, may be due to the rather different sets of attributes in BLESS and in our image captions. Many of the attributes used in BLESS rarely occur in image captions, examples are *antarctic*, *amphibious*, *aquatic*, and *noisy*.

In order to statistically validate these findings, we applied a Gaussian Location-Scale Generalized Additive Mixed Model (GAMM) (Wood, 2017), with word as random-effect factor, and main effects for *embedding type* and *relation* for both mean and variance. This analysis revealed that the grounded English embeddings (monolingual grounding) had the highest mean score, followed by the grounded English embeddings generated by integrating English and German, followed closely by the English + Arabic embeddings. Interestingly, compared to the textual embeddings, the variance for grounded embeddings is reduced, and even more reduced for inter-lingual grounded embeddings with Arabic and German. Thus, there seems to be a trade-off between mean and variance. While monolingual grounding had the highest mean score, inter-lingual grounding helped more in reducing the variance, resulting in more refined clusters of semantically related words.

Comparing the mean of scores with respect to the different relations, with the *random* relation as the baseline, we noticed that the mean decreases for *attri*, but increases for all other relations, and noticeably so for the *hyper* and *mero* relations. The variance, on the other hand, increases for all relations and to the greatest extent for *attr* and *coord*. These statistical results dovetail well with our previously mentioned conclusions about visually different word pairs in *coord* category and the difference in *attributes* between the BLESS data and our image captions. Overall, the boxplots indicate that inter-lingual visual grounding creates more refined clusters of word vectors in the vector space based on visual clues in the training sets.

7 Discussion

We proposed an inter-lingual visual grounding model on textual word embeddings. Our model thus far supports the benefit of visual grounding and inter-lingual visual grounding on various word similarity and word categorization benchmarks. Some of the results in Section 6 however are hard to interpret. In this section, we will discuss possible explanations for the model's behavior on different tasks across different languages.

On the word similarity benchmarks (Tables 1, 2, and 3) we observe that German and English seem to interact more efficiently than Arabic with either. We believe the slight degradation in performance when adding Arabic might be due to the fact that the Arabic language structure is quite different: much more information is packed into its verbs, and pronouns are used differently and more sparingly. Moreover, its orthography leaves out a lot of phonological information (hardly any vowels), so word embeddings are much more ambiguous relative to English or German. Therefore, the semantic spaces that are constructed are much less similar to that in the two other languages. Apart from the evident differences between Arabic and the other two languages, it is worth mentioning that adding Arabic is far from detrimental. That is, the resulting embeddings (Arabic added) still outperform the textual embeddings significantly. This implies that there exists a linearly aligned common core between the three languages (vector spaces) which as observed in section 6.3, yielded the lowest variance and more pure vector space. Table 4 further supports these findings. Interestingly, the monolingual grounding of English does not seem to improve the categorization performance, inter-lingual knowledge, on the other hand, results in obvious improvements with respect to the mean score. The opposing impact of adding Arabic on the similarity/relatedness results in contrast to the categorization results indicates the need for further investigation on the evaluation criteria of inter-lingual embeddings.

Furthermore, it is not clear why monolingual visual grounding is more beneficial for word similarity compared to word categorization. We think cultural biases might play a role. For example, our training set (the COCO image dataset) is likely culture-specific, with a strong bias toward the US culture, and our benchmarks are compiled with various purposes across different languages. We, therefore, believe that current evaluation benchmarks only shine light on some facets of the complex interplay of different languages in visual grounding, and further investigation is required for more coherent interpretations.

8 Conclusions

The main purpose of this study is to shed light on the problem of inter-lingual visual grounding. We stated the importance of grounding in language understanding and the cognitive plausibility of text representations. We also suggested a baseline architecture for inter-lingual visual grounding and analyzed the performance of the resulting embeddings on word similarity and categorization benchmarks.

Our findings indicate that inter-lingual features lead to improvements on both similarity and categorization benchmarks with a more significant effect on categorization. Our results on the similarity benchmarks indicate that inter-lingual visual grounding is more beneficial for related languages such as English and German, but can lead to reduced performance when unrelated languages, such as English and Arabic, or German and Arabic, are considered jointly. On the other hand, Arabic provided the most improvement on categorization benchmarks for grounded English embeddings.

We hope that these initial steps towards inter-lingual visual grounding inspire further research. Low-resourced languages might benefit from joint processing with high-resourced languages in multilingual models but one has to make sure that their unique characteristics are not overwhelmed and masked by datasets acquired in different cultural settings.

Limitations

The architecture that we made use of for exploring multi-lingual visual grounding has the limitation that embeddings from different languages, which define high-dimensional spaces that are in all likelihood not congruent, constitute the input for visual grounding. One direction for future research is to first align the embeddings of different languages. A large multilingual language model such as XLM (Lample and Conneau, 2019) may help to better capture shared inter-lingual features, while at the same time retaining the linear alignment that restricts the extent to which vision can affect text-based semantics. Another possibility is to use an unsupervised technique (Conneau et al., 2017) to generate cross-lingual embeddings, which can then be used as initializers for our grounding architecture.

Acknowledgements

This work has been supported by EXC number 2064/1 – Project num- ber 390727645, the German Federal Ministry of Education and Research (BMBF): Tübingen AI Center, FKZ: 01IS18039A, and the European research council, project WIDE-742545. The authors thank the International Max Planck Research School for Intelligent Systems (IMPRS-IS) for supporting Hassan Shahmohammadi. We appreciate the contribution of (Biswas et al., 2021) from the German Research Center of Artificial Intelligence (DFKI) who have provided us with the German COCO captions upon request.

References

Julien Abadji, Pedro Ortiz Suarez, Laurent Romary, and Benoît Sagot. 2022. Towards a Cleaner Document-Oriented Multilingual Crawled Corpus. *arXiv e-prints*, page arXiv:2201.06642.

Faaza A Almarsoomi, James D OShea, Zuhair Bandar, and Keeley Crockett. 2013. Awss: An algorithm for measuring arabic word semantic similarity. In *2013 IEEE international conference on systems, man, and cybernetics*, pages 504–509. IEEE.

Abdulrahman Almuhareb and Massimo Poesio. 2005. Concept learning and categorization from the web. In *proceedings of the annual meeting of the Cognitive Science society*, volume 27.

Jordi Armengol-Estapé, Casimiro Pio Carrino, Carlos Rodriguez-Penagos, Ona de Gibert Bonet, Carme Armentano-Oller, Aitor Gonzalez-Agirre, Maite Melero, and Marta Villegas. 2021. Are multilingual models the best choice for moderately under-resourced languages? a comprehensive assessment for catalan. *arXiv preprint arXiv:2107.07903*.

Marco Baroni and Alessandro Lenci. 2011. How we blessed distributional semantic evaluation. In *Proceedings of the GEMS 2011 Workshop on GEometrical Models of Natural Language Semantics*, pages 1–10.

William F Battig and William E Montague. 1969. Category norms of verbal items in 56 categories a replication and extension of the connecticut category norms. *Journal of experimental Psychology*, 80(3p2):1.

Rajarshi Biswas, Michael Barz, Mareike Hartmann, and Daniel Sonntag. 2021. Improving german image captions using machine translation and transfer learning. In *International Conference on Statistical Language and Speech Processing*, pages 3–14. Springer.

Elia Bruni, Nam-Khanh Tran, and Marco Baroni. 2014. Multimodal distributional semantics. *Journal of artificial intelligence research*, 49:1–47.

Andrea Burns, Donghyun Kim, Derry Wijaya, Kate Saenko, and Bryan A Plummer. 2020. Learning to scale multilingual representations for vision-language tasks. In *European Conference on Computer Vision*, pages 197–213. Springer.

Jose Camacho-Collados, Mohammad Taher Pilehvar, Nigel Collier, and Roberto Navigli. 2017. Semeval-2017 task 2: Multilingual and cross-lingual semantic word similarity. Association for Computational Linguistics.

Xi Chen, Xiao Wang, Soravit Changpinyo, AJ Piergiovanni, Piotr Padlewski, Daniel Salz, Sebastian Goodman, Adam Grycner, Basil Mustafa, Lucas Beyer, et al. 2022. Pali: A jointly-scaled multilingual language-image model. *arXiv preprint arXiv:2209.06794*.

Alexis Conneau, Guillaume Lample, Marc'Aurelio Ranzato, Ludovic Denoyer, and Hervé Jégou. 2017. Word translation without parallel data. *arXiv preprint arXiv:1710.04087*.

Jia Deng, Wei Dong, Richard Socher, Li-Jia Li, Kai Li, and Li Fei-Fei. 2009. Imagenet: A large-scale hierarchical image database. In *2009 IEEE conference on computer vision and pattern recognition*, pages 248–255. Ieee.

Timothy Dozat. 2016. Incorporating nesterov momentum into adam.

ESSLLI. 2009. https://esslli2009.labri.fr/.

ESSLLI-a. 2009. http://wordspace.collocations.de/doku.php/data:esslli2008:concrete_nouns_categorization.

ESSLLI-b. 2009. http://wordspace.collocations.de/doku.php/data:esslli2008:abstract_concrete_nouns_discrimination.

ESSLLI-c. 2009. http://wordspace.collocations.de/doku.php/data:esslli2008:verb_categorization.

Lev Finkelstein, Evgeniy Gabrilovich, Yossi Matias, Ehud Rivlin, Zach Solan, Gadi Wolfman, and Eytan Ruppin. 2001. Placing search in context: The concept revisited. In *Proceedings of the 10th international conference on World Wide Web*, pages 406–414.

Daniela Gerz, Ivan Vulić, Felix Hill, Roi Reichart, and Anna Korhonen. 2016. Simverb-3500: A large-scale evaluation set of verb similarity. *arXiv preprint arXiv:1608.00869*.

Stevan Harnad. 1990. The symbol grounding problem. *Physica D: Nonlinear Phenomena*, 42(1-3):335–346.

Mika Hasegawa, Tetsunori Kobayashi, and Yoshihiko Hayashi. 2017. Incorporating visual features into word embeddings: A bimodal autoencoder-based approach. In *IWCS 2017—12th International Conference on Computational Semantics—Short papers*.

Muhammad Hashim. 2020. Arabic coco. https://github.com/canesee-project/Arabic-COCO.

Samer Hassan and Rada Mihalcea. 2009. Cross-lingual semantic relatedness using encyclopedic knowledge. In *Proceedings of the 2009 conference on empirical methods in natural language processing*, pages 1192–1201.

Felix Hill, Roi Reichart, and Anna Korhonen. 2015. Simlex-999: Evaluating semantic models with (genuine) similarity estimation. *Computational Linguistics*, 41(4):665–695.

Yu Huang, Chenzhuang Du, Zihui Xue, Xuanyao Chen, Hang Zhao, and Longbo Huang. 2021. What makes multi-modal learning better than single (provably). *Advances in Neural Information Processing Systems*, 34:10944–10956.

Jamie Kiros, William Chan, and Geoffrey Hinton. 2018. Illustrative language understanding: Large-scale visual grounding with image search. In *Proceedings of the 56th Annual Meeting of the Association for Computational Linguistics (Volume 1: Long Papers)*, pages 922–933.

Karol Kurach, Sylvain Gelly, Michal Jastrzebski, Philip Haeusser, Olivier Teytaud, Damien Vincent, and Olivier Bousquet. 2017. Better text understanding through image-to-text transfer. *arXiv preprint arXiv:1705.08386*.

Guillaume Lample and Alexis Conneau. 2019. Cross-lingual language model pretraining. *arXiv preprint arXiv:1901.07291*.

Ira Leviant and Roi Reichart. 2015. Separated by an un-common language: Towards judgment language informed vector space modeling. *arXiv preprint arXiv:1508.00106*.

Aristidis Likas, Nikos Vlassis, and Jakob J Verbeek. 2003. The global k-means clustering algorithm. *Pattern recognition*, 36(2):451–461.

Tsung-Yi Lin, Michael Maire, Serge Belongie, James Hays, Pietro Perona, Deva Ramanan, Piotr Dollár, and C Lawrence Zitnick. 2014. Microsoft coco: Common objects in context. In *European conference on computer vision*, pages 740–755. Springer.

Minh-Thang Luong, Richard Socher, and Christopher D. Manning. 2013. Better word representations with recursive neural networks for morphology. In *CoNLL*, Sofia, Bulgaria.

Alireza Mohammadshahi, Rémi Lebret, and Karl Aberer. 2019. Aligning multilingual word embeddings for cross-modal retrieval task. *arXiv preprint arXiv:1910.03291*.

Minheng Ni, Haoyang Huang, Lin Su, Edward Cui, Taroon Bharti, Lijuan Wang, Dongdong Zhang, and Nan Duan. 2021. M3p: Learning universal representations via multitask multilingual multimodal pre-training. In *Proceedings of the IEEE/CVF conference on computer vision and pattern recognition*, pages 3977–3986.

Jeffrey Pennington, Richard Socher, and Christopher D Manning. 2014. Glove: Global vectors for word representation. In *Proceedings of the 2014 conference on empirical methods in natural language processing (EMNLP)*, pages 1532–1543.

Kira Radinsky, Eugene Agichtein, Evgeniy Gabrilovich, and Shaul Markovitch. 2011. A word at a time: computing word relatedness using temporal semantic analysis. In *Proceedings of the 20th international conference on World wide web*, pages 337–346.

A Saif, MJ Ab Aziz, and N Omar. 2014. Evaluating knowledge-based semantic measures on arabic. *International Journal on Communications Antenna and Propagation*, 4(5):180–194.

Hassan Shahmohammadi, Maria Heitmeier, Elnaz Shafaei-Bajestan, Hendrik Lensch, and Harald Baayen. 2022. Language with vision: a study on grounded word and sentence embeddings. *arXiv preprint arXiv:2206.08823*.

Hassan Shahmohammadi, Hendrik Lensch, and R Harald Baayen. 2021. Learning zero-shot multifaceted visually grounded word embeddings via multi-task training. *arXiv preprint arXiv:2104.07500*.

Carina Silberer and Mirella Lapata. 2014. Learning grounded meaning representations with autoencoders. In *Proceedings of the 52nd Annual Meeting of the Association for Computational Linguistics (Volume 1: Long Papers)*, pages 721–732.

Christian Szegedy, Vincent Vanhoucke, Sergey Ioffe, Jon Shlens, and Zbigniew Wojna. 2016. Rethinking the inception architecture for computer vision. In *Proceedings of the IEEE conference on computer vision and pattern recognition*, pages 2818–2826.

S. N. Wood. 2017. *Generalized Additive Models*. Chapman & Hall/CRC, New York.

Mingyang Zhou, Luowei Zhou, Shuohang Wang, Yu Cheng, Linjie Li, Zhou Yu, and Jingjing Liu. 2021. Uc2: Universal cross-lingual cross-modal vision-and-language pre-training. In *Proceedings of the IEEE/CVF Conference on Computer Vision and Pattern Recognition*, pages 4155–4165.

A Subspace-Based Analysis of Structured and Unstructured Representations in Image-Text Retrieval

Erica K. Shimomoto[1], Edison Marrese-Taylor[1], Hiroya Takamura[1], Ichiro Kobayashi[1,2], Yusuke Miyao[1,3]
National Institute of Advanced Industrial Science and Technology[1]
Ochanomizu University[2], The University of Tokyo[3]
{kidoshimomoto.e,edison.marrese,takamura.hiroya}@aist.go.jp
koba@is.ocha.ac.jp, yusuke@is.s.u-tokyo.ac.jp

Abstract

In this paper, we specifically look at the image-text retrieval problem. Recent multimodal frameworks have shown that structured inputs and fine-tuning lead to consistent performance improvement. However, this paradigm has been challenged recently with newer Transformer-based models that can reach zero-shot state-of-the-art results despite not explicitly using structured data during pre-training. Since such strategies lead to increased computational resources, we seek to better understand their role in image-text retrieval by analyzing visual and text representations extracted with three multimodal frameworks: SGM, UNITER, and CLIP. To perform such analysis, we represent a single image or text as low-dimensional linear subspaces and perform retrieval based on subspace similarity. We chose this representation as subspaces give us the flexibility to model an entity based on feature sets, allowing us to observe how integrating or reducing information changes the representation of each entity. We analyze the performance of the selected models' features on two standard benchmark datasets. Our results indicate that heavily pre-training models can already lead to features with critical information representing each entity, with zero-shot UNITER features performing consistently better than fine-tuned features. Furthermore, while models can benefit from structured inputs, learning representations for objects and relationships separately, such as in SGM, likely causes a loss of crucial contextual information needed to obtain a compact cluster that can effectively represent a single entity.

1 Introduction

The integration of techniques from Natural Language Processing (NLP) and Computer Vision (CV) has led to the development of multimodal approaches, which have quickly attracted the scientific community's attention. Examples include tasks such as image captioning (Hossain et al., 2019), machine translation (Specia et al., 2016; Elliott et al., 2017), word sense disambiguation (Bevilacqua et al., 2021), and visual question answering (Antol et al., 2015). Great progress in these tasks has been made by using massive amounts of training data with deeper models, leading to rapidly increasing computational costs.

In this paper, we specifically look at the image-text retrieval task, where the goal is to retrieve an image from a text query (image retrieval) or a text from an image query (text retrieval) from a database containing images and texts. In this context, we see a line of works encoding local and global structures to learn representations for both modalities, extracted using object detectors (Qu et al., 2020) and large pre-trained language models (Diao et al., 2021). To further understand the relationship between such structures, several works also encoded visual (Shi et al., 2019) and textual (Wang et al., 2020) scene-graphs or designed their pipelines to learn such graphs (Schroeder and Tripathi, 2020).

A more recent trend has been to use Transformer-based models to learn the representations for each modality and to model their interaction (Chen et al., 2020), also making use of such structured data (Messina et al., 2021; Dong et al., 2022). While these frameworks have resulted in state-of-the-art performance in multiple downstream tasks, including image-text retrieval, the inference is computationally expensive for this task as it requires a forward pass of each image-text pair in the database to perform retrieval.

Although structured inputs and fine-tuning have shown consistent performance improvement across all the aforementioned models, this paradigm has been challenged recently with newer Transformer-based models, such as CLIP (Radford et al., 2021). This model, for example, can not only reduce the computational inference overhead by allowing the images and texts to be processed individually, but

Proceedings of the Workshop on Unimodal and Multimodal Induction of Linguistic Structures (UM-IoS), pages 29 - 44
December 7, 2022 ©2022 Association for Computational Linguistics

it also achieves zero-shot state-of-the-art results for image-text retrieval despite not explicitly using structured data during its pre-training.

In light of these issues, this paper analyzes visual and text representations produced by several multimodal frameworks in the task of image-text retrieval. We are particularly interested in studying the ability of these models in encoding relevant information to perform retrieval in a variety of scenarios, including model fine-tuning versus zero-shot performance for models that require pre-training, as well as how the addition or removal of structure information from images (e.g., scene-graphs) and texts (e.g., semantic triplets), affects such representations. We find it pivotal to understand the role of such strategies as their integration ultimately leads to increased computational resources.

To perform such an analysis, we set a common ground by looking at subspace representations in the context of image-text retrieval. In the subspace setting, the idea is to represent a single entity, e.g., an image or a sentence, as a low-dimensional linear subspace in the original high-dimensional feature space and to perform retrieval based on subspace similarity. Such representation is based on the empirical evidence that patterns of the same entity (e.g., pictures of the same person) tend to cluster in high-dimensional space (Watanabe and Pakvasa, 1973; Iijima et al., 1974). We expect features from the same entity learned by such multimodal frameworks also form these compact clusters, and therefore their distribution can be represented by linear subspaces. Furthermore, as most image-text retrieval frameworks rely on the cosine similarity between feature vectors to compare two entities, the subspace similarity comes in handy as it is equivalent to cosine similarity when we have one-dimensional subspaces (i.e., a single vector representing an entity). Finally, subspaces give us the flexibility to model an entity based on a set of vectors, e.g., a set of object embeddings in an image or set of entities in a sentence, allowing us to observe how integrating more information by fine-tuning or adding structure data, changes the representation of each entity.

This paper focuses on frameworks that explicitly incorporate or capture structured inputs, either from the visual or textual side. Concretely, we evaluate and compare the text-image retrieval performance using the subspace representation of features extracted using three frameworks: SGM (Wang et al., 2020), UNITER (Chen et al., 2020), and CLIP (Radford et al., 2021). We chose these three models based on the distinct way they treat multimodal data: SGM, a scene graph-based model, heavily relies on structured data, generating object-level and relationship-level cross-modal features; UNITER, a pre-trained Transformer-based model that generates joint visual and textual embeddings relying on objects detected on the input images; and CLIP, a pre-trained contrastive model which is trained by simply pairing whole images with complete sentences and without making explicit use of structure, which also allows us to extract of image and text embeddings individually in a zero-shot fashion, overcoming the limitations of previous models such as UNITER.

We analyze the performance of feature subspaces of selected models on two standard benchmark datasets, COCO (Lin et al., 2014) and Flickr30k (Young et al., 2014; Plummer et al., 2015), focusing on the tasks of image-to-text and text-to-image retrieval. Furthermore, we observe how results change when modeling pre-trained and fine-tuned features from UNITER and introducing or removing structure information from SGM and CLIP features. Our results indicate that UNITER's pre-training leads to features with critical information representing each entity during pre-training, with zero-shot features performing consistently better than fine-tuned features. Moreover, we observed that learning representations for objects and relationships separately, such as in SGM, likely causes a loss of crucial contextual information needed to effectively represent a single entity, whereas using only SGM's object representations led to better performance. This result might explain why CLIP features can better characterize entities when features are extracted based on global features, where we observed that explicitly considering local structure information harms retrieval performance.

2 Background

2.1 Subspace representation

Given a set of entities (i.e., images, sentences) whose representations lie on a rich high-dimensional feature space, subspace-based methods aim to encode a set of features representing a given entity (i.e., CNN features from an image, word vectors from a sentence) by a lower-dimensional linear subspace in the original feature space. While there are several ways to obtain the subspace representation, we focus on the formulation based on principal component analysis (PCA). The reason that leads us to consider this method is that PCA can compactly represent the distribution of the features in a set based on the directions of highest variance. Such characteristics lead to a model that can discard irrelevant information, such as noise, while effectively representing variations, e.g., rotation and illumination in images.

Formally, consider a set of N feature vectors $\{\boldsymbol{x}_i\}_{i=1}^N$ representing an entity, stacked as the columns of the matrix $\boldsymbol{X} \in \mathbb{R}^{p\times N}$, where p is the dimension of the original feature space. We apply PCA without data centering to model a subspace from this set of features. The orthonormal basis vectors of the m-dimensional subspace $\mathcal{Y}$ are obtained as the eigenvectors with the m largest eigenvalues $\{\lambda_l\}_{l=1}^m$ of the matrix $\boldsymbol{R} = \boldsymbol{X}\boldsymbol{X}^\top$. The entity is finally represented as $\boldsymbol{Y} = [\boldsymbol{\Phi}_1 \ldots \boldsymbol{\Phi}_m] \in \mathbb{R}^{p\times m}$, which has the corresponding orthonormal basis vectors as its column vectors. For simplicity, we will refer to the subspaces by their bases matrices. Such basis vectors can be interpreted as the main hidden features representing the distribution of the features in the set.

Though several subspace-based methods have been developed over the course of the past 50 years, mainly for image classification, the most relevant variations for this work are the Subspace Method (SM) and the Mutual Subspace Method (MSM; Maeda, 2010), as they establish two important similarity measures that we need to perform image-text retrieval.

Vector-subspace similarity in SM: Consider we have k reference classes represented as m_i-dimensional subspaces $\{\boldsymbol{Y}_i\}_{i=1}^k$ in a p-dimensional vector space, where $m_i < p$. SM seeks to classify an input entity represented by a single feature vector $\boldsymbol{v}_{in}$ normalized to have norm 1. To measure the similarity between the input feature vector $\boldsymbol{v}_{in}$ and a class reference subspace $\boldsymbol{Y}_i$, defined as $S^{in,i} = \boldsymbol{v}_{in}^\top \boldsymbol{P}_i \boldsymbol{v}_{in}$, where $\boldsymbol{P}_i = \boldsymbol{Y}_i\boldsymbol{Y}_i^\top$ is the projection matrix onto the subspace $\boldsymbol{Y}_i$.

Subspace-subspace similarity in MSM: MSM is a generalization of SM, where both input and references are represented as subspaces. Such an approach has been shown to improve the robustness when applied to image-set classification tasks (Maeda, 2010; Fukui and Maki, 2015).

In MSM, the input is represented by a subspace $\boldsymbol{Y}_{in}$ modeled from a set of feature vectors $\{\boldsymbol{x}_i\}_{i=1}^N$. To perform classification, it is necessary to calculate the similarity between the input subspace $\boldsymbol{Y}_{in}$ and the i-th class subspace $\boldsymbol{Y}_i$. This similarity is measured by using the canonical angles between them (Chatelin, 2012). We can calculate them by using the singular value decomposition (SVD) (Fukui and Yamaguchi, 2005).

Consider two subspaces, $\boldsymbol{Y}_{in} \in \mathbb{R}^{p\times m_{in}}$ and $\boldsymbol{Y}_i \in \mathbb{R}^{p\times m_i}$, with m_{in} and m_i dimensions respectively, and $m_{in} \leq m_i$. We first calculate the SVD $\boldsymbol{Y}_{in}^\top \boldsymbol{Y}_i = \boldsymbol{U}\boldsymbol{\Sigma}\boldsymbol{V}^\top$, where $\boldsymbol{\Sigma} = \mathrm{diag}(\kappa_1, \ldots, \kappa_{m_{in}})$, $\{\kappa_j\}_{j=1}^{m_{in}}$ represents the set of singular values, and $(\kappa_1 \geq \ldots \geq \kappa_{m_{in}})$. The similarity can then be calculated as $S^{in,i}(t) = \frac{1}{t}\sum_{j=1}^t \kappa_j^2$, where $1 \leq t \leq m_{in}$. This similarity is equivalent to taking the average of the squared cosine of t canonical angles.

Vector-vector similarity: In the special case where both input and reference subspaces have only one dimension, i.e., $\boldsymbol{Y}_{in} = \boldsymbol{\Phi}_{in} \in \mathbb{R}^{p\times 1}$ and $\boldsymbol{Y}_i = \boldsymbol{\Phi}_i \in \mathbb{R}^{p\times 1}$, the subspace similarity is equivalent to the cosine similarity $S^{in,i} = \boldsymbol{\Phi}_{in}^\top \boldsymbol{\Phi}_i$, where both $\boldsymbol{\Phi}_{in}$ and $\boldsymbol{\Phi}_i$ have norm equal to 1.

2.2 Multimodal retrieval frameworks

We used features obtained from three multimodal frameworks that can generate sets of features representing each entity in each modality. As all of our selected models achieve outstanding performance in image-text retrieval while leveraging different types of information, we are interested in studying how varying such input affects the representation of each entity by assessing their performance when using the subspace representation. We briefly introduce our selected models below, referring the reader to the original papers for more details.

2.2.1 SGM

Wang et al. (2020) proposed a scene-graph matching framework (SGM) for image-text retrieval. Concretely, they encode visual and textual scene-graphs in a joint embedding space, resulting in a representation vector for each object and relationship in both modalities. This framework has four main parts, which we describe below.

Scene-graph parsers: Images are fed to a pre-trained scene-graph generator, such as MSDN (Li et al., 2017) and Neural Motifs (Zellers et al., 2018). The obtained visual scene-graphs contain both object and relationship nodes, and each of them has a text label. On the textual side, scene-graphs also contain object and relationship nodes; In addition, textual scene-graphs also have two types of edges: *Word order edge*, which follows the order of the words in the texts; and *Semantic edge*, which is obtained by parsing semantic triplets using SPICE (Anderson et al., 2016), relating objects by their relationships.

Visual graph encoder: Visual features are extracted by encoding the image regions into feature vectors by using a Faster-RCNN. The feature vectors from **object nodes** are extracted from its corresponding image region, and the feature vectors from **relationship nodes** are extracted from the union of the image region of the two object nodes that are connected by the relationship node. Then, these visual features are fused with the word embedding corresponding to the node's label through a multimodal fusion layer. Finally, this graph is encoded by a Graph Convolutional Network, generating one feature vector for each object and each relationship nodes. This results in the feature sets $\boldsymbol{O} = \{\boldsymbol{h}_{o_i}\}_{i=1}^{N_o} \in \mathbb{R}^{1024 \times N_o}$, and $\boldsymbol{P} = \{\boldsymbol{h}_{p_i}\}_{i=1}^{N_p} \in \mathbb{R}^{1024 \times N_p}$.

Textual graph encoder: It consists of a word embedding layer, a word-level bi-GRU encoder, and a path-level bi-GRU. The word-level bi-GRU processes the nodes following the word order in the caption, while the path-level processes the nodes following the semantic paths. The final feature vector for each node is obtained by averaging the representation given by both bi-GRUs, resulting in the feature sets $\boldsymbol{W} = \{\boldsymbol{h}_{w_t}\}_{i=1}^{N_w} \in \mathbb{R}^{1024 \times N_w}$, and $\boldsymbol{R} = \{\boldsymbol{h}_{r_i}\}_{i=1}^{N_r} \in \mathbb{R}^{1024 \times N_r}$.

Similarity calculation: Images and texts are compared based on two similarities: Between the visual and textual object nodes (S^o) and between the visual and textual relationship nodes (S^r), defined in Equations 1 and 2. The final graph-based similarity is obtained by summing S^o and S^r.

$$S^o = \frac{1}{N_w} \sum_{t=1}^{N_w} \max_{i \in [1, N_o]} \boldsymbol{h}_{w_t}^T \boldsymbol{h}_{o_i} \tag{1}$$

$$S^r = \frac{1}{N_p} \sum_{t=1}^{N_p} \max_{i \in [1, N_r]} \boldsymbol{h}_{p_t}^T \boldsymbol{h}_{r_i} \tag{2}$$

2.2.2 UNITER

UNiversal Image-TExt Representation (Chen et al., 2020) (UNITER) is a Transformer-based large-scale pre-trained model for joint multimodal embedding. UNITER first goes through a designed pre-training task and learns generalizable contextualized embeddings for each region in an image and each word in an input text, and can be further fine-tuned for image-text retrieval. The model contains mainly two parts: image and text embedders and the transformer module.

Image and text embedders: For images, they first use Faster R-CNN (Ren et al., 2015) to extract visual features for each image region. Next, they encode this information along with the location of the features through a fully-connected layer and then project them into the joint embedding space. For text, they tokenize following BERT (Devlin et al., 2019). Finally, they sum the word embedding and position embedding to generate the final text representation on the joint embedding space.

Transformer module: A transformer module further processes both image and text embeddings, learning generalizable contextualized embeddings for each region and word. In our experiments, we use the output from this module to represent images and texts.

2.2.3 CLIP

Contrastive Language–Image Pre-training (Radford et al., 2021) is also a Transformer-based model which uses a simple contrastive pre-training to predict which caption matches a given caption. In this manner, the model can efficiently construct image and text representations. Natural language supervision is later used to ask the model to name learned visual concepts (or describe new ones), allowing zero-shot transfer to downstream tasks with state-of-the-art performance in many cases.

3 Subspace-based image-text retrieval

The goal of image-text retrieval is to find an image based on a text query (image retrieval) or a text passage based on an image query (text retrieval) from a database containing images and texts. Formally, given a query entity q in one modality, we seek to find the most similar entity e in the other modality.

In this paper, we represent entities and queries by the sets of features extracted from the multimodal frameworks described in the previous section and perform retrieval using subspace-based similarities. In doing so, we assume that the entities in the database are represented as subspaces $\{\boldsymbol{Y}_d\}_{d=1}^{N_d}$

modeled from each entity's feature set, and that the query entity is represented by a set of feature vectors $\{\boldsymbol{q}_i\}_{i=1}^{N_q}$, or by its subspace. Then, we compare the query and each database entity subspace using subspace similarity. We highlight that such setting is equivalent to comparing two feature vectors based on the cosine similarity when we only have one feature vector representing each entity.

We explore the two fundamental subspace similarities described in Section 2.1, performing image-text retrieval in two different ways: Retrieval based on SM and based on MSM.

3.1 SM-based retrieval

In this case, we use the vector-subspace similarity. Since SM assumes single vector inputs, we propose a modification so that the similarity between a set of features and a subspace is defined by the mean similarity between the query features $\{\boldsymbol{q}_i\}_{i=1}^{N_q}$ and the database entity subspace $\boldsymbol{Y}_d$:

$$S^{q,d} = \frac{1}{N_q} \sum_{j=1}^{N_q} \boldsymbol{q}_j^\top \boldsymbol{P}_d \boldsymbol{q}_j, \tag{3}$$

where $\boldsymbol{P}_d = \boldsymbol{Y}_d \boldsymbol{Y}_d^\top$ is the projection matrix onto the subspace of entity d in the database.

When using this similarity, we assume each feature vector of the query is equally important for retrieval.

3.2 MSM-based retrieval

In this case, we use the subspace-subspace similarity. First, we model the query subspace $\boldsymbol{Y}_q$ from its set of features. Then, we perform the search based on the subspace similarity defined in section 2.1.

Using this similarity, we find the closest hidden features in each subspace and measure the angles between them, i.e., the canonical angles. As PCA is used to model the subspaces, features that do not contribute to representing each entity vector set are considered less important to perform retrieval.

4 Experimental Framework

We experimented with image-text retrieval on two datasets, Flickr30k (Young et al., 2014; Plummer et al., 2015) (FLICKR30K) and COCO (Young et al., 2014; Lin et al., 2014) (COCO). Both datasets contain 5 captions (i.e., text passages) for each image. However, they differ in one order of magnitude regarding the number of examples (approx. 300K images on COCOand approx. 30K on FLICKR30K). Because of this reason, in order to keep computational costs within our budget, we used FLICKR30K to extensively study multiple settings and selected only the best configurations for our experiments with COCO.

In all cases, each image and caption is represented by a single or several feature vectors, and retrieval is performed using SM and MSM as defined earlier.

Our evaluation is performed based on the R@k metric, the percentage of queries whose ground-truth is ranked within the top k, which is the standard for the task. We experimented using different subspaces' dimensions and report the best results. Below, we give details about how our multi-modal features are extracted for each model.

SGM With this model, we are particularly interested in understanding how considering objects and their relationships affects retrieval. To extract the features, we use the model checkpoints trained on both datasets provided by the authors. Each image is represented by one set of visual object features $\boldsymbol{O} \in \mathbb{R}^{1024 \times N_o}$, and one set of visual relation features $\boldsymbol{P} \in \mathbb{R}^{1024 \times N_p}$. Each caption is represented by one set of textual object features $\boldsymbol{W} \in \mathbb{R}^{1024 \times N_w}$ and one set of textual relation features $\boldsymbol{R} \in \mathbb{R}^{1024 \times N_r}$.

Considering we have two sets of features representing each visual and textual entity, we followed the same strategy taken by SGM when performing retrieval by calculating S^o and S^r based on subspace similarity, and then summing both to achieve the final similarity for the pair $S^{o,r}$. To better understand the role of each set of features in representing an entity, we also performed retrieval based only on S^o, only on S^r, and on S^g, which represents each entity by the concatenation of the object and relation features.

UNITER As UNITER's excellent performance is due mostly to its extensive pre-training and fine-tuning, we are interested in comparing the retrieval performance of pre-trained features versus fine-tuned features in image-text retrieval. We feed positive image-caption pairs through the model to obtain their joint representations (i.e., sequence of vectors). We split each sequence to obtain one set of features $\boldsymbol{I} \in \mathbb{R}^{768 \times N_i}$ for each image, and one set of features $\boldsymbol{C} \in \mathbb{R}^{768 \times N_c}$ for each caption. For the captions, we disregarded the representation for the [SEP] token.

While we understand that processing only positive image-caption pairs is not the ideal approach to perform retrieval, we reckon this is a limitation of UNITER, as it requires an image and a text passage to be fed simultaneously. Ideally, we would like to be able to forward each image and text only once and perform a ranking on top of the obtained representations. We performed preliminary experiments feeding only captions and only images, but the results showed that this approach does not create meaningful representations. Therefore, since we want to observe the effects of fine-tuning on the multi-modal representations, we primarily focus on the performance difference between them rather than the actual numbers.

We use the pre-trained UNITER released by the authors and test it on three different settings: zero-shot (ZS) where we directly use the pre-trained UNITER to extract our representations; Fine-tuned (FT), where we further train the pre-trained model on the downstream dataset with the default sampling strategy; and another fine-tuned model where the final training is performed using an improved technique for hard negative example mining (FT_{HN}). We note that the latter strategy has resulted in the best retrieval performance for the original model.

CLIP: We use the pre-trained model released by OpenAI. Different from SGM, CLIP does not explicitly use structured inputs and represents each image and text as a single feature vector $\boldsymbol{h} \in \mathbb{R}^{512}$.

In this scenario, we seek to understand if processing structured information with CLIP could help improve retrieval performance. To verify this point, we use the co-reference chains and manually annotated bounding boxes for each of the images and captions in the FLICKR30K dataset provided by Plummer et al. (2017) to input structured information and verify how the resulting features perform in contrast with the original CLIP features.

We follow the standard CLIP pipeline and extract an image vector $\boldsymbol{v}_{img} \in \mathbb{R}^{512}$ for each image (Img_G), and a caption vector $\boldsymbol{v}_{cap} \in \mathbb{R}^{512}$ for each caption (Text_G). Retrieval, in this case, is performed by using simple cosine similarity. We further crop the images following the annotated bounding boxes and process each cropped portion, which results in a set of vectors $\boldsymbol{I} \in \mathbb{R}^{512 \times N_i}$ with N_i representations of local objects for each image (Img_L). Analogously, we use the annotated entities in the captions to obtain a set of features

Method	Sim	Dim	Mean	R@1	R@5	R@10
			Text Retrieval			
SGM	S^o	-	85.96	70.40	92.10	95.40
	S^r	-	2.43	0.40	2.40	4.50
	$S^{o,r}$	-	**86.33**	71.80	91.70	95.50
SM	S^g	5	**40.40**	20.40	45.10	55.70
	S^o		38.20	18.80	42.10	53.70
	S^r	5	0.33	0.10	0.40	0.50
	$S^{o,r}$		33.80	16.00	37.00	48.40
MSM	S^g	10	59.03	40.20	63.60	73.30
	S^o		**60.53**	40.60	65.70	75.30
	S^r	5	0.80	0.10	0.90	1.13
	$S^{o,r}$		20.80	11.10	22.20	29.10
			Image Retrieval			
SGM	S^o	-	72.54	52.72	78.92	86.00
	S^r	-	1.74	0.40	1.76	3.08
	$S^{o,r}$	-	**73.20**	53.52	79.62	86.46
SM	S^g	5	**39.90**	18.44	44.12	57.14
	S^o		38.48	17.52	42.70	55.24
	S^r	5	1.20	0.28	1.20	2.12
	$S^{o,r}$		36.51	16.30	40.34	52.90
MSM	S^g	5	46.08	26.40	50.60	61.24
	S^o		**47.21**	27.70	51.82	61.10
	S^r	5	1.13	0.20	1.20	2.00
	$S^{o,r}$		42.00	23.68	46.30	56.02

Table 1: Results with SGM-Subspace on the Flickr30k dataset. Best results for each method are shown in bold. Mean denotes the mean of the R@1, R@5, and R@10, and Dim denotes the dimensions of the subspaces in SM and MSM. Results for the baseline were taken from our reproduction of the original model.

$\boldsymbol{C} \in \mathbb{R}^{512 \times N_c}$ with N_c textual entities representations (Text_L). In this case, retrieval is performed based on subspace similarity. We evaluate the performance by using both global (G) and local (L) features, as well as their combination.

4.1 Choice of subspace dimension

In general, for single modality problems, it is possible to get an idea of the suitable subspace dimension by observing the variance contribution ratio with each additional dimension.

The amount of variance retained by the basis vectors of the subspace can be determined by using the cumulative contribution rate $\mu(m)$. Considering that we want to keep a minimum of μ_{min} of the text variance, we can determine m by ensuring that $\mu(m)_d \geq \mu_{min}$, where $\mu(m)_d = \sum_{l=1}^{m}(\lambda_l)/\sum_{l=1}^{p}(\lambda_l)$. However, preliminary experiments showed us that this metric alone is not suitable to choose the dimension of subspaces modeled from artificially generated multimodal fea-

Method	Sim	Dim	Mean	R@1	R@5	R@10
			Text Retrieval			
SGM	$S^{o,r}$	-	58.56	35.30	64.90	75.50
SM	S^g	5	21.20	7.20	21.20.	35.20
	S^o		**26.40**	9.60	27.6	42.00
	S^r	1	0.40	0.00	0.40	0.80
	$S^{o,r}$		16.70	4.80	16.80	28.40
MSM	S^g	5	42.90	24.40	46.40	58.00
	S^o		**44.90**	24.00	50.40	60.40
	S^r	5	0.10	0.00	0.00	0.40
	$S^{o,r}$		17.10	10.00	18.00	23.20
			Image Retrieval			
SGM	$S^{o,r}$	-	58.90	35.30	64.90	76.50
SM	S^g	5	19.30	4.20	20.20	33.40
	S^o		**21.10**	7.50	22.00	33.80
	S^r	5	0.00	0.00	0.00	0.00
	$S^{o,r}$		21.10	7.70	21.80	33.80
MSM	S^g	5	34.30	16.70	37.10	49.00
	S^o		**35.10**	17.40	38.50	49.40
	S^r	5	0.00	0.00	0.00	0.00
	$S^{o,r}$		34.50	17.70	37.00	48.60

Table 2: Results with SGM-Subspace on the COCO dataset. Best results for each method are shown in bold. Mean denotes the mean of the R@1, R@5, and R@10, and Dim denotes the dimensions of the subspaces in SM and MSM. Results for the baseline were taken from the original SGM paper.

Method	Type	Dim	Mean	R@1	R@5	R@10
			Text Retrieval			
UNITER	ZS⋆	-	91.43	80.70	95.70	98.00
	ZS	-	91.50	80.80	95.70	98.00
	$\text{FT}^{\star}_{HN}$	-	**93.93**	85.90	97.10	98.80
	FT_{HN}	-	93.36	83.10	95.50	98.50
SM	ZS	20	**91.60**	86.10	93.30	95.40
	FT	20	80.80	69.70	84.50	88.30
	FT_{HN}	20	44.20	27.70	48.90	56.10
MSM	ZS	1	**76.00**	63.10	80.10	84.90
	FT	5	56.80	0.40	80.60	89.50
	FT_{HN}	5	56.20	1.60	79.00	87.90
			Image Retrieval			
UNITER	ZS⋆	-	-	66.16	88.40	92.94
	ZS	-	-	66.14	88.36	92.94
	$\text{FT}^{\star}_{HN}$	-	**84.17**	75.52	92.36	96.08
	FT_{HN}	-	-	68.02	89.54	94.54
SM	ZS	1	**48.00**	35.00	51.60	57.40
	FT	5	47.40	34.50	51.20	56.50
	FT_{HN}	5	28.40	17.10	31.10	37.10
MSM	ZS	1	**75.00**	63.70	78.60	82.70
	FT	15	53.60	32.40	60.50	67.90
	FT_{HN}	15	55.30	42.90	58.90	64.10

Table 3: Results with UNITER on FLICKR30K. Best results for each method are shown in bold. Mean denotes the mean of the R@1, R@5, and R@10, and Dim denotes the dimensions of the subspaces in SM and MSS, and ⋆ denotes results taken from Chen et al. (2020).

Method	Type	Dim	Mean	R@1	R@5	R@10
			Text Retrieval			
UNITER	ZS	-	**81.71**	64.10	87.74	93.30
	$\text{FT}^{\star}_{HN}$	-	81.62	64.40	87.40	93.08
SM	ZS	10	**68.30**	51.30	73.60	79.90
MSM	ZS	5	58.20	38.60	63.80	72.20
			Image Retrieval			
UNITER	ZS	-	70.45	48.79	76.72	85.84
	FT_{HN}	-	72.00	50.33	78.52	87.16
SM	ZS	1	24.50	17.00	26.30	30.00
MSM	ZS	1	**38.00**	31.20	40.00	42.80

Table 4: Results with UNITER on COCO, on the full 5k images test set. Mean denotes the mean of the R@1, R@5, and R@10, Dim denotes the dimensions of the subspaces in SM and MSM, and indicates results taken from Chen et al. (2020).

tures. Therefore, in this work we performed a grid search by assessing the image-text retrieval performance with different subspace dimensions, reporting the best results. We refer the readers to the supplementary material for results with all tested dimensions.

5 Results and Discussions

SGM-subspace: Tables 1 and 2 show the results when using SGM features. In this case, the best subspace performance was achieved by MSM for both tasks, which indicates that leveraging the distribution of the features for both input and references leads to more robust representations.

Furthermore, we can see that while SGM benefits from considering both S^o and S^r with $S^{o,r}$, the subspace-based methods performed better when considering only the objects (S^o) or when considering both globally (S^g), where the information from relationships helped improve results over $S^{o,r}$. Such contrast in results could be due to how SGM calculates the similarity between two entities: It leverages vector-vector relationships, possibly leading the model to focus on local structures and ignore the global context. However, such contextual information is crucial for the subspaces to effectively represent the features from the entity, thus leading to degraded performance.

Features	Method	Dim	Text retrieval				Image Retrieval			
			Mean	R@1	R@5	R@10	Mean	R@1	R@5	R@10
Text_G & Img_G	CLIP	-	**90.30**	77.80	95.00	98.10	**76.60**	58.10	82.50	89.40
Text_L & Img_L	SM	1	**47.90**	27.30	52.30	64.10	**36.80**	19.00	40.60	50.70
	MSM	1	47.30	27.00	51.70	63.10	35.40	19.90	38.30	47.90
Text_L & Img_G	SM	1	61.40	37.40	68.10	78.60	42.00	24.60	45.90	55.50
Text_G & Img_L		5	75.70	59.10	81.00	87.00	67.70	46.10	74.50	82.40
Text_G & Img_{G+L}		5	**83.70**	69.90	87.90	93.30	**74.90**	54.50	81.30	88.80
Text_{G+L} & Img_G		5	83.40	67.00	89.20	93.90	70.40	49.90	76.30	84.80
Text_{G+L} & Img_{G+L}	SM	5	**70.00**	50.30	75.50	84.20	**61.90**	38.40	68.60	78.70
	MSM	1	63.90	44.30	69.70	77.80	61.10	41.10	66.40	75.90

Table 5: Results of our experiments with for CLIP-subspace on FLICKR30K, where the sub-indices G and L indicate the use of global and local features to represent each image and/or caption.

UNITER-subspace: Tables 3 and 4 show the best results for retrieval when using UNITER features. The best subspace performance was achieved using SM in caption retrieval and MSM in image retrieval. We can observe that while the performance of the original UNITER increases after fine-tuning, our best results were achieved using ZS UNITER features, performing about 33.70% and 19.65% better in caption and image retrieval, respectively, in terms of mean R@k compared to hard-negative features in the FLICKR30K dataset.

We can also observe that the best results for both FLICKR30K and COCO were achieved using subspaces with dimensions ranging from 1 to 20, much smaller than the original 768-dimensional feature space, even when ZS features are used. Such low-dimensional subspaces could indicate that the UNITER has already compressed critical information to represent each entity during pre-training.

CLIP-subspace: Table 5 shows the best retrieval results when using CLIP features. Out of the three chosen models, the original CLIP is the closest to the subspace-based retrieval, as it is equivalent to using one-dimensional subspaces of the global G features and, therefore, direct comparison with the subspace-based retrieval is adequate.

We can see that using only G features, i.e., CLIP's original performance, leads to the best results. On the other hand, using only local L features leads to the worst performance. However, we can observe that image representation can better benefit from L features than the captions, leading to the best subspace performance when both G and L features are used to represent images. While considering the structure information does not lead to better performance, this result indicates that G image features are better aligned with the L image features than text features. This result could be explained by the fact that processing isolated textual entities could lead to a loss of context as the subspace representation cannot handle word order.

6 Conclusions and Future Work

The main goal of this paper was to better understand the role of structured inputs and fine-tuning in image-text retrieval. We analyzed visual and text representations extracted with SGM, UNITER, and CLIP by representing a single image or text as low-dimensional linear subspaces and performing retrieval based on subspace similarity. We analyzed how the performance of the selected models' features changed when considering fine-tuning versus zero-shot performance for models that require pre-training, as well as the addition or removal of structure information from images (e.g., scene-graphs) and texts (e.g., semantic triplets).

Our results indicate that UNITER's pre-training leads to features with critical information representing each entity during pre-training, with zero-shot features performing consistently better than fine-tuned features. Moreover, we observed that using only SGM's object representations led to better performance than when considering the relationship representations. Finally, considering structure information with CLIP does not improve the retrieval results. However, we could observe that global information from the text side seems more critical than text local information.

A natural progression of this work is to analyze these features from a geometrical perspective, using the well-established literature on subspace representation.

Acknowledgements

This paper is based on results obtained from a project JPNP20006, commissioned by the New Energy and Industrial Technology Development Organization (NEDO). For experiments, computational resource of AI Bridging Cloud Infrastructure (ABCI) provided by National Institute of Advanced Industrial Science and Technology (AIST) was used.

References

Peter Anderson, Basura Fernando, Mark Johnson, and Stephen Gould. 2016. Spice: Semantic propositional image caption evaluation. In *European conference on computer vision*, pages 382–398. Springer.

Stanislaw Antol, Aishwarya Agrawal, Jiasen Lu, Margaret Mitchell, Dhruv Batra, C Lawrence Zitnick, and Devi Parikh. 2015. Vqa: Visual question answering. In *Proceedings of the IEEE international conference on computer vision*, pages 2425–2433.

Michele Bevilacqua, Tommaso Pasini, Alessandro Raganato, Roberto Navigli, et al. 2021. Recent trends in word sense disambiguation: A survey. In *Proceedings of the Thirtieth International Joint Conference on Artificial Intelligence, IJCAI-21*. International Joint Conference on Artificial Intelligence, Inc.

Françoise Chatelin. 2012. *Eigenvalues of Matrices: Revised Edition*. SIAM.

Yen-Chun Chen, Linjie Li, Licheng Yu, Ahmed El Kholy, Faisal Ahmed, Zhe Gan, Yu Cheng, and Jingjing Liu. 2020. Uniter: Universal image-text representation learning. In *European conference on computer vision*, pages 104–120. Springer.

Jacob Devlin, Ming-Wei Chang, Kenton Lee, and Kristina Toutanova. 2019. BERT: Pre-training of Deep Bidirectional Transformers for Language Understanding. In *Proceedings of the 2019 Conference of the North American Chapter of the Association for Computational Linguistics: Human Language Technologies, Volume 1 (Long and Short Papers)*, pages 4171–4186, Minneapolis, Minnesota. Association for Computational Linguistics.

Haiwen Diao, Ying Zhang, Lin Ma, and Huchuan Lu. 2021. Similarity reasoning and filtration for image-text matching. In *Proceedings of the AAAI Conference on Artificial Intelligence*, volume 35, pages 1218–1226.

Xinfeng Dong, Huaxiang Zhang, Lei Zhu, Liqiang Nie, and Li Liu. 2022. Hierarchical feature aggregation based on transformer for image-text matching. *IEEE Transactions on Circuits and Systems for Video Technology*.

Desmond Elliott, Stella Frank, Loïc Barrault, Fethi Bougares, and Lucia Specia. 2017. Findings of the second shared task on multimodal machine translation and multilingual image description. In *Proceedings of the Second Conference on Machine Translation*, pages 215–233.

Kazuhiro Fukui and Atsuto Maki. 2015. Difference subspace and its generalization for subspace-based methods. *IEEE Transactions on Pattern Analysis and Machine Intelligence*, 37(11):2164–2177.

Kazuhiro Fukui and Osamu Yamaguchi. 2005. Face recognition using multi-viewpoint patterns for robot vision. *Robotics Research, The Eleventh International Symposium, ISRR*, pages 192–201.

MD Zakir Hossain, Ferdous Sohel, Mohd Fairuz Shiratuddin, and Hamid Laga. 2019. A comprehensive survey of deep learning for image captioning. *ACM Computing Surveys (CsUR)*, 51(6):1–36.

Taizo Iijima, Hiroshi Genchi, and Ken-ichi Mori. 1974. A theory of character recognition by pattern matching method. In *Learning systems and intelligent robots*, pages 437–450. Springer.

Yikang Li, Wanli Ouyang, Bolei Zhou, Kun Wang, and Xiaogang Wang. 2017. Scene graph generation from objects, phrases and region captions. In *Proceedings of the IEEE international conference on computer vision*, pages 1261–1270.

Tsung-Yi Lin, Michael Maire, Serge Belongie, James Hays, Pietro Perona, Deva Ramanan, Piotr Dollár, and C. Lawrence Zitnick. 2014. Microsoft COCO: Common Objects in Context. In *Computer Vision – ECCV 2014*, Lecture Notes in Computer Science, pages 740–755, Cham. Springer International Publishing.

Ken-ichi Maeda. 2010. From the subspace methods to the mutual subspace method. In *Computer Vision*, pages 135–156. Springer.

Nicola Messina, Fabrizio Falchi, Andrea Esuli, and Giuseppe Amato. 2021. Transformer reasoning network for image-text matching and retrieval. In *2020 25th International Conference on Pattern Recognition (ICPR)*, pages 5222–5229. IEEE.

Bryan A. Plummer, Liwei Wang, Chris M. Cervantes, Juan C. Caicedo, Julia Hockenmaier, and Svetlana Lazebnik. 2015. Flickr30k Entities: Collecting Region-to-Phrase Correspondences for Richer Image-to-Sentence Models. In *Proceedings of the IEEE International Conference on Computer Vision*, pages 2641–2649.

Bryan A. Plummer, Liwei Wang, Christopher M. Cervantes, Juan C. Caicedo, Julia Hockenmaier, and Svetlana Lazebnik. 2017. Flickr30k entities: Collecting region-to-phrase correspondences for richer image-to-sentence models. *IJCV*, 123(1):74–93.

Leigang Qu, Meng Liu, Da Cao, Liqiang Nie, and Qi Tian. 2020. Context-aware multi-view summarization network for image-text matching. In *Proceedings of the 28th ACM International Conference on Multimedia*, pages 1047–1055.

Alec Radford, Jong Wook Kim, Chris Hallacy, Aditya Ramesh, Gabriel Goh, Sandhini Agarwal, Girish Sastry, Amanda Askell, Pamela Mishkin, Jack Clark, Gretchen Krueger, and Ilya Sutskever. 2021. Learning Transferable Visual Models From Natural Language Supervision. In *Proceedings of the 38th International Conference on Machine Learning*, pages 8748–8763. PMLR.

Shaoqing Ren, Kaiming He, Ross Girshick, and Jian Sun. 2015. Faster r-cnn: Towards real-time object detection with region proposal networks. *Advances in neural information processing systems*, 28.

Brigit Schroeder and Subarna Tripathi. 2020. Structured query-based image retrieval using scene graphs. In *Proceedings of the IEEE/CVF Conference on Computer Vision and Pattern Recognition Workshops*, pages 178–179.

Botian Shi, Lei Ji, Pan Lu, Zhendong Niu, and Nan Duan. 2019. Knowledge aware semantic concept expansion for image-text matching. In *IJCAI*, volume 1, page 2.

Lucia Specia, Stella Frank, Khalil Sima'An, and Desmond Elliott. 2016. A shared task on multimodal machine translation and crosslingual image description. In *Proceedings of the First Conference on Machine Translation: Volume 2, Shared Task Papers*, pages 543–553.

Sijin Wang, Ruiping Wang, Ziwei Yao, Shiguang Shan, and Xilin Chen. 2020. Cross-modal scene graph matching for relationship-aware image-text retrieval. In *Proceedings of the IEEE/CVF Winter Conference on Applications of Computer Vision*, pages 1508–1517.

Satosi Watanabe and Nikhil Pakvasa. 1973. Subspace method of pattern recognition. In *Proc. 1st. IJCPR*, pages 25–32.

Peter Young, Alice Lai, Micah Hodosh, and Julia Hockenmaier. 2014. From image descriptions to visual denotations: New similarity metrics for semantic inference over event descriptions. *Transactions of the Association for Computational Linguistics*, 2:67–78.

Rowan Zellers, Mark Yatskar, Sam Thomson, and Yejin Choi. 2018. Neural motifs: Scene graph parsing with global context. In *Proceedings of the IEEE conference on computer vision and pattern recognition*, pages 5831–5840.

A Hardware specifications

For all the experiments conducted in this paper, we used three different machines:

1. For fine-tuning and extracting features from UNITER, we used a server machine with an Intel Xeon E5-2630 CPU, and two NVIDIA RTX-2080 (Driver 418.56, CUDA 10.1) GPUs, running Ubuntu 20.04.

2. For extracting features from SGM and running the experiments with UNITER and SGM features, we used a machine with an Intel Core i7-6800K CPU, with one NVIDIA GeForce GTX 1070 (Driver 471.41, CUDA 11.4), running Ubuntu 18.04 on Windows Subsystem for Linux version 2.

3. For extracting and running experiments with CLIP features, we used a node on large cluster equipped with a 16-GB NVIDIA V100 GPU (CUDA 11.3).

However, we highlight that all experiments using the subspace-based methods can be performed using the second machine listed above.

B Results using different subspace dimensions

In Tables 6 to 12, we show the results with varying subspace dimensions for all three models.

C Replication of original models' results

In Tables 13 to 14, we show our reproduction of UNITER and CLIP's results.

Feature	Dim	Text retrieval Mean	R@1	R@5	R@10	Image Retrieval Mean	R@1	R@5	R@10
ZS	1	76.00	63.10	80.00	84.90	**48.00**	35.00	51.60	57.40
	5	84.10	74.60	87.20	90.50	44.20	31.60	47.60	53.50
	10	90.00	84.10	92.00	94.00	42.20	29.20	45.50	52.00
	20	**91.60**	86.10	93.30	95.40	41.30	28.10	44.60	51.30
FT	1	43.70	29.10	47.20	54.80	39.60	28.30	42.50	48.10
	5	71.00	56.80	74.70	81.60	**47.40**	34.50	51.20	56.50
	10	77.40	66.00	80.90	85.40	45.90	33.70	49.20	54.90
	20	**80.80**	69.70	84.50	88.30	44.90	32.40	48.50	53.80
FT_{HN}	1	22.40	12.90	24.20	30.10	13.10	6.10	14.40	18.90
	5	43.50	26.50	47.10	56.80	**28.40**	17.10	31.10	37.10
	10	42.50	23.40	46.70	57.50	27.70	16.50	30.10	36.40
	20	**44.20**	27.70	48.90	56.10	28.10	17.00	30.60	36.70

Table 6: Results with UNITER-subspace on the Flickr30k dataset using SM. Best results for each method are shown in bold. Mean denotes the mean of the R@1, R@5, and R@10, and Dim denotes the dimensions of the subspaces in SM.

Feature	Dim	Text retrieval Mean	R@1	R@5	R@10	Image Retrieval Mean	R@1	R@5	R@10
ZS	1	**76.00**	63.10	80.10	84.90	**75.00**	63.70	78.60	82.70
	5	54.40	0.10	75.80	87.40	39.80	23.70	43.50	52.20
	10	1.80	0.10	0.80	4.40	60.40	43.70	64.70	72.70
	15	1.80	0.10	0.90	4.30	57.20	32.90	64.80	73.90
FT	1	43.70	29.10	47.20	54.80	43.10	32.30	45.70	51.20
	5	**56.80**	0.40	80.60	89.50	18.10	9.60	19.50	25.30
	10	2.50	0.10	1.10	6.30	50.10	36.00	54.10	60.10
	15	1.90	0.10	1.30	4.30	**53.60**	32.40	60.50	67.90
FT_{HN}	1	22.40	12.90	24.20	30.10	13.60	7.30	14.90	18.70
	5	**56.20**	1.60	79.00	87.90	22.40	14.60	24.00	28.60
	10	1.60	0.10	0.90	3.90	49.30	36.70	52.50	58.50
	15	1.80	0.10	1.20	4.00	**55.30**	42.90	58.90	64.10

Table 7: Results with UNITER-subspace on the Flickr30k dataset using MSM. Best results for each method are shown in bold. Mean denotes the mean of the R@1, R@5, and R@10, and Dim denotes the dimensions of the subspaces MSM.

Feature	Dim	Text retrieval Mean	R@1	R@5	R@10	Image Retrieval Mean	R@1	R@5	R@10
ZS	1	52.80	35.30	57.50	65.60	**24.50**	17.00	26.30	30.00
	5	61.10	43.10	66.50	73.70	23.40	16.10	25.10	28.90
	10	**68.30**	51.30	73.60	79.90	22.50	15.40	24.20	28.00

Table 8: Results with UNITER-subspace on the MSCOCO dataset using SM, using all 5k test images. Best results for each method are shown in bold. Mean denotes the mean of the R@1, R@5, and R@10, and Dim denotes the dimensions of the subspaces in SM.

Feature	Dim	Text retrieval Mean	R@1	R@5	R@10	Image Retrieval Mean	R@1	R@5	R@10
ZS	1	52.80	35.30	57.50	65.70	**38.00**	31.20	40.00	42.80
	5	**58.20**	38.60	63.80	72.20	24.90	15.90	26.90	31.90
	10	50.70	28.20	56.70	67.10	32.80	22.30	35.40	40.70

Table 9: Results with UNITER-subspace on the MSCOCO dataset using MSM, using all 5k test images. Best results for each method are shown in bold. Mean denotes the mean of the R@1, R@5, and R@10, and Dim denotes the dimensions of the subspaces MSM.

Method	Dim	Sim	Text retrieval Mean	R@1	R@5	R@10	Image Retrieval Mean	R@1	R@5	R@10
SM	1	S^g	12.03	4.70	13.20	18.20	31.90	13.08	34.84	47.78
		S^o	17.47	6.10	19.10	27.20	35.04	14.74	38.72	51.68
		S^r	1.27	0.40	1.10	2.30	2.28	0.62	2.28	3.96
		$S^{o,r}$	13.00	5.50	13.40	20.10	35.53	14.74	39.16	52.70
	5	S^g	**40.40**	20.40	45.10	55.70	**39.90**	18.44	44.12	57.14
		S^o	38.20	18.80	42.10	53.70	38.48	17.52	42.70	55.24
		S^r	0.33	0.10	0.40	0.50	1.20	0.28	1.20	2.12
		$S^{o,r}$	33.80	16.00	37.00	48.40	36.51	16.30	40.34	52.90
	10	S^g	**29.23**	13.00	32.10	42.60	**31.42**	13.08	34.86	56.34
		S^o	32.03	14.80	35.40	45.90	30.36	12.62	33.38	45.08
		S^r	0.40	0.00	0.30	0.90	1.19	0.26	1.20	2.12
		$S^{o,r}$	27.03	12.40	29.80	38.90	28.80	11.56	31.58	43.26
MSM	1	S^g	0.63	0.20	0.60	1.10	1.21	0.24	1.18	2.22
		S^o	**17.57**	6.60	18.80	27.30	**31.77**	15.54	34.70	45.06
		S^r	1.23	0.40	1.10	2.20	1.29	0.32	1.36	2.20
		$S^{o,r}$	15.50	5.90	16.20	24.40	31.60	15.30	34.60	44.90
	5	S^g	58.03	37.20	63.60	75.30	46.08	26.40	50.60	61.24
		S^o	**60.53**	40.60	65.70	75.30	**47.21**	27.70	51.82	62.10
		S^r	0.80	0.10	0.90	1.40	1.13	0.20	1.20	2.00
		$S^{o,r}$	20.80	11.10	22.20	29.10	42.00	23.68	46.30	56.02
	10	S^g	**59.03**	40.20	63.60	73.30	**41.71**	23.50	45.72	55.92
		S^o	52.20	31.60	57.10	67.90	41.44	23.26	45.52	55.54
		S^r	0.87	0.10	1.00	1.50	0.97	0.24	0.84	1.82
		$S^{o,r}$	12.00	6.60	13.20	16.20	29.39	14.26	32.38	41.54

Table 10: Results with SGM-subspace on the Flickr30k dataset using SM and MSM. Best results for each method are shown in bold. Mean denotes the mean of the R@1, R@5, and R@10, and Dim denotes the dimensions of the subspaces in SM and MSM.

Method	Dim	Sim	Text retrieval Mean	R@1	R@5	R@10	Image Retrieval Mean	R@1	R@5	R@10
SM	1	S^g	13.10	4.40	14.00	20.80	10.60	0.40	8.50	23.00
		S^o	**26.40**	9.60	27.6	42.00	20.70	7.40	22.40	32.20
		S^r	0.40	0.00	0.40	0.80	0.00	0.00	0.00	0.00
		$S^{o,r}$	16.70	4.80	16.80	28.40	20.70	7.50	22.30	32.20
	5	S^g	**21.20**	7.20	21.20	35.20	19.30	4.20	20.20	33.40
		S^o	21.10	7.70	21.80	33.80	**21.10**	7.50	22.00	33.80
		S^r	0.00	0.00	0.00	0.00	0.00	0.00	0.00	0.00
		$S^{o,r}$	16.10	5.20	15.60	27.60	**21.10**	7.70	21.80	33.80
	10	S^g	12.90	5.20	14.00	19.60	17.00	1.80	17.60	31.80
		S^o	**13.30**	5.60	12.80	21.60	20.90	7.80	21.80	33.10
		S^r	0.00	0.00	0.00	0.00	0.00	0.00	0.00	0.00
		$S^{o,r}$	10.70	4.40	10.00	17.60	**21.00**	7.70	21.80	33.50
MSM	1	S^g	19.20	6.80	20.00	30.80	21.20	9.10	22.50	32.00
		S^o	**26.10**	9.60	27.60	41.20	**29.20**	13.40	31.40	42.80
		S^r	0.40	0.00	0.40	0.80	0.00	0.00	0.00	0.00
		$S^{o,r}$	19.60	4.80	20.80	33.20	**29.20**	13.40	31.40	42.90
	5	S^g	42.90	24.40	46.40	58.00	34.30	16.70	37.10	49.00
		S^o	**44.90**	24.00	50.40	60.40	**35.10**	17.40	38.50	49.40
		S^r	0.10	0.00	0.00	0.40	0.00	0.00	0.00	0.00
		$S^{o,r}$	17.10	10.00	18.00	23.20	34.50	17.70	37.00	48.60
	10	S^g	**42.90**	22.00	48.40	58.40	**33.70**	16.70	37.40	47.00
		S^o	39.70	20.40	44.80	54.00	32.80	15.10	36.40	46.80
		S^r	0.10	0.00	0.00	0.40	0.20	0.00	0.20	0.30
		$S^{o,r}$	6.40	4.00	6.00	9.20	31.80	14.50	35.40	45.60

Table 11: Results with SGM-subspace on the MSCOCO dataset using SM and MSM, using all 5k test images. Best results for each method are shown in bold. Mean denotes the mean of the R@1, R@5, and R@10, and Dim denotes the dimensions of the subspaces in SM and MSM.

Table 12: Results of our experiments with for CLIP-subspace on FLICKR30K, where the sub-indices G and L indicate the use of global and local features to represent each image and/or caption.

Features	Method	Dim	Text retrieval				Image Retrieval			
			Mean	R@1	R@5	R@10	Mean	R@1	R@5	R@10
Text$_G$ & Img$_G$	CLIP	-	**90.30**	77.80	95.00	98.10	**76.60**	58.10	82.50	89.40
Text$_L$ & Img$_G$	CLIP	-	54.70	29.30	60.40	74.50	42.40	24.80	46.40	55.90
Text$_G$ & Img$_L$	CLIP	-	71.80	55.10	76.10	84.10	57.70	34.20	63.80	75.20
Text$_G$& Img$_{G+L}$	CLIP	-	79.10	62.20	84.20	90.90	63.80	40.20	70.50	90.70
Text$_{G+L}$ & Img$_G$	CLIP	-	74.40	52.10	81.00	90.00	65.80	45.40	71.90	80.20
Text$_L$ & Img$_L$	SM	1	**47.90**	27.30	52.30	64.10	**36.80**	19.00	40.60	50.70
	SM	5	47.20	21.90	54.30	65.40	35.90	17.40	39.10	51.30
	SM	10	39.60	20.00	43.10	55.70	35.90	17.60	39.00	51.10
	MSM	1	**47.30**	27.00	51.70	63.10	**35.40**	19.90	38.30	47.90
	MSM	5	23.40	12.00	24.70	33.60	31.30	14.10	34.70	45.20
	MSM	10	26.40	12.60	27.30	39.30	24.10	11.60	25.90	34.80
Text$_L$ & Img$_G$	SM	1	**61.40**	37.40	68.10	78.60	**42.00**	24.60	45.90	55.50
	SM	5	42.10	23.70	45.10	57.50	35.10	17.40	38.20	49.80
	SM	10	39.40	21.40	42.30	54.40	34.90	17.30	38.00	49.50
Text$_G$ & Img$_L$	SM	1	70.40	54.00	74.00	83.20	62.00	40.60	68.20	77.00
	SM	5	**75.70**	59.10	81.00	87.00	**67.70**	46.10	74.50	82.40
	SM	10	72.40	55.20	77.00	85.10	59.30	37.50	64.90	75.50
Text$_G$ & Img$_{G+L}$	SM	1	77.90	60.90	82.90	89.90	68.20	47.50	74.60	82.60
	SM	5	**83.70**	69.90	87.90	93.30	**74.90**	54.50	81.30	88.80
	SM	10	78.50	61.90	83.60	90.10	66.70	44.40	73.30	82.50
Text$_{G+L}$ & Img$_G$	SM	1	77.30	57.00	83.80	91.10	63.80	43.40	69.70	78.40
	SM	5	**83.40**	67.00	89.20	93.90	**70.40**	49.90	76.30	84.80
	SM	10	78.50	58.20	85.60	91.60	69.80	49.20	75.90	84.30
Text$_{G+L}$ & Img$_{G+L}$	SM	1	64.70	44.70	70.70	78.80	59.80	37.20	65.70	76.40
	SM	5	**70.00**	50.30	75.50	84.20	**61.90**	38.40	68.60	78.70
	SM	10	60.50	40.00	65.80	75.70	61.20	37.60	67.90	78.20
	MSM	1	**63.90**	44.30	69.70	77.80	**61.10**	41.10	66.40	75.90
	MSM	5	62.10	38.50	67.50	80.40	56.20	34.80	61.70	72.20
	MSM	10	56.40	34.20	62.00	73.00	37.70	21.30	40.80	50.90

Dataset	Model	Text retrieval			Image Retrieval		
		R@1	R@5	R@10	R@1	R@5	R@10
Flickr30k	ZS	80.70	95.70	98.00	66.16	88.40	92.94
	ZS (ours)	80.80	95.70	98.00	66.14	88.36	92.94
	Ft*	-	-	-	-	-	-
	Ft (ours)	76.40	92.00	96.20	63.00	86.62	91.98
	Ft-HN	85.90	97.10	98.80	72.52	92.36	96.08
	Ft-HN (ours)	83.10	95.50	98.50	68.02	89.54	94.54
COCO	ZS*	-	-	-	-	-	-
	ZS (ours)	64.10	87.74	93.30	48.79	76.72	85.84
	Ft*	-	-	-	-	-	-
	Ft (ours)	54.22	81.30	88.86	42.97	72.26	82.17
	Ft-HN	64.40	87.40	93.08	50.33	78.52	87.16
	Ft-HN (ours)	60.64	84.68	91.70	46.42	74.78	84.40

Table 13: Results of our replication of UNITER on the Flickr30k and COCO datasets, where $*$ indicates results not reported by the original paper.

Method	Dim	Text retrieval Mean	R@1	R@5	R@10	Image Retrieval Mean	R@1	R@5	R@10
Reported	-	-	88.0	98.7	99.4	-	68.7	90.6	95.2
Ours	-	90.6	78.8	94.9	98.2	77.4	58.8	83.5	90.0

Table 14: Results of CLIP retrieval on the Flickr30k dataset. Reported indicates the result reported in the original paper, and Ours indicates our replication. Mean denotes the mean of the R@1, R@5, and R@10.

Discourse Relation Embeddings: Representing the Relations between Discourse Segments in Social Media

Youngseo Son **Vasudha Varadarajan** **H. Andrew Schwartz**
Department of Computer Science, Stony Brook University
{yson,vvaradarajan,has}@cs.stonybrook.edu

Abstract

Discourse relations are typically modeled as a discrete class that characterizes the relation between segments of text (e.g. causal explanations, expansions). However, such predefined discrete classes limit the universe of potential relations and their nuanced differences. Adding higher-level semantic structure to modern contextual word embeddings, we propose representing discourse relations as points in high dimensional continuous space. However, unlike words, discourse relations often have no surface form (relations are *inbetween two segments*, often with no explicit word or phrase marker), presenting a challenge for existing embedding techniques. We present a novel method for automatically creating *discourse relation embeddings* (DiscRE), addressing the embedding challenge through a weakly supervised, multitask approach. Results show DiscRE representations obtain the best performance on Twitter discourse relation classification (macro $F1 = 0.76$) and social media causality prediction (from $F1 = .79$ to $.81$), performing beyond modern sentence and word transformers, and capturing novel nuanced relations (e.g. relations at the intersection of causal explanations and counterfactuals).

1 Introduction

Relations between discourse segments (i.e., phrases rooted by a main verb phrases or clauses) have mostly been studied as discrete classes; most notably Penn Discourse Treebank (PDTB) (Prasad et al., 2008) and Rhetorical Structure Theory Discourse Treebank (RST DT) (Carlson et al., 2001) contain 43 and 72 types of discourse relations respectively. At the same time, such work has taken place over newswire, the domain of both the PDTB and RST. With many different relation classes over sophisticated schema, annotation is non-trivial prohibiting extensive development in new domains (e.g., social media). Thus, progress in developing,

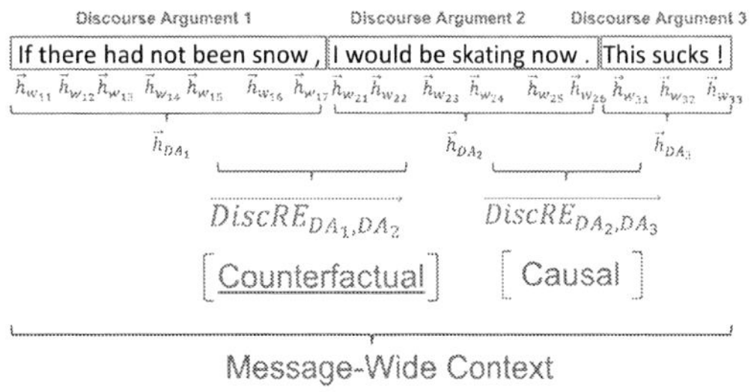

Figure 1: Our model DiscRE predicts relations of adjacent discourse arguments based on other text spans of the whole message as context. By learning and embedding fine-grained properties of discourse relation with the posteriors from PDTB into a continuous vector space, DiscRE may learn existing discourse relation tagsets like 'causal' relations, but also new latent discourse relations such as 'counterfactual' relations.

training and evaluating discourse relation identifiers has happened over *discrete-class* models with *labeled newswire* corpora (Pitler et al., 2009; Park and Cardie, 2012; Ji and Eisenstein, 2014; Lin et al., 2014; Popa et al., 2019).

To address this challenge and enable expansion of discourse work to social media, we propose a weakly supervised learning method which does not require any explicit labels. Instead, it adds a semantic structure that can effectively capture various types of discourse relations, even in other domains leveraging a multitask learning method called "Discourse Relation Embeddings (DiscRE)". Our DiscRE model represents discourse relations as continuous vectors rather than single discrete classes.

As the first study of *embedding* discourse relations into high dimensional continuous spaces, we mainly focus on social media. Social media is a challenging domain because it contains many acronyms, emojis, unicode, and informal variations of grammatical structure, but its personal nature provides diverse and psychologically-relevant dis-

Proceedings of the Workshop on Unimodal and Multimodal Induction of Linguistic Structures (UM-IoS), pages 45 - 55
December 7, 2022 ©2022 Association for Computational Linguistics

course patterns which are not often found from newswire text. According to our best knowledge, there are only relatively small datasets for specific types of discourse relations for causal relation (Son et al., 2018) and counterfactual relations (Son et al., 2017), but they are not diverse and large enough to learn general discourse relations.

In this paper, we propose a novel weakly supervised learning method for deriving discourse relation embeddings on social media. We created a social media discourse relation dataset and validated our new approach. Furthermore, we conducted visual investigations on continuous discourse relation spaces and thorough qualitative analysis on the behaviors of DiscRE in both PDTB and social media. Then, we also validated how well our learning method can generalize across different domains by applying DiscRE as transfer learning features for discourse relation downstream tasks.

Our contributions include: (1) a novel model structure which, when weakly supervised, creates embeddings capturing discourse relations (DiscRE), (2) the creation of new Twitter discourse relation dataset and the validation of our approach for the discourse relation classification on the dataset, (3) quantitative and qualitative evaluation of DiscRE on PTDB and downstream social media discourse relation tasks in which DiscRE outperformed strong modern contextual word and sentence embeddings, obtaining a new state-of-the-art performance for causality and counterfactuals, and (4) the release of all of our datasets and models.

2 Related Work

Our work builds on previous studies in discourse relations with two key distinctions: (1) the predominant set of work on discourse relations has focused on annotated newswire datasets (PDTB and RST DT) rather than social media; (2) work to improve discourse parsing has focused either on feature engineering or models for better predicting *predefined* discourse relations rather than embeddings (or latent relations). Such work takes pre-segmented clauses as input (Pitler et al., 2009; Park and Cardie, 2012) or builds full end-to-end discourse parsers (Ji and Eisenstein, 2014; Lin et al., 2014). Kishimoto et al. (2020) looked into adapting BERT for relation classification by pretraining with domain text and connective prediction. Other methods have zeroed-in on implicit discourse relations (those without a connective token) and also used a hierarchical model but for discourse classification rather than embedding (Bai and Hai, 2018). Some work from Varia et al. (2019); Ma et al. (2021); Zhang et al. (2021) leverage CNNs and graph networks to capture relationships between adjacent discourse units for implicit discourse relation classification.

Some have studied *single* discourse relations over social media. Son et al. (2017) used a hybrid rule-based and feature based supervised classifier to capture counterfactual statements from tweets. Bhatia et al. (2015) and Ji and Smith (2017) applied RST discourse parsing to social media movie review sentiment analysis, showing a pretrained model which was optimized for RST DT, suffered from domain differences when it was run on different domains (e.g., legislative bill). Son et al. (2018) developed a causal relation extraction model using hierarchical RNNs to parse social media. In general, hierarchical RNN-based models have worked well in general for capturing specific relations in social media and other discourse relations outside social media (Bhatia et al., 2015; Son et al., 2018; Ji and Smith, 2017).

Our work is related to modern multi-purpose contextual word embeddings (Devlin et al., 2018; Peters et al., 2018) in the motivation to utilize latent representations in order to capture context-specific meaning. However, our model generates contextual discourse relation embeddings by learning probabilities rather than discrete labels and, it can learn all possible relations even from the same text leveraging posterior probabilities from well-established study (Prasad et al., 2008).

We also build on research that has assembled custom discourse relation datasets or created training instances from existing datasets using discourse connectives (Jernite et al., 2017; Nie et al., 2019; Sileo et al., 2019). Jernite et al. (2017) designed an objective function to learn discourse relation categories (conjunction) based on discourse connectives along with other discourse coherence measurements while Nie et al. (2019) and Sileo et al. (2019) used objectives to predict discourse connectives. Here, we devised an objective function for learning posterior probabilities of discourse relations of the given discourse connectives, so the model can capture more fine-grained senses and discourse relation properties of the connectives[1]. Also, all of them used sentence encoders to learn sentence

[1] e.g., 'since' can signal a temporal relation in 'I have been working for this company since I graduated', but might signal a causal relation 'I like him since he is very kind to me'.

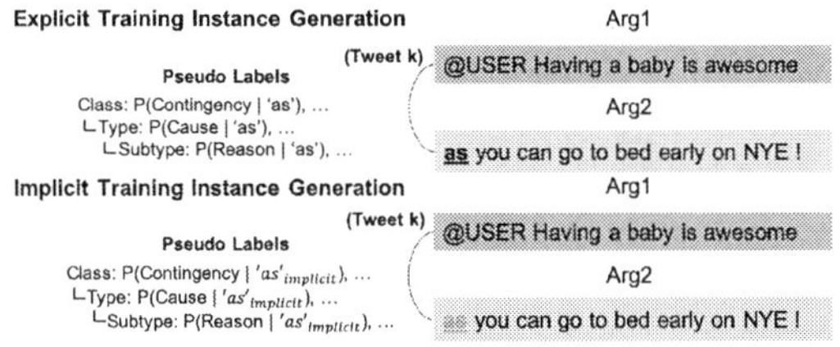

Figure 2: Training instance generation example. For explicit relation training, the training instance is labeled with the posterior probabilities of all possible *Class*, *Type*, and *Subtype* given the explicit connective 'as' from PDTB.

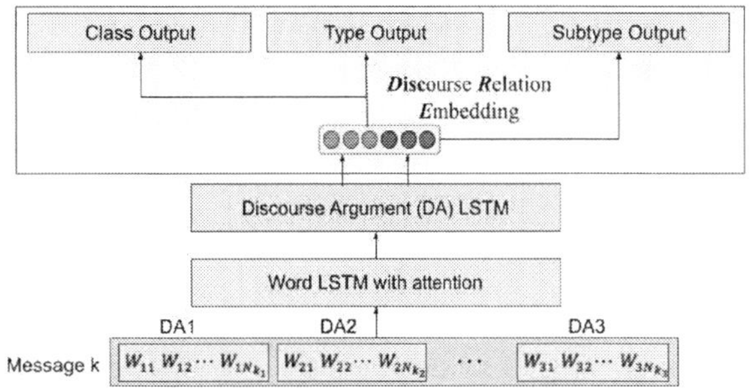

Figure 3: Our model learns different nuances and high dimensional contextual discourse relations by learning probabilities of all possible discourse relations in the relation hierarchy (*Class*, *Type*, and *Subtype*).

representations and compared their learned representations with other state-of-the-art sentence embeddings such as Infersent (Conneau et al., 2017). However, our DiscRE model learns a "discourse relation" representation (i.e. embedding) between discourse arguments rather than the representation of a respective text span of the pair (Figure 1).

Finally, some have studied an RNN-attention-based approach to multitask learning for discourse relation predictions in PDTB (Lan et al., 2017; Ji et al., 2016) and a sentence encoder with multi-purpose learning for discourse-based objectives (Jernite et al., 2017). Also, Liu et al. (2016) leveraged a multi-task neural network for discourse parsing across existing discourse trees and discourse connectives. Shi and Demberg (2019) used next sentence prediction to get better at implicit discourse relation classification.

A particular challenge of these prior works has been to improve performance when no connective is explicitly mentioned in the text. All of these works utilized predefined discrete classes of possible discourse relations. While we were inspired and build on some of their techniques, our task is more broadly defined as producing vector representations of the relationship between discourse segments *not limited to predefined discourse relations* (whether defined with explicit connectives or conventional discourse signals exist or not) and is evaluated over a broad diversity of discourse relation tasks as well as downstream applications.

3 Methods

The base for our model is a hierarchical BiRNN, following work on capturing causal relations in social media (Son et al., 2018), but we have added word-level attention, reflecting the necessity to keep word-level markers while parsing higher-order discourse relations (e.g., word pairs, modality, or N-grams) (Pitler et al., 2009).

3.1 Data Collection

DiscRE Weakly-Supervised Learning Training Set. No existing annotated discourse relation dataset exists for social media. Thus, we collected random tweets from December 2018 through January 2019 for training. Non-English tweets were filtered out, and URLs and user mentions were replaced with separate special tokens respectively. For training, we collected only messages which contained at least one of the most frequent discourse connectives from each PDTB discourse sense (*Type*) annotation[2] among random tweets from January 2019: up to 3,000 messages for each type of discourse relation which is similar to the numbers in existing social media discourse relation datasets. With this process, we 1) balance our training set to have similar effect sizes of target datasets, 2) minimize potential biases towards a few dominant discourse relations in Twitter, and 3) keep the minimal numbers of discourse relation data samples to validate the effectiveness of the computationally efficient objective function for directly capturing discourse relations. Originally we found 20,787 tweets with our keyword search, but our discourse connective disambiguation process (see details in Section 3.2) left us 11,517 tweets. We chose random 10% of them as our development set to tune hyperparameters.

Qualitative Analysis Evaluation Set. For our qualitative analysis, we separately collected 10,000 random tweets from December 2018 without any

[2]after, before, when, but, though, nevertheless, however, because, if, and, for example, or, except, also.

restrictions so we can test our model on an unseen and unbiased natural social media test set as possible. This setting also allows us to conduct qualitative analysis with minimized potential biases which might exaggerate the capabilities of our model (e.g., our model would be evaluated on discourse relations and discourse connectives it had never seen during its training, so it would not be able to depend only on posterior probabilities of certain discourse connectives used as keywords for training set collection to obtain coherent qualitative analysis results).

PDTB-style Twitter Discourse Relation Dataset. As an additional social media evaluation, we created a Twitter discourse relation classification dataset. We collected 360 tweets from September 2020 using the same preprocessing methods for DiscRE training set. Specifically, first, we collected 30 tweets using all discourse connectives of each discourse relation class (i.e., *Contingency*, *Temporal*, *Comparison*, and *Expansion*) as search keywords from random tweets, so 120 tweets in total. Then, three well-trained annotators annotated whether each set of 30 tweets have its target relations as a binary classification. Finally, we randomly shuffled 120 keyword tweets and 240 non-keyword random tweets, and annotators classified four discourse relation classes. Pairwise inter-rater agreement was 85%, with three-way reliable in the moderate range (Fleiss $\kappa = 0.49$). We used majority vote as our discourse relation labels. Among 360 tweets, there were 36 *Contingency*, 8 *Temporal*, 22 *Comparison*, and 43 *Expansion* relations. The rest of the tweets were annotated with *None*.

3.2 Discourse Argument Extraction

We adopted the PDTB-style argument extraction method as it is relatively simple and thus more robust in noisy texts of social media. For argument extraction, we combined approaches of Biran and McKeown (2015) and Son et al. (2018).

We extract the sentences and use the Tweebo parser Kong et al. (2014) to extract discourse arguments (we identified discourse connectives only if there are verb phrases[3]). If there is discourse connective in a sentence, we identify an argument to which a discourse connective attached as *Arg2* , and the other as *Arg1* (Prasad et al., 2007). For discourse connectives at the beginning of a tweet, we identify the text from the beginning until the end of the first verb phrase separated by punctuation Tweet POS tags or other discourse connectives as *Arg2*, and the rest as *Arg1*; if a discourse connective or coordinating conjunction Tweet POS tag is in the middle, we identify the text from start to the middle connective as *Arg1*, and from the connective to the end as *Arg2* (Biran and McKeown, 2015). We also identify emojis as separate discourse arguments as suggested by (Son et al., 2018) since they play a critical role in signaling implicit relations.

3.3 Training

We use weakly supervised multitask learning with a hierarchy of PDTB-style discourse relation learners (Figure 2). Note that this method, as opposed to entirely self-supervised (i.e. predict next discourse argument), enables us to capture the relationships beyond the likelihood of one discourse argument to appear after another (i.e. how BERT models sentences), which would not necessarily distinguish one relationship from another.

Pseudo Labeling and Training Instance Generation. For each discourse argument pair, the discourse connectives were extracted, and the pair was labelled with all of the possible relations that are found in PDTB. We use the ratio of these possible discourse relations given the discourse connective as a weight within binary cross-entropy loss – this idea of using probabilistic labels follows the work in *pseudo labeling* for image recognition (Lee, 2013). More specifically, two types of training instances were used for the weakly supervised learning of DiscRE: explicit relation pairs and implicit relation pairs. For explicit relation training pairs, the discourse argument which contains discourse connectives is defined as *Arg2* and the rest text span of the pair is defined as *Arg1*. This segmentation method obtained state-of-the-art performances for previous discourse relation tasks (Biran and McKeown, 2015; Son et al., 2018). For implicit relation training pairs, the discourse connective is removed from *Arg2* of each pair; Rutherford and Xue (2015) found this approach can learn strong additional signals quite well, although it is not perfectly equivalent to learning implicit discourse relations[4]. Next, each of these generated pairs were input along with its whole tweet as its context to our DiscRE model

[3]minimal discourse units defined in Prasad et al. (2008)

[4]Among the discourse connectives we used for our training, only 'if' belongs to the *'Non-omissible'* discourse connective class and even this class showed relatively high effectiveness for implicit relation training when omitted (Rutherford and Xue, 2015).

optimize the model towards the objective function to learn the posterior distributions of all possible relations given the discourse connective in PDTB (Figure 3). Importantly, this mode of labeling is self scalable, yet it also enables a relatively delicate learning objective which considers all possible discourse relations rather than predicting just discourse connectives.

3.4 Discourse Relation Embeddings

We used a hierarchical bidirectional LSTM model; the first layer LSTM (Word LSTM) captures interaction between words of each discourse argument with attention. The second layer LSTM (Discourse Argument LSTM) captures relations among all discourse arguments across the whole tweet. This architecture was inspired by Son et al. (2018) and Ji and Smith (2017) as they found that their similar hierarchical model architecture performed well in related discourse relation tasks. As the first work to attempt embedding relations, we choose RNNs because the sequences of discourse units are of a similar size as where RNNs have been successful over transformers elsewhere (Matero and Schwartz, 2020). Discourse relations, by their definition, describe relations between neighboring or close discourse units, and thus do not have the same motivations for attention-based architectures as long distance dependencies in sequences of words.

This model was optimized on each tweet for training towards the following objective function:

$$J(\theta) = -\sum_{i}\sum_{j=1}^{N_i} w_{ij} y_{ij} log(f_i(x_{ij})))$$

where i is three levels of discourse relation hierarchy from PDTB (*Class*, *Type*, and *Subtype*) and N_i is the dimension of all existing relations in each level and w_{ij} is the posterior from PDTB of the relations given the discourse connective in the current pair of arguments. This can be viewed as multitask learning of shared RNN layers for three different level outputs (Figure 3). The hidden vectors of *Arg1* and *Arg2* from Discourse Argument LSTM were concatenated to learn *Class* output and *Type* output, as these are relations between two arguments. Whereas, only the hidden vector of *Arg2* from Discourse Argument LSTM was used for learning *Subtype* as it is rather a role of *Arg2*, given the *Class* and *Type* relations (Figure 3). There is a dropout layer with a dropout rate of 0.3 (as suggested in Ji and Smith (2017) and Son et al. (2018)) between Word LSTM and Discourse Argument LSTM.

Finally, for generating DiscRE, the hidden vectors of *Arg1* and *Arg2*, and the output vectors of *Class*, *Type*, and *Subtype* were concatenated. With this structure, DiscRE can capture latent features of discourse relations between any given argument pair, based on the context across all other discourse arguments in addition to probabilities of predefined discourse relations with contextual nuances (Figure 3).

Model Configuration. DiscRE is implemented in PyTorch (Paszke et al., 2019). For hyperparameter tuning, we explored the dimensions of pretrained word embeddings (Glove) and hidden vectors 25, 50, 100, and 200 with SGD and Adam (Kingma and Ba, 2014). We chose the models which obtain best performances on our development set, which used Adam with 200 dimensions and typically 50 epochs. We implemented a word-level attention as defined in (Yang et al., 2016) but with ReLU function for its activation. We compare with other similar models such as: (1) BERT, for which we used BERT base uncased model (12 layers, 768 hidden dimensions, and 12 heads) by HuggingFace [5]and (2) InferSent, for which we used a pretrained model trained with 300 dimension glove vectors as inputs and 2,048 LSTM hidden dimensions.

4 Results

DiscRE was validated on both newswire and social media discourse relation tasks. Additionally, qualitative analysis on the DiscRE representations were explore for both the domains.

4.1 Evaluations

First, we examined whether DiscRE can capture discourse relations in PDTB, even though grammatical properties and general text formats of newswire and social media are quite different. Then, we evaluated our model for social media discourse relation tasks: causal relation prediction and Twitter discourse relation classification. We used linear SVMs for all transfer learner classifiers for evaluation as this model obtained the best performance from the previous related work (Son et al., 2018).

[5] https://huggingface.co/bert-base-uncased

Models	CON.	TEM.	COM.	EXP.	Mic.	Mac.
Ngrams	0.575	0.693	0.757	0.757	0.709	0.695
BERT	**0.612**	0.724	0.746	0.748	0.714	0.708
Inferse.	0.604	0.670	0.738	0.726	0.693	0.685
DiscRE	0.598	**0.736**	**0.768**	**0.768**	**0.726**	**0.718**

Table 1: F1 scores of the four-way PDTB discourse class prediction ('CON.': *Contingency*, 'TEM.': *Temporal*, 'COM.': *Comparison*, 'EXP.': *Expansion*). We report both micro F1 and macro F1. DiscRE obtained the best performances across all four discourse relation classes except for the second best performance for Contingency class prediction F1.

Transfer Learning on PDTB. In order to measure how well our model can generalize to different domains and capture predefined newswire discourse relations, we conducted transfer learning experiments for predicting the four senses of Level-1 discourse relation classes: *Contingency*, *Temporal*, *Comparison*, and *Expansion*.

We extract DiscRE from the pairs: *Arg1* and *Arg2* from the PDTB dataset, and used them as transfer learning features to a linear classifier. The PDTB dataset was created with the annotators first segmenting the texts into discourse arguments, and then annotating a discourse relation between each pair of neighboring discourse arguments (marked as *Arg1* and *Arg2*). To make a fair comparison, we extracted BERT, Ngrams, and Infersent from *Arg1* and *Arg2* and the concatenation of *Arg1* and *Arg2* to use as separate features, so that the transfer learned model can recognize the notion of *Arg1* and *Arg2* and utilize the whole context as well. The classifiers were trained with each of these embeddings and we report the performances.

As suggested in Prasad et al. (2007), we used Sections 2 to 21 for training and Section 23 for testing in PDTB. Despite the relatively small number of the training set and larger domain differences with newswire target domains in its pretraining procedures, DiscRE still obtained the best performance for overall discourse relation predictions except for *Contingency* classification F1. This may indicate that DiscRE learns domain-agnostic signals for discourse relations leveraging discourse connectives in the weakly supervised multitask learning settings. (Table 1).

Causal Relation Prediction on Social Media. We evaluated our model on a causality prediction task on social media messages collected by Son et al. (2018). The DiscRE embeddings of the messages were extracted and for each message, the embeddings were averaged over for the transfer learning features for causality prediction. For comparison, BERT embeddings were also extracted for each discourse unit, and averaged for each message in the dataset, and Infersent sentence embeddings were directly extracted from the messages. The transfer learned classifier from DiscRE embeddings can be used to improve over the best results reported in the previous work on causality prediction (Son et al., 2018). DiscRE obtained better performances ($F1 = 0.752$) than BERT ($F1 = 0.746$) and Infersent (F1=0.709) and overall, this simple transfer learning approach using obtained a comparable performance to the models used in Son et al. (2018) ($F1 = 0.791$) (Table 2). On further exploration, we found that fine-tuning BERT for the causality prediction task improved the performance to $F1 = 0.789$. Furthermore, when DiscRE was used along with best performing text features from Son et al. (2018) (N-grams, Tweet POS tags, Word Pairs (Pitler et al., 2009), sentiment tags) of the messages for transfer learning, we obtained a new state-of-the-art performance (See Table 2)

Model	F1
(Son et al., 2018)	0.791
BERT	0.746
Infersent	0.709
DiscRE	0.752
BERT Fine-Tuned	0.789
DiscRE + ALL	**0.807**

Table 2: Causality prediction performance of DiscRE compared to other models. DiscRE-based classifier obtained the new state-of-the-art performance.

[6]Interestingly, on Twitter, the attention weights of social-media-specific variations of 'because' obtained similar weights even though the DiscRE model was not systematically designed to capture domain differences of discourse connectives: 'because': 0.16, 'bcuz': 0.18, 'cos': 0.16, 'cuz': 0.15, 'cause': 0.16.

Models	CON.	TEM.	COM.	EXP.	None	Mic.	Mac.
Ngrams	0.386	0.386	0.353	0.119	0.813	0.686	0.407
BERT	0.412	0.000	0.426	0.086	0.857	0.706	0.316
Inferse.	0.390	0.111	0.566	0.324	0.867	0.719	0.452
DiscRE	**0.478**	**0.421**	**0.591**	**0.400**	**0.883**	**0.758**	**0.554**

Table 3: F1 scores of the discourse class prediction on Twitter ('CON.': *Contingency*, 'TEM.': *Temporal*, 'COM.': *Comparison*, 'EXP.': *Expansion*). Then, we report both micro F1 and macro F1. DiscRE obtained the best performance across all relations.

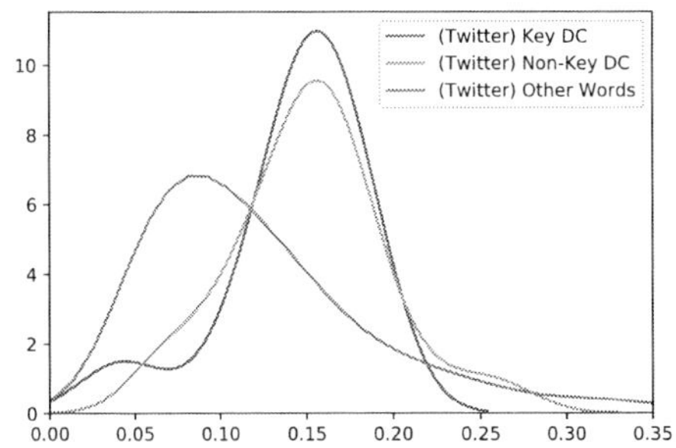

(a) Average Attention Weights on Twitter

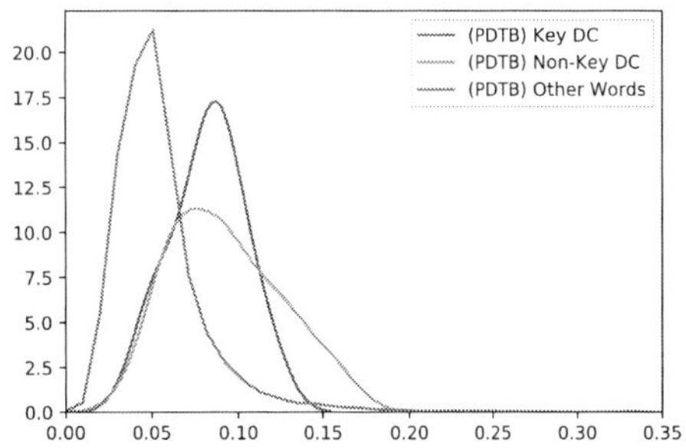

(b) Average Attention Weights on PDTB

Figure 4: Distribution plot with attention weights as a variable in x-axis, 'Key DC': discourse connectives used as keywords for the training set collection, 'Non-Key DC': discourse connectives which were not included in the keywords. We analyzed the average attention weight distributions of discourse connectives vs other words. Discourse connectives tend to receive higher attention on both PDTB and Twitter[6].

Discourse Relation Classification on Social Media. To validate DiscRE beyond the existing corpus of newswire domain, it was applied to a discourse relation classification task on our new Twitter discourse relation dataset. We extracted DiscRE, BERT, Ngrams, and Infersent from tweets with the same methods used in the causality task. We conducted 10-fold cross validation and report F1 scores of the models on each class in Table 3. The result showed that DiscRE obtains the best performance across all the classes. (Micro F1=0.758).

4.2 Qualitative Analysis on DiscRE model

Attention Analysis. First, we ran pretrained DiscRE on the evaluation tweet dataset (Section 3.1) and investigated average attention weights. Discourse connectives gained higher attention than non-discourse-connective words (Figure 4).[7] This suggests that discourse connectives play a quite significant role in DiscRE.

Furthermore, we observed that both, the discourse connectives used as keywords for training set collection, as well as the relatively less frequent discourse connectives obtained higher attention weights than other words on the random tweet evaluation set. This pattern supports that our model was not biased towards only prevailing discourse connectives it has already seen from the training set, but generalized quite well on unseen discourse connectives.

When we analyzed attention weights on the DiscRE model for the PDTB dataset, it showed a similar pattern. Although all words in the PDTB vocabulary generally obtained lower attention, the discourse connectives still obtained higher attention weights than other words, and relatively high attention weights were distributed on both keyword and non-keyword discourse connectives in PDTB as well. These results suggest that DiscRE can capture words with important discourse signals even on the other domains.

DiscRE Analysis. We evaluated DiscRE on social media discourse relations datasets which are publicly available: causality (Son et al., 2017) and

[7]Beyond some outliers due to noisy unigrams and social-media-specific discourse arguments (e.g., emojis or verb phrases with omitted subjects)

counterfactual (Son et al., 2018). We averaged the DiscRE embeddings of all adjacent pairs of discourse arguments per message and visualized using tSNE (Figures 5, 6). In general, discourse relations are diverse and even the same *Type* show up in various different forms in both explicit and implicit relations, so the distinctions between them are very hard to be captured within just two dimensions. Nevertheless, we found fairly clear patterns that distinguish two different discourse relations; majority counterfactual messages tend to cluster separately towards the left, as compared to causality messages (Figure 5). *Conjunctive Normal* and *Conjunctive Converse* forms of counterfactuals are especially clustered at the left side separately (e.g., "I would be healthier, if I had worked out regularly") (Son et al., 2017).

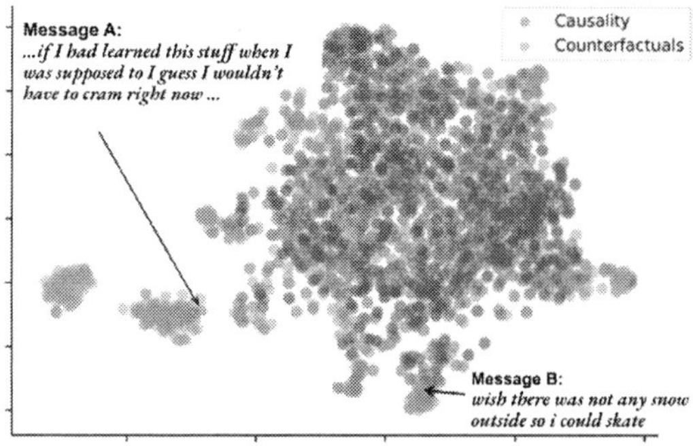

Figure 5: DiscRE differences between counterfactual messages and causality messages. Counterfactual messages are generally positioned at the left side compared to causality messages. When we investigated edge cases of causality messages that clustered closely with counterfactuals, we found causality messages which contained counterfactual relations inside ('Message A': 'is doing great.... lol. If I had learned this stuff when I was supposed to I guess I wouldn't have to cram right now. Oh well. There's always next year... or grade 12.' 'Message B': 'i wish there was not any snow outside so i could skate').

It is noteworthy that the counterfactual relation does not exist as a discourse relation tag in PDTB, but DiscRE still captures its distinguishable properties and even different forms of it (i.e., *Wish verb* forms and *Conjunctive* forms). While this visualization provides significant insights about semantic differences of discourse relations, further analysis over coherent clusters helps us see some discourse-based properties in common (e.g., see 'Message A' and 'Message B' on Figure 5).

Additionally, we investigated how well DiscRE can generalize to newswire domain by projecting DiscRE embeddings of discourse relations in the PDTB testset into 2D tSNE, similar to the visualization of causal and counterfatual relations (Figure 6). Even though we used most coarse-grained discourse relation classes, DiscRE captured quite coherent patterns of clusters for different relations. Nevertheless, many implicit discourse relations were clustered together on the upper left part as they are generally harder to be captured (Pitler et al., 2008; Rutherford and Xue, 2015).

5 Conclusion

This paper suggests a difference in how semantics is modeled in NLP, moving beyond word-level embeddings to embeddings that capture the semantics of discourse relations. We explored a new task of creating latent discourse relation embeddings, designing a novel weakly supervised multitask learning method and evaluating it both quantitatively and qualitatively over social media and newswire domains. While we built on previous work over discourse relation classes, our results suggest the *continuous* discourse relation embeddings (DiscRE) has certain benefits over manual categorizations. Continuous representations of relations between segments of text have been relatively unexplored yet they can yield subtle attributes of discourse relations, yielding strong performance in applications and perhaps new organizations of functional discourse relations.

Our model obtained the best performance on the discourse relation classification tasks in both PDTB and our new Twitter discourse dataset. Our model also obtained a new state-of-the-art performance using DiscRE in the social media causal relation prediction task. Further, for predicting discourse relations over PDTB, we found DiscRE achieved the higher performance than other embeddings, suggesting a focus on embedding *relations* can capture information not available in other types of modern embeddings which focus on representing particular word or phrase instances rather than their relationships. We release our dataset, code and pretrained models, for others to explore this new task, better develop continuous representations of discourse relations, as well as to extend discourse relation parsing beyond newswire to other domains.

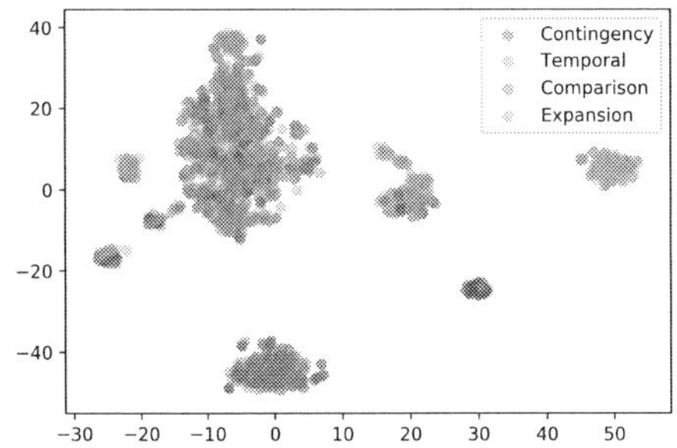

Figure 6: DiscRE differences between the four discourse relation classes of the PDTB dataset. Many examples of implicit discourse relations were clustered on the upper left side. Expansion is a quite general class which may overlap semantically with other types of relations, so they were more widely spread than other relations.

6 Limitations

The model delineated in this work is scalable with large amounts of unsupervised data, but still orders of magnitude less than what modern language models require. The social media validation was performed on a small annotated dataset with a high inter-annotator agreement, limited to 360 tweets that had examples from each relation class . The model was trained on a single 12GB memory GPU (we used a NVIDIA Titan XP graphics card). The approach should be expected to work best with languages that have limited morphology, like English.

The weakly supervised approach has a small limitation in that it still aligns the model, to some degree, with an existing tagset (i.e. the PDTB discourse relation tagset), but our results suggested we were able to capture relations beyond it (e.g. capturing a relation that is a mix of causal explanation and counterfactuals).

7 Ethical Considerations

All of our work is restricted to document-level information; No user-level information is used.

Acknowledgements

This work was supported by DARPA via Young Faculty Award grant #W911NF-20-1-0306 to H. Andrew Schwartz at Stony Brook University; the conclusions and opinions expressed are attributable only to the authors and should not be construed as those of DARPA or the U.S. Department of Defense. This work was also supported in part by NIH R01 AA028032-01.

References

Hongxiao Bai and Zhao Hai. 2018. Deep enhanced representation for implicit discourse relation recognition. In *COLING*.

Parminder Bhatia, Yangfeng Ji, and Jacob Eisenstein. 2015. Better document-level sentiment analysis from rst discourse parsing. In *Proceedings of the 2015 Conference on Empirical Methods in Natural Language Processing*, pages 2212–2218.

Or Biran and Kathleen McKeown. 2015. Pdtb discourse parsing as a tagging task: The two taggers approach. In *Proceedings of the 16th Annual Meeting of the Special Interest Group on Discourse and Dialogue*, pages 96–104.

Lynn Carlson, Daniel Marcu, and Mary Ellen Okurovsky. 2001. Building a discourse-tagged corpus in the framework of rhetorical structure theory. In *Proceedings of the Second SIGdial Workshop on Discourse and Dialogue*.

Alexis Conneau, Douwe Kiela, Holger Schwenk, Loïc Barrault, and Antoine Bordes. 2017. Supervised learning of universal sentence representations from natural language inference data. In *Proceedings of the 2017 Conference on Empirical Methods in Natural Language Processing*, pages 670–680.

Jacob Devlin, Ming-Wei Chang, Kenton Lee, and Kristina Toutanova. 2018. Bert: Pre-training of deep bidirectional transformers for language understanding. *arXiv preprint arXiv:1810.04805*.

Yacine Jernite, Samuel R Bowman, and David Sontag. 2017. Discourse-based objectives for fast unsupervised sentence representation learning. *arXiv preprint arXiv:1705.00557*.

Yangfeng Ji and Jacob Eisenstein. 2014. Representation learning for text-level discourse parsing. In *Proceedings of the 52nd Annual Meeting of the Association for Computational Linguistics (Volume 1: Long Papers)*, volume 1, pages 13–24.

Yangfeng Ji, Gholamreza Haffari, and Jacob Eisenstein. 2016. A latent variable recurrent neural network for discourse relation language models. In *Proceedings of NAACL-HLT*, pages 332–342.

Yangfeng Ji and Noah A Smith. 2017. Neural discourse structure for text categorization. In *Proceedings of the 55th Annual Meeting of the Association for Computational Linguistics (Volume 1: Long Papers)*, pages 996–1005.

Diederik P Kingma and Jimmy Ba. 2014. Adam: A method for stochastic optimization. *arXiv preprint arXiv:1412.6980*.

Yudai Kishimoto, Yugo Murawaki, and Sadao Kurohashi. 2020. Adapting BERT to implicit discourse relation classification with a focus on discourse connectives. In *Proceedings of the 12th Language Resources and Evaluation Conference*, pages 1152–1158, Marseille, France. European Language Resources Association.

Lingpeng Kong, Nathan Schneider, Swabha Swayamdipta, Archna Bhatia, Chris Dyer, and Noah A. Smith. 2014. A dependency parser for tweets. In *Proceedings of the 2014 Conference on Empirical Methods in Natural Language Processing (EMNLP)*, pages 1001–1012, Doha, Qatar. Association for Computational Linguistics.

Man Lan, Jianxiang Wang, Yuanbin Wu, Zheng-Yu Niu, and Haifeng Wang. 2017. Multi-task attention-based neural networks for implicit discourse relationship representation and identification. In *Proceedings of the 2017 Conference on Empirical Methods in Natural Language Processing*, pages 1299–1308.

Dong-Hyun Lee. 2013. Pseudo-label: The simple and efficient semi-supervised learning method for deep neural networks. In *Workshop on Challenges in Representation Learning, ICML*, volume 3, page 2.

Ziheng Lin, Hwee Tou Ng, and Min-Yen Kan. 2014. A pdtb-styled end-to-end discourse parser. *Natural Language Engineering*, 20(2):151–184.

Yang Liu, Sujian Li, Xiaodong Zhang, and Zhifang Sui. 2016. Implicit discourse relation classification via multi-task neural networks. In *Thirtieth AAAI Conference on Artificial Intelligence*.

Yuhao Ma, Yu Yan, and Jie Liu. 2021. *Implicit Discourse Relation Classification Based on Semantic Graph Attention Networks*. Association for Computing Machinery, New York, NY, USA.

Matthew Matero and H. Andrew Schwartz. 2020. Autoregressive affective language forecasting: A self-supervised task. In *Proceedings of the 28th International Conference on Computational Linguistics*, pages 2913–2923, Barcelona, Spain (Online). International Committee on Computational Linguistics.

Allen Nie, Erin Bennett, and Noah Goodman. 2019. Dissent: Learning sentence representations from explicit discourse relations. In *Proceedings of the 57th Annual Meeting of the Association for Computational Linguistics*, pages 4497–4510.

Joonsuk Park and Claire Cardie. 2012. Improving implicit discourse relation recognition through feature set optimization. In *Proceedings of the 13th Annual Meeting of the Special Interest Group on Discourse and Dialogue*, pages 108–112. Association for Computational Linguistics.

Adam Paszke, Sam Gross, Francisco Massa, Adam Lerer, James Bradbury, Gregory Chanan, Trevor Killeen, Zeming Lin, Natalia Gimelshein, Luca Antiga, et al. 2019. Pytorch: An imperative style, high-performance deep learning library. In *Advances in Neural Information Processing Systems*, pages 8024–8035.

Matthew Peters, Mark Neumann, Mohit Iyyer, Matt Gardner, Christopher Clark, Kenton Lee, and Luke Zettlemoyer. 2018. Deep contextualized word representations. In *Proceedings of the 2018 Conference of the North American Chapter of the Association for Computational Linguistics: Human Language Technologies, Volume 1 (Long Papers)*, pages 2227–2237.

Emily Pitler, Annie Louis, and Ani Nenkova. 2009. Automatic sense prediction for implicit discourse relations in text. In *Proceedings of the Joint Conference of the 47th Annual Meeting of the ACL and the 4th International Joint Conference on Natural Language Processing of the AFNLP: Volume 2-Volume 2*, pages 683–691. Association for Computational Linguistics.

Emily Pitler, Mridhula Raghupathy, Hena Mehta, Ani Nenkova, Alan Lee, and Aravind K Joshi. 2008. Easily identifiable discourse relations. *Technical Reports (CIS)*, page 884.

Diana Nicoleta Popa, Julien Perez, James Henderson, and Eric Gaussier. 2019. Implicit discourse relation classification with syntax-aware contextualized word representations. In *The Thirty-Second International Flairs Conference*.

Rashmi Prasad, Nikhil Dinesh, Alan Lee, Eleni Miltsakaki, Livio Robaldo, Aravind K Joshi, and Bonnie L Webber. 2008. The penn discourse treebank 2.0. In *LREC*. Citeseer.

Rashmi Prasad, Eleni Miltsakaki, Nikhil Dinesh, Alan Lee, Aravind Joshi, Livio Robaldo, and Bonnie L Webber. 2007. The penn discourse treebank 2.0 annotation manual.

Attapol Rutherford and Nianwen Xue. 2015. Improving the inference of implicit discourse relations via classifying explicit discourse connectives. In *Proceedings of the 2015 Conference of the North American Chapter of the Association for Computational Linguistics: Human Language Technologies*, pages 799–808.

Wei Shi and Vera Demberg. 2019. Next sentence prediction helps implicit discourse relation classification within and across domains. In *Proceedings of the 2019 Conference on Empirical Methods in Natural Language Processing and the 9th International Joint Conference on Natural Language Processing (EMNLP-IJCNLP)*, pages 5790–5796, Hong Kong, China. Association for Computational Linguistics.

Damien Sileo, Tim Van de Cruys, Camille Pradel, and Philippe Muller. 2019. Mining discourse markers for unsupervised sentence representation learning. In *Proceedings of the 2019 Conference of the North American Chapter of the Association for Computational Linguistics: Human Language Technologies, Volume 1 (Long and Short Papers)*, pages 3477–3486.

Youngseo Son, Nipun Bayas, and H Andrew Schwartz. 2018. Causal explanation analysis on social media. In *Proceedings of the 2018 Conference on Empirical Methods in Natural Language Processing*, pages 3350–3359.

Youngseo Son, Anneke Buffone, Joe Raso, Allegra Larche, Anthony Janocko, Kevin Zembroski, H Andrew Schwartz, and Lyle Ungar. 2017. Recognizing counterfactual thinking in social media texts. In *Proceedings of the 55th Annual Meeting of the Association for Computational Linguistics (Volume 2: Short Papers)*, pages 654–658.

Siddharth Varia, Christopher Hidey, and Tuhin Chakrabarty. 2019. Discourse relation prediction: Revisiting word pairs with convolutional networks. In *Proceedings of the 20th Annual SIGdial Meeting on Discourse and Dialogue*, pages 442–452, Stockholm, Sweden. Association for Computational Linguistics.

Zichao Yang, Diyi Yang, Chris Dyer, Xiaodong He, Alex Smola, and Eduard Hovy. 2016. Hierarchical attention networks for document classification. In *Proceedings of the 2016 Conference of the North American Chapter of the Association for Computational Linguistics: Human Language Technologies*, pages 1480–1489.

Yingxue Zhang, Fandong Meng, Peng Li, Ping Jian, and Jie Zhou. 2021. Context tracking network: Graph-based context modeling for implicit discourse relation recognition. In *Proceedings of the 2021 Conference of the North American Chapter of the Association for Computational Linguistics: Human Language Technologies*, pages 1592–1599, Online. Association for Computational Linguistics.

Understanding Cross-modal Interactions in V&L Models that Generate Scene Descriptions

Michele Cafagna[1] **Kees van Deemter**[2] **Albert Gatt**[1,2]

[1]University of Malta, Institute of Linguistics and Language Technology
[2]Universiteit Utrecht, Information and Computing Sciences
michele.cafagna@um.edu.mt
{a.gatt, c.j.vandeemter}@uu.nl

Abstract

Image captioning models tend to describe images in an object-centric way, emphasising visible objects. But image descriptions can also abstract away from objects and describe the type of scene depicted. In this paper, we explore the potential of a state of the art Vision and Language model, VinVL, to caption images at the scene level using (1) a novel dataset which pairs images with both object-centric and scene descriptions. Through (2) an in-depth analysis of the effect of the fine-tuning, we show (3) that a small amount of curated data suffices to generate scene descriptions without losing the capability to identify object-level concepts in the scene; the model acquires a more holistic view of the image compared to when object-centric descriptions are generated. We discuss the parallels between these results and insights from computational and cognitive science research on scene perception.

Figure 1: Image from the MS-COCO 2014 validation set. One reference caption is: *a man in a chefs hat chopping food.*

1 Introduction

When humans view images, they can quickly capture their 'gist'. For example, it is immediately evident that Figure 1 is a kitchen. Such judgments are fast and are informed by expectations about which objects occur in typical scenes ('scene semantics') and their configuration ('syntax') (Malcolm et al., 2016; Võ, 2021; Self et al., 2019). This knowledge affects the deployment of attentional resources (Torralba et al., 2006; Oliva and Torralba, 2007; Wu et al., 2014; Henderson and Hayes, 2017). Scene understanding and object recognition constrain the selection of attended locations in human visual attention (Itti and Koch, 2001).

In this paper, we explore the implications of these findings for image captioning models. There are at least two levels at which an image can be appraised. An **object-centric** perspective focuses primarily on individual objects and actions (e.g. the example caption in Fig 1). This has dominated captioning models (see Hodosh et al., 2013, for an early, influential statement of this view) and has informed the design of widely-used datasets, which pair images with captions that explicitly mention at least some of the objects in a picture (e.g. Young et al., 2014; Chen et al., 2015; Pont-Tuset et al., 2020; Gurari et al., 2019; Sharma et al., 2018; Agrawal et al., 2019). In contrast, a **scene-level** caption (e.g. 'a kitchen' for Figure 1) contains less object-specific detail. Such captions are less redundant with respect to the image they describe, but convey enough information to generate inferences about content and structure (e.g. kitchens typically contain cupboards, but not birds; etc).

Most image captioning datasets contain object-centric captions and no currently available resource pairs both scene-level and object-centric captions with images. In this paper, we address this gap and ask (i) whether captioning models can be adapted both for object-centric and scene-level captioning and (ii) whether the two strategies rely on different types of interplay between the visual and linguistic modalities. Addressing these questions can shed light on the ability of V&L models to reason about the relationship between scenes and their components. In addition, it is desirable for mod-

Proceedings of the Workshop on Unimodal and Multimodal Induction of Linguistic Structures (UM-IoS), pages 56 - 72
December 7, 2022 ©2022 Association for Computational Linguistics

els to generate scene-level descriptions as well as object-centric ones. In many communicative contexts, scene-level captions are informative and non-redundant, recalling the quality and the quantity discourse maxims defined by Grice (1975).

We present a study of object-centric versus scene-level captioning. We focus on VinVL (Zhang et al., 2021), a BERT-based model in the OSCAR family (Li et al., 2020b) of models, which have recently dominated the state of the art in image captioning.[1] Our main contributions are:

i) We introduce a novel dataset, HL-Scenes (Sec 3) extending part of the COCO dataset (Chen et al., 2015) with scene-level descriptions.

ii) We perform an in-depth investigation of the impact of fine-tuning on the pre-trained model. The analysis is designed to thoroughly inspect object-scene relations by exploiting cross-modal attention (Sec 5), coupled with probing (Sec 7) and ablation studies (Sec 6).

iii) We show that (i) VinVL's pre-trained representations are rich enough to support scene-level captioning, but that (ii) fine-tuning results in a different deployment of attentional resources. This bears parallels to the findings in research on human scene perception.

2 Related work

Datasets Existing image-caption datasets emphasise object-centric captions (an early exception, using abstract scenes, is Ortiz et al., 2015). This is also true of web-sourced datasets such as Conceptual Captions (CC; Sharma et al., 2018). For example, the CC filtering pipeline explicitly checks for overlaps between caption tokens and objects identified in the image. The `nocaps` benchmark (Agrawal et al., 2019) tests models' ability to generalise to out-of-domain objects. There are several V&L datasets and tasks which introduce knowledge-rich annotations and address models' ability to reason with linguistic and visual cues (Zellers et al., 2019, 2018; Suhr et al., 2017, 2019; Park et al., 2020; Pezzelle et al., 2020). In this paper, we take this line of work further by introducing the novel HL-Scenes dataset, which pairs object-centric and scene-level captions to images.

[1] At the time of this work, three OSCAR-based models (OSCAR, VinVL, LEMON) are among the top 5 in the leaderboard of the COCO image captioning task.

Models Transformer-based V&L models are usually divided into *single-stream* (Li et al., 2020a; Chen et al., 2020; Li et al., 2020b; Su et al., 2020) and *dual-stream* (Tan and Bansal, 2019; Lu et al., 2019; Radford et al., 2021) architectures. It has been shown that single- and dual- stream models perform roughly at par under the same training settings (Bugliarello et al., 2021). On the other hand Hendricks et al. (2021) showed that model performance is highly impacted by dataset curation, attention, and loss function definition.

Most V&L single-stream models are inspired by BERT (Devlin et al., 2019). They incorporate the visual modality in the form of features extracted using a visual backbone, typically a Faster-RCNN (Ren et al., 2015) pre-trained on an object labelling task such as ImageNet (Deng et al., 2009; Russakovsky et al., 2015). From the perspective of caption generation, the Oscar (Li et al., 2020b) single-stream architecture has emerged as an influential model. Oscar enforces grounding between image-caption pairs by using object labels as anchor points (a strategy also adopted by Hu et al., 2021). This makes it particularly suited to the goals of this paper, namely, in-depth analysis of the cross-modal interactions in the treatment of objects during generation. Oscar and its successors, VinVL (Zhang et al., 2021) and LEMON (Hu et al., 2022) achieved SOTA performance on captioning tasks such as COCO and `nocaps`.

Methods In this paper, we focus on three techniques for model analysis: attention analysis, multimodal ablation and probing. Analyses of attention in pre-trained V&L models include both quantitative methods (e.g. Abnar and Zuidema, 2020) and qualitative analysis (e.g. Li et al., 2020a; Wei et al., 2021). We use both methods to study how VinVL deploys attention during the generation, of object-centric, versus scene-level captions (Section 5).

Several methods have been proposed to study the extent to which V&L models exploit both visual and textual information (Shekhar et al., 2017; Parcalabescu et al., 2022; Gat et al., 2021; Hessel and Lee, 2020). Ablation methods analyse model behaviour when portions of the input are masked or deleted (Bugliarello et al., 2021; Cafagna et al., 2021). We use the ablation of diagnostic objects in scenes (Section 6), to study the reliance of VinVL on such objects during scene-level caption generation.

Probes are well-suited to test for the presence

of task-relevant information in model representations (Belinkov and Glass, 2019; Belinkov, 2022). Cao et al. (2020) develop a probe-based benchmark centred around different V&L tasks. Salin et al. (2022) analyse models' reliance on text versus vision to capture colour information. Hendricks and Nematzadeh (2021) rely on probes to study lexical and syntactic understanding in V&L models. In our approach, similar in spirit, we develop probes to identify and measure the extend to which scene information is present in the model's representations before and after fine-tuning on scene-level caption generation.

3 Data

We developed the new High Level Scenes (HL-scenes) dataset, which is explicitly designed to pair images with both object-centric and scene-level captions. To this end, we sampled 15k images from the 2014 COCO train split (Chen et al., 2015), with the constraint that each image depicts at least one person. Captions in COCO are highly object-centric (Lin et al., 2014). We crowd-sourced three scene-level annotations per image on Amazon Mechanical Turk[2], from workers with at least an 85% approval rating. Crowd workers saw an image and wrote a description in response to the question: *Where is the picture taken?* Annotators were encouraged to use their knowledge of typical scenes in writing their descriptions. Finally, we paired our scene-level HL captions with the previously available COCO (Lin et al., 2014) captions.

Figure 2 shows an example of an image with the two types of captions. See Appendix E for more examples. We collected a total of 14,997 image-caption pairs, and we reserve 11,999 for training and 1,499 each for validation and testing.

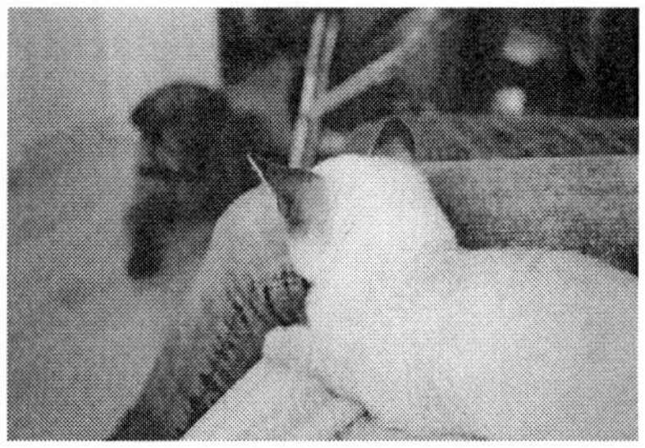

COCO
Reference: a close-up of a kitten looking at a dog laying in the background.
Generated: a cat and a dog sitting next to each other.

HL-scenes
Reference: in the home.
Generated: the picture is taken in a house.

Figure 2: Scene-level captions in HL-Scenes, with corresponding object-centric COCO caption. The generated captions are outputs from VinVL before and after fine-tuning (see Section 4).

4 Model

VinVL (Zhang et al., 2021) is a single-stream BERT-based model with a Faster-RCNN (Ren et al., 2015) visual backbone. It is an extension of Oscar (Li et al., 2020b). VinVL implements a training strategy where object tags are used as anchor points between the visual and textual modality to facilitate cross-modal alignment. As pointed out by Li et al. (2020b), this strategy is motivated by the fact that in the datasets used to pre-train multimodal models, between 1 and 3 of the objects detected by the visual backbone are mentioned in the caption. However, the object labels are provided by an off-the-self object detector separately trained on Visual Genome (Krishna et al., 2017). VinVL was pre-trained on a combination of COCO (Chen et al., 2015), Conceptual Captions (Sharma et al., 2018), SBU captions (Ordonez et al., 2011) and Flickr30k (Young et al., 2014), as well as additional VQA data.

VinVL has been shown to perform well on understanding tasks, including VQA, NLVR2, image-text and text-image retrieval (Goyal et al., 2017; Suhr et al., 2019; Lin et al., 2014), and on generative tasks, including COCO (Chen et al., 2015) and `nocaps` (Agrawal et al., 2019).

In the Oscar family of models, the use of labels as anchors makes the models ideal for our experiments, in that it explicitly enables us to study the interaction between object-level information (captured by labels and visual features) and scene-level description generation.

4.1 Fine-tuning

We first establish that VinVL can generate scene descriptions after fine-tunning, before turning to an in-depth analysis of the model's attention and internal representations.

We note that since the HL-scenes dataset extends the COCO dataset, the model has been exposed to the images of the HL-scenes dataset during pre-

[2]Workers were paid at the rate of €0.03 per item, an amount we consider equitable for the work involved, and in line with rates for similar tasks.

Epoch.	B4	M	RL	CIDEr	SPICE
2	49.3	29.3	67.1	161.8	32.6
4	49.7	30.1	68.1	168.5	34.0
6	48.5	29.8	67.3	164.9	33.5
8	48.9	30.2	67.6	165.8	33.9
10	49.1	30.4	67.7	168.0	34.4

Table 1: Automatic metrics computed over different epochs on the HL-Scenes validation set. B4: Bleu-4; M: METEOR; RL: ROUGE-L.

training on COCO. On the other hand, the scene descriptions are completely novel.

We fine-tune on scene-descriptions for 10 epochs. We use the standard configuration used by Zhang et al. (2021) for image captioning. At inference time, we fix the maximum generation length to 20 tokens and use a beam size of 5.

VinVL shows a quick adaptation to the scene-level descriptions from the first epoch. This adaptability recalls observations made for other transformer-based generative models (e.g. Brown et al., 2020). We show an example in Figure 2. For completeness, Table 1 reports the automatic evaluation metrics computed on the validation set over 10 epochs. For more details see Appendix A.

5 How does attention to objects change from object-centric to scene-level generation?

We first investigate the model's self-attention before and after fine-tuning on the scene-level caption generation task.

Method We focus on the self-attention patterns in the first layer, as they are directly connected to the inputs and do not depend on higher-level interactions which might obscure the fundamental changes in attention across the two modalities (visual features and labels) in VinVL. A discussion of attention patterns at higher layers can be found in Appendix (B). We select 100 random samples from the HL-Scenes test-set and extract the attention matrices before and after fine-tuning on scene descriptions. We aggregate the attention values by taking the maximum across all the heads, as it allows us to observe where the model tends to assign a significant amount of attention, giving us a better view of the potential impact of fine-tuning on scene-level captions. VinVL prevents textual inputs from directly interacting with the other modalities during generation; therefore there is no interaction between caption tokens and visual features. On the other hand, the model includes object tags as anchors and this allows us to study the multimodal interactions between the visual features and these object labels.

VinVL acquires a holistic view of the scene after pre-training Figure 3 is a representative example of self-attention matrices extracted from the pre-trained (3a) and fine-tuned (3b) model with the image in Figure 2. The pre-trained model, which generates an object-centric caption, focuses attention on individual input tokens in the vision-to-vision, vision-to-label and label-to-vision sub-blocks.

After fine-tuning, as the model generates a scene-level caption, the self-attention appears to be more evenly distributed over the inputs (3b). This suggests that when generating scene-level captions, the model leverages a wider range of visual features with less exclusive focus on individual objects or labels.

We perform a quantitative analysis of the self-attention in the sub-blocks of the matrix involving visual regions and object labels, computing a kernel density estimate of the distributions of the standard deviations and attention masses for each of the 100 samples. The result is shown in Figure 4. It is clear that the fine-tuned model has overall a lower standard deviation than the pre-trained model. This confirms that a similar attention mass is distributed more evenly after fine-tuning. We take this as evidence that in the process of generating scene descriptions, the fine-tuned model acquires a more holistic view of the input image, in contrast to the highly object-centred deployment of attentional resources evident in the pre-trained model.

VinVL relies on diagnostic objects when generating scene-level captions VinVL redistributes self-attention over a wider range of visual features after fine-tuning. Nevertheless, previous work on scene perception (Self et al., 2019; Võ, 2021) leads us to expect that in describing a scene, the model needs to rely on highly diagnostic objects. We compute diagnosticity empirically, based on the occurrence of objects in scenes in our dataset. Let S be the set of the k most frequent scene types mentioned in scene-level captions in the HL-Scenes dataset.[3] We proceed as follows:

1. $\forall\ s \in S$ we build $O_M^s = [o_1^s, o_2^s, ..., o_n^s]$, the ranked list of the n most attended objects by

[3] Since our dataset consists of captions, we extract scene labels from these captions. See Appendix (B).

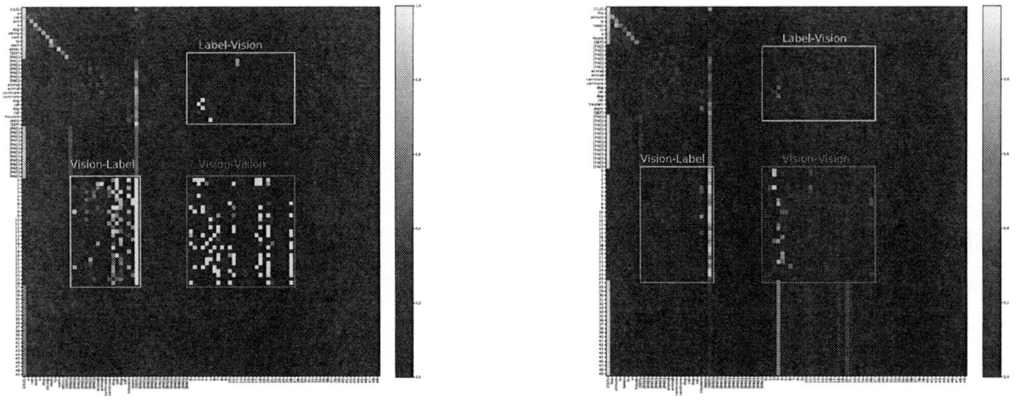

(a) Attention matrix of the pre-trained model

(b) Attention matrix of the fine-tuned model

Figure 3: Attention matrices comparison for the image in Figure 2. We highlight the sub-blocks corresponding to vision-to-vision, vision-to-label and label-to-vision. In the pre-trained model, attention mass is sharply focused on individual portions of the input; after fine-tuning, a more even distribution is observed.

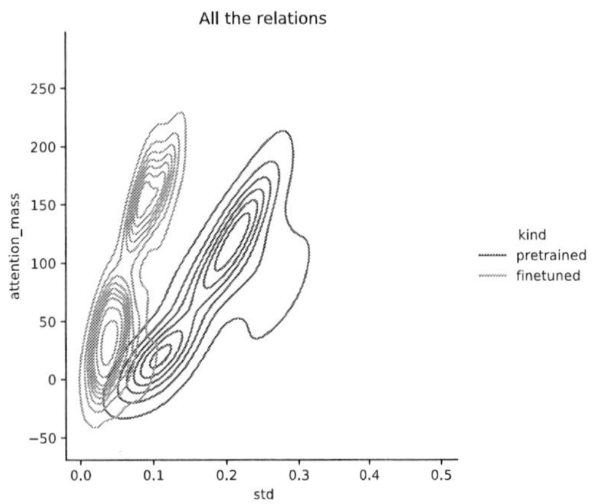

Figure 4: Kernel density estimate of distributions of standard deviations against attention mass for pre-trained and fine-tuned VinVL.

Scene	RBO @			IoU @		
	3	5	7	3	5	7
station	0.88	0.84	0.87	0.5	0.66	1.0
road	1.0	0.9	0.91	1.0	0.66	1.0
room	0.27	0.25	0.24	0.2	0.11	0.18
sea	0.88	0.84	0.8	0.5	0.66	0.55
resort	0.72	0.7	0.7	0.5	0.42	0.55
house	0.38	0.5	0.53	0.5	0.42	0.55
restaurant	0.55	0.55	0.54	0.5	0.42	0.53

Table 2: Rank Biased Overlap (RBO) and Intersection over Union (IoU) of the most attended objects and the most frequent objects for the top seven common scenes. Both metrics range from 0 (no overlap) to 1 (perfect correspondence).

the model M when generating a description of a scene of type s.

2. Similarly, $\forall\ s \in S$ we collect $O_D^s = [o_1^s, o_2^s, ..., o_n^s]$, the ranked list of the most frequent objects in images depicting scenes of type s in the dataset D.

We measure the overlap between O_M^s and O_D^s by computing their Intersection over Union (IoU), which is only sensitive to overlap in content, as well as their Rank Biased Overlap (RBO; Webber et al., 2010)[4], which computes the similarity of two ranked lists. More details about this metric are given in Appendix B. Table 2 shows RBO and IoU for the top 3, 5 and 7 objects in the lists. We observe that the two metrics correlate strongly ($r(19) = .81, p < .001$). From this we conclude that during generation of scene-level captions, the model attends more to diagnostic objects, i.e. those which are common in a scene of a given type. Moreover, we observe high scores for scene types such as *station, road, resort, sea*. In our dataset, these are characterised by frequently occurring objects, which are therefore highly diagnostic of scene type. In contrast, for scenes like *room, house, restaurant* we observe lower scores. We hypothesise that this is due to the fact that such scenes can contain a wider variety of objects, which individually have lower diagnosticity with respect to the scene type.

6 How reliant is the model on diagnostic objects?

The results from the previous sections established that, following fine-tuning on scene-level descrip-

[4]https://github.com/changyaochen/rbo

tions, VinVL distributes attention more evenly over objects in a scene. Nevertheless, the objects which are most likely to be present in a scene attract the highest proportion of the attention mass. This raises the question whether, by removing highly diagnostic objects from an image, the model representations are still informative enough to detect what type of scene is represented in an image.

We first address this issue from the perspective of generation: does a model fine-tuned on scene descriptions still manage to correctly describe a picture at the scene level, when highly diagnostic objects are unavailable? Given the more even distribution of attention observed across scene components in the fine-tuned model, our hypothesis would be that even in the absence of such highly diagnostic objects, the model can rely on other information to detect the scene type. Hence, we expect the fine-tuned model to be more robust to object ablation in the visual modality, compared to the model pre-trained on object-level captions.

6.1 Method

As explained in Section 4, in VinVL, two separate models are used to (i) extract visual features corresponding to regions via the model's visual backbone; and (ii) to determine the object labels that function as anchors between the visual and textual modalities. This means we do not have an exact correspondence between object labels and visual features.

Visual feature tagging For simplicity we will refer to *vf* as the bounding box a visual feature corresponds to, and *ot* as the bounding box an object label corresponds to. To perform an ablation, we first establish an approximate correspondence betweeen *ot* and *vf*, using *ot* as reference to assign an object label to the visual features.

We compute the IoU[5] between *vf* and *ot* and empirically assign a label to a visual feature if $IoU(vf, ot) >= 0.6$. Moreover, if *vf* is contained by or overlaps with *ot* by at least 80% of its area, we assign to *vf* the label of *ot*. With this heuristic we cover 74% of the visual features of every image of our sample.

Computing object diagnosticity We use the scene labels extracted from captions in Section 5, and compute the Pointwise Mutual Information (PMI) between scene types and object labels. Examples of the most informative objects for some scenes are shown in Table 3.

[5]Note that in this section we refer to the Intersection Over Union to compute the overlap between two bounding boxes, not the metric used to compute the overlap between two sets of items as done in Section 5.

Scene	Top informative objects
restaurant	french fries, fork, submarine sandwich
road	vehicle number plate, traffic sign, traffic light
sea	surfboard, watercraft, boat
room	computer mouse, nightstand, tablet computer
station	train, suitcase, luggage and bags

Table 3: Most informative objects for some scenes ranked using PMI.

the picture is shot in a ski resort → the picture is taken in a snowfield *(jacket, tree, footwear)*
the picture is shot in a baseball field → the picture is taken in a ground *(sports uniform, man, boy)*
in a kitchen → in the kitchen *(kitchen appliance, countertop, cabinetry)*

Figure 5: Changes to scene-level captions generated by the fine-tuned model after ablation of three diagnostic objects. Ablated objects are shown in parentheses.

Ablation Ablation of an object is performed similarly to (Frank et al., 2021), by removing its corresponding label from the list of object tags, along with every visual feature assigned to that object. We replace them with a `[PAD]` token. We compare captions generated by both the pre-trained and fine-tuned model with and without ablation of the top 1, 2 and 3 most informative objects for a given scene in the test-set. For more details on the sample sizes see Appendix C.

6.2 Results

We expect to observe some differences in the generations when ablation is applied, especially in the pre-trained model, as the ablation removes information which is explicitly verbalised in object-centric captions. For the pre-trained model, object-centric captions change 41% of the time after ablation, compared to 13% of the time for the scene-level captions by the fine-tuned model.

A manual inspection on a sample of items suggested that the changes in the captions involve minimal semantic shifts, often due to minor function word changes or a more generic term being generated for the noun denoting the scene type. Some examples are shown in Figure 5.

In summary, the model is resilient to ablation in the visual modality, suggesting that its representations are robust for both types of generation task,

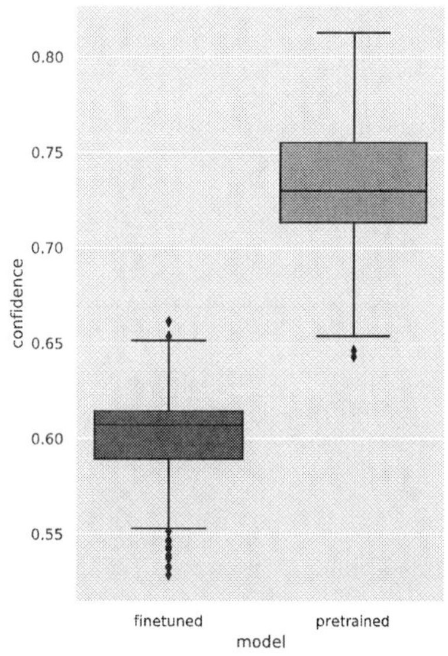

Figure 6: Confidence scores of the unchanged caption after ablation. On the left, the model generating scene-level descriptions (fine-tuned); on the right, the model generating objective descriptions (pre-trained).

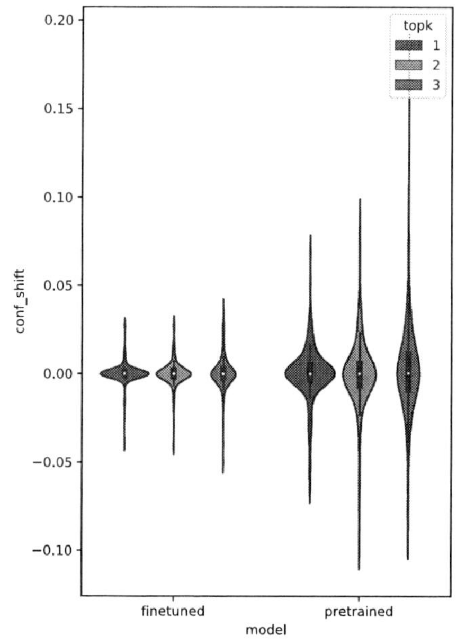

Figure 7: Confidence shift of the unchanged captions when ablating the top 1, 2 and 3 most informative objects from the scene. A negative shift means that the caption was generated with higher confidence after ablation. On the left, the model generating scene-descriptions (fine-tuned); on the right, the model generating object-centric descriptions (pre-trained).

but more so for scene-level captioning. We study robustness of representations in more detail using probes, in Section 7.

Confidence scores We also analyse the confidence score produced at generation time by the model for those captions which do not change after ablation. As shown in Figure 6, after ablation pre-trained VinVL generates object-centric descriptions with higher confidence than fine-tuned VinVL does with scene-level descriptions. However, the variance in the confidence score after ablation is lower for the fine-tuned model generating scene-level captions (Figure 7), suggesting greater robustness to ablation during scene-level caption generation.

7 Can we disentangle the role of attention and model representation?

The results so far suggest that there are significant changes in the model's self-attention, though it relies on diagnostic objects to generate scene-level captions. It is also somewhat more robust to object ablation, especially in the fine-tuned case. At this point, we probe the model's representations to address to what extent the knowledge required for scene-level caption generation is already present after pre-training. This would imply that the primary change to the model after fine-tuning is in the self-attention mechanism.

Method Given a pair (V, L) consisting of visual features V and object labels L, we train a probe to classify scene type based on VinVL encodings, before and after fine-tuning. We also repeat the procedure on inputs ablated as described in Section 6. For this experiment, we identify 1426 images from HL-scenes, representing 8 types of scene, downsampling the more frequent classes (see Appendix D for details). The class distribution is shown in Figure 8. For every image in the probing dataset we extract the model's feature representations from the last layer and we average across the inputs, obtaining a single vector.

We train both a neural and a random forest probe. We report results from the latter which is the best performing; full details of the neural probe are in Appendix D.

Results Probes are tested on different train/test proportions, up to a 50/50 split. In Figure 9 we report results for the 50/50 train/test split, which is also the most challenging (for results on other splits see Appendix D). The baseline performs a

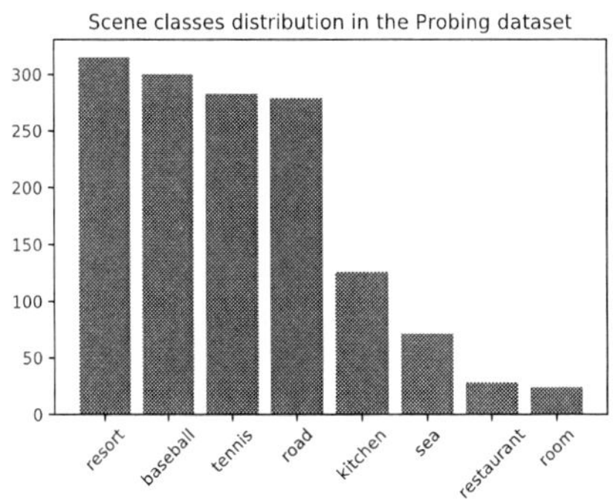

Figure 8: Scene distribution in the probing dataset

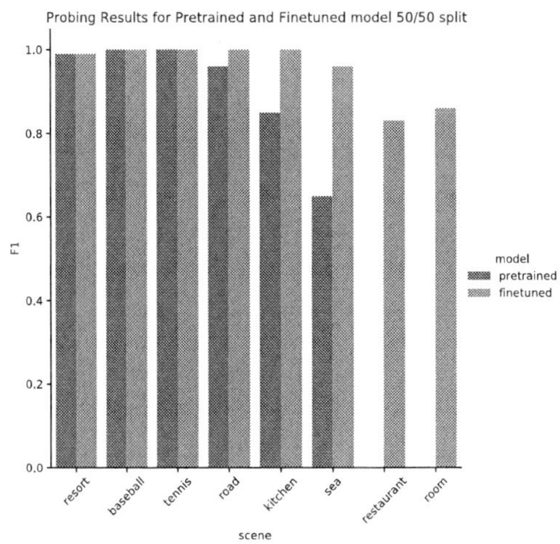

Figure 9: F1-scores of the scene classification task for the pre-trained in (blue) and the fine-tuned model (orange).

random assignment of the labels to the features. For both pre-trained and fine-tuned models, probes perform at ceiling for scenes with a high support (cf. Figure 8). For scene types with a very low frequency, like *restaurant* and *room*, the probe trained on features from the pre-trained model fails. In contrast, probing features from the fine-tuned model still performs at ceiling. These results suggest that the information to detect the scene type is already present to some extent in the pre-trained model. Nevertheless, fine-tuning proves effective in closing the gap for low-support scenes.

When trained on features extracted from ablated inputs in Table 4, the probe is not particularly affected by the ablation, confirming the robustness of the model's representations as observed in the ablation study (Section 6).

Model	micro-F1	macro-F1	weighted-F1
Random	0.16	0.12	0.16
Pretrained	0.94	0.67	0.92
Finetuned	**0.99**	**0.96**	**0.99**
Pretrained (A)	0.92	0.66	0.90
Finetuned (A)	0.98	0.88	0.97

Table 4: F1-scores for the scene classification task in the 50/50 split using a random forest. The first row (Random) corresponds to the performance of random baseline while (A) is the performance on the features obtained by the ablating the input.

8 Conclusion

In this paper, we addressed scene-level caption generation. Taking a cue from prior work on scene semantics and syntax, our goal was to assess V&L models' ability to reason about the link between scenes and their components and exploit this to generate informative captions with less redundancy.

Findings and Contributions We contributed a new dataset pairing object-centric and scene-level captions, and showed that VinVL is able to generate scene-level descriptions with minimal fine-tuning.

Our analysis showed that the fine-tuning results in a more even distribution of attention mass over the image, suggesting a more 'holistic' view of the scene which nevertheless makes use of diagnostic object information. Using a combination of ablation and probing methods, we also show that much of the relevant information for scene-level captioning is present after pre-training. Hence, the model's ability to generate scene-level captions is primarily acquired through a change in its self-attention.

Limitations In this work we draw conclusions from an analysis of a single model, this can be considered a limitation. Nevertheless, VinVL is representative of a larger family of SOTA models in the field, based on Oscar, which are dominating the scene in V&L tasks. Moreover, Oscar pretraining using object tags makes the model well-suited to an in-depth analysis of cross-modal interactions in a generative context.

We acknowledge also that the results of the ablation analysis (Section 6) could in part be affected by the approximate nature of our tagging method. Furthermore, as noted by Frank et al. (2021), visual feature deletion may still leave relevant contextual information in the remaining feature vectors, due to the Faster-RCNN's wide field of view.

Acknowledgements

Contribution from the ITN project NL4XAI (*Natural Language for Explainable AI*). This project has received funding from the European Union's Horizon 2020 research and innovation programme under the Marie Skłodowska-Curie grant agreement No 860621. This document reflects the views of the author(s) and does not necessarily reflect the views or policy of the European Commission. The REA cannot be held responsible for any use that may be made of the information this document contains.

References

Samira Abnar and Willem Zuidema. 2020. Quantifying attention flow in transformers. In *Proceedings of the 58th Annual Meeting of the Association for Computational Linguistics*, pages 4190–4197, Online. Association for Computational Linguistics.

Harsh Agrawal, Karan Desai, Yufei Wang, Xinlei Chen, Rishabh Jain, Mark Johnson, Dhruv Batra, Devi Parikh, Stefan Lee, and Peter Anderson. 2019. Nocaps: Novel object captioning at scale. In *Proceedings of the IEEE/CVF International Conference on Computer Vision*, pages 8948–8957.

Yonatan Belinkov. 2022. Probing classifiers: Promises, shortcomings, and advances. *Computational Linguistics*, 48(1):207–219.

Yonatan Belinkov and James Glass. 2019. Analysis Methods in Neural Language Processing: A Survey. *Transactions of the Association for Computational Linguistics*, 7:49–72.

Tom Brown, Benjamin Mann, Nick Ryder, Melanie Subbiah, Jared D Kaplan, Prafulla Dhariwal, Arvind Neelakantan, Pranav Shyam, Girish Sastry, Amanda Askell, et al. 2020. Language models are few-shot learners. *Advances in neural information processing systems*, 33:1877–1901.

Emanuele Bugliarello, Ryan Cotterell, Naoaki Okazaki, and Desmond Elliott. 2021. Multimodal pretraining unmasked: A meta-analysis and a unified framework of vision-and-language berts. *Transactions of the Association for Computational Linguistics*, 9:978–994.

Michele Cafagna, Kees van Deemter, Albert Gatt, et al. 2021. What vision-language models 'see' when they see scenes. *ArXiv preprint 2109.07301*.

Jize Cao, Zhe Gan, Yu Cheng, Licheng Yu, Yen-Chun Chen, and Jingjing Liu. 2020. Behind the scene: Revealing the secrets of pre-trained vision-and-language models. In *European Conference on Computer Vision*, pages 565–580. Springer.

Xinlei Chen, Hao Fang, Tsung-yi Lin, Ramakrishna Vedantam, C Lawrence Zitnick, Saurabh Gupta, and Piotr Doll. 2015. Microsoft COCO Captions : Data Collection and Evaluation Server. *arXiv preprint 1504.00325*, pages 1–7.

Yen-Chun Chen, Linjie Li, Licheng Yu, Ahmed El Kholy, Faisal Ahmed, Zhe Gan, Yu Cheng, and Jingjing Liu. 2020. Uniter: Universal image-text representation learning. In *Computer Vision – ECCV 2020*, pages 104–120, Cham. Springer International Publishing.

Kevin Clark, Urvashi Khandelwal, Omer Levy, and Christopher D. Manning. 2019. What does BERT look at? an analysis of BERT's attention. In *Proceedings of the 2019 ACL Workshop BlackboxNLP: Analyzing and Interpreting Neural Networks for NLP*, pages 276–286, Florence, Italy. Association for Computational Linguistics.

Jia Deng, Wei Dong, Richard Socher, Li-Jia Li, Kai Li, and Li Fei-Fei. 2009. Imagenet: A large-scale hierarchical image database. In *2009 IEEE conference on computer vision and pattern recognition*, pages 248–255. Ieee.

Jacob Devlin, Ming-Wei Chang, Kenton Lee, and Kristina Toutanova. 2019. BERT: Pre-training of deep bidirectional transformers for language understanding. In *Proceedings of the 2019 Conference of the North American Chapter of the Association for Computational Linguistics: Human Language Technologies, Volume 1 (Long and Short Papers)*, pages 4171–4186, Minneapolis, Minnesota. Association for Computational Linguistics.

Stella Frank, Emanuele Bugliarello, and Desmond Elliott. 2021. Vision-and-language or vision-for-language? on cross-modal influence in multimodal transformers. In *Proceedings of the 2021 Conference on Empirical Methods in Natural Language Processing*, pages 9847–9857, Online and Punta Cana, Dominican Republic. Association for Computational Linguistics.

Itai Gat, Idan Schwartz, and Alexander Schwing. 2021. Perceptual Score: What Data Modalities Does Your Model Perceive? In *35th Conference on Neural Information Processing Systems (NeurIPS 2021)*, Sydney, Australia.

Yash Goyal, Tejas Khot, Douglas Summers-Stay, Dhruv Batra, and Devi Parikh. 2017. Making the v in vqa matter: Elevating the role of image understanding in visual question answering. In *Proceedings of the IEEE conference on computer vision and pattern recognition*, pages 6904–6913.

Herbert P Grice. 1975. Logic and conversation. In Peter Cole and Jerry Morgan (eds), editors, *Speech acts*, pages 41–58. New York: Academic Press.

Danna Gurari, Qing Li, Chi Lin, Yinan Zhao, Anhong Guo, Abigale Stangl, and Jeffrey P. Bigham. 2019.

Vizwiz-priv: A dataset for recognizing the presence and purpose of private visual information in images taken by blind people. *2019 IEEE/CVF Conference on Computer Vision and Pattern Recognition (CVPR)*, pages 939–948.

John M. Henderson and Taylor R. Hayes. 2017. Meaning-based guidance of attention in scenes as revealed by meaning maps. *Nature Human Behaviour*, 1:743–747.

Lisa Anne Hendricks, John Mellor, Rosalia Schneider, Jean-Baptiste Alayrac, and Aida Nematzadeh. 2021. Decoupling the role of data, attention, and losses in multimodal transformers. *Transactions of the Association for Computational Linguistics*, 9:570–585.

Lisa Anne Hendricks and Aida Nematzadeh. 2021. Probing image-language transformers for verb understanding. In *Findings of the Association for Computational Linguistics: ACL-IJCNLP 2021*, pages 3635–3644, Online. Association for Computational Linguistics.

Jack Hessel and Lillian Lee. 2020. Does my multimodal model learn cross-modal interactions? It's harder to tell than you might think! In *Proceedings of the 2020 Conference on Empirical Methods in Natural Language Processing (EMNLP'20)*, pages 861–877, Online. Association for Computational Linguistics.

Micah Hodosh, Peter Young, and Julia Hockenmaier. 2013. Framing image description as a ranking task: Data, models and evaluation metrics. *Journal of Artificial Intelligence Research*, 47:853–899.

Xiaowei Hu, Zhe Gan, Jianfeng Wang, Zhengyuan Yang, Zicheng Liu, Yumao Lu, and Lijuan Wang. 2022. Scaling up vision-language pre-training for image captioning. In *Proceedings of the IEEE/CVF Conference on Computer Vision and Pattern Recognition (CVPR)*, pages 17980–17989.

Xiaowei Hu, Xi Yin, Kevin Lin, Lei Zhang, Jianfeng Gao, Lijuan Wang, and Zicheng Liu. 2021. Vivo: Visual vocabulary pre-training for novel object captioning. *Proceedings of the AAAI Conference on Artificial Intelligence*, 35(2):1575–1583.

Laurent Itti and Christof Koch. 2001. Computational modelling of visual attention. *Nature reviews neuroscience*, 2(3):194–203.

Ranjay Krishna, Yuke Zhu, Oliver Groth, Justin Johnson, Kenji Hata, Joshua Kravitz, Stephanie Chen, Yannis Kalantidis, Li-Jia Li, David A Shamma, et al. 2017. Visual genome: Connecting language and vision using crowdsourced dense image annotations. *International journal of computer vision*, 123(1):32–73.

Liunian Harold Li, Mark Yatskar, Da Yin, Cho-Jui Hsieh, and Kai Wei Chang. 2020a. What does BERT with vision look at? In *Proceedings of the 58th Annual Meeting of the Association for Computational Linguistics*, pages 5265–5275, Online. Association for Computational Linguistics.

Xiujun Li, Xi Yin, Chunyuan Li, Pengchuan Zhang, Xiaowei Hu, Lei Zhang, Lijuan Wang, Houdong Hu, Li Dong, Furu Wei, et al. 2020b. Oscar: Object-semantics aligned pre-training for vision-language tasks. In *European Conference on Computer Vision*, pages 121–137. Springer.

Tsung-Yi Lin, Michael Maire, Serge Belongie, James Hays, Pietro Perona, Deva Ramanan, Piotr Dollár, and C Lawrence Zitnick. 2014. Microsoft coco: Common objects in context. In *European conference on computer vision*, pages 740–755. Springer.

Jiasen Lu, Dhruv Batra, Devi Parikh, and Stefan Lee. 2019. Vilbert: Pretraining task-agnostic visiolinguistic representations for vision-and-language tasks. *Advances in neural information processing systems*, 32.

George L. Malcolm, Iris I.A. Groen, and Chris I. Baker. 2016. Making Sense of Real-World Scenes. *Trends in Cognitive Sciences*, 20(11):843–856.

Aude Oliva and Antonio Torralba. 2007. The role of context in object recognition. *Trends in cognitive sciences*, 11(12):520–527.

Vicente Ordonez, Girish Kulkarni, and Tamara Berg. 2011. Im2text: Describing images using 1 million captioned photographs. In *Proceedings of the 2011 Conference on Advances in Neural Information Processing Systems (NIPS'11)*, pages 1143–1151, Granada, Spain. Curran Associates Ltd.

Luis Gilberto Mateos Ortiz, Clemens Wolff, and Mirella Lapata. 2015. Learning to Interpret and Describe Abstract Scenes. In *Proceedings of the 2015 Annual Conference of the North American Chapter of the ACL (NAACL'15)*, pages 1505–1515, Denver, Colorado. Association for Computational Linguistics.

Letitia Parcalabescu, Michele Cafagna, Lilitta Muradjan, Anette Frank, Iacer Calixto, and Albert Gatt. 2022. VALSE: A task-independent benchmark for vision and language models centered on linguistic phenomena. In *Proceedings of the 60th Annual Meeting of the Association for Computational Linguistics (Volume 1: Long Papers)*, pages 8253–8280, Dublin, Ireland. Association for Computational Linguistics.

Jae Sung Park, Chandra Bhagavatula, Roozbeh Mottaghi, Ali Farhadi, and Yejin Choi. 2020. VisualCOMET: Reasoning About the Dynamic Context of a Still Image. In *Proceedings of the European Conference on Computer Vision*, pages 508–524, Berlin and Heidelberg. Springer.

Sandro Pezzelle, Claudio Greco, Greta Gandolfi, Eleonora Gualdoni, and Raffaella Bernardi. 2020. Be Different to Be Better! A Benchmark to Leverage the Complementarity of Language and Vision. In *Findings ofthe Association for Computational Linguistics: EMNLP 2020*, pages 2751–2767, Online. Association for Computational Linguistics.

Jordi Pont-Tuset, Jasper Uijlings, Soravit Changpinyo, Radu Soricut, and Vittorio Ferrari. 2020. Connecting vision and language with localized narratives. In *European Conference on Computer Vision*, pages 647–664. Springer.

Alec Radford, Jong Wook Kim, Chris Hallacy, Aditya Ramesh, Gabriel Goh, Sandhini Agarwal, Girish Sastry, Amanda Askell, Pamela Mishkin, Jack Clark, et al. 2021. Learning transferable visual models from natural language supervision. In *International Conference on Machine Learning*, pages 8748–8763. PMLR.

Shaoqing Ren, Kaiming He, Ross Girshick, and Jian Sun. 2015. Faster r-cnn: Towards real-time object detection with region proposal networks. *Advances in neural information processing systems*, 28.

Olga Russakovsky, Jia Deng, Hao Su, Jonathan Krause, Sanjeev Satheesh, Sean Ma, Zhiheng Huang, Andrej Karpathy, Aditya Khosla, Michael Bernstein, et al. 2015. Imagenet large scale visual recognition challenge. *International journal of computer vision*, 115(3):211–252.

Emmanuelle Salin, Badreddine Farah, Stéphane Ayache, and Benoit Favre. 2022. Are Vision-Language Transformers Learning Multimodal Representations? A probing perspective. In *Proceedings of the 36th AAAI Conference on Artificial Intelligence*, Vancouver, BC. Association for the Advancement of Artificial Intelligence.

Julie S. Self, Jamie Siegart, Munashe Machoko, Enton Lam, and Michelle R Greene. 2019. Diagnostic Objects Contribute to Late – But Not Early– Visual Scene Processing. *Journal of Vision*, 19:227.

Piyush Sharma, Nan Ding, Sebastian Goodman, and Radu Soricut. 2018. Conceptual captions: A cleaned, hypernymed, image alt-text dataset for automatic image captioning. In *Proceedings of the 56th Annual Meeting of the Association for Computational Linguistics (ACL'18)*, pages 2556–2565, Melbourne, Australia. Association for Computational Linguistics.

Ravi Shekhar, Sandro Pezzelle, Yauhen Klimovich, Aurelie Herbelot, Moin Nabi, Enver Sangineto, and Raffaella Bernardi. 2017. FOIL it! Find One mismatch between Image and Language caption. In *Proceedings of the 55th Annual Meeting of the Association for Computational Linguistics (ACL'17)*, pages 255–265, Vancouver, BC. Association for Computational Linguistics.

Weijie Su, Xizhou Zhu, Yue Cao, Bin Li, Lewei Lu, Furu Wei, and Jifeng Dai. 2020. VL-BERT: pre-training of generic visual-linguistic representations. In *8th International Conference on Learning Representations, ICLR 2020, Addis Ababa, Ethiopia, April 26-30, 2020*. OpenReview.net.

Alane Suhr, Mike Lewis, James Yeh, and Yoav Artzi. 2017. A Corpus of Natural Language for Visual Reasoning. In *Proceedings ofthe 55th Annual Meeting ofthe Association for Computational Linguistics (ACL'17)*, pages 217–223, Vancouver, BC. Association for Computational Linguistics.

Alane Suhr, Stephanie Zhou, Ally Zhang, Iris Zhang, Huajun Bai, and Yoav Artzi. 2019. A corpus for reasoning about natural language grounded in photographs. In *Proceedings of the 57th Annual Meeting of the Association for Computational Linguistics*, pages 6418–6428, Florence, Italy. Association for Computational Linguistics.

Hao Tan and Mohit Bansal. 2019. LXMERT: Learning cross-modality encoder representations from transformers. In *Proceedings of the 2019 Conference on Empirical Methods in Natural Language Processing and the 9th International Joint Conference on Natural Language Processing (EMNLP-IJCNLP)*, pages 5100–5111, Hong Kong, China. Association for Computational Linguistics.

Antonio Torralba, Aude Oliva, Monica S. Castelhano, and John M. Henderson. 2006. Contextual guidance of eye movements and attention in real-world scenes: The role of global features in object search. *Psychological Review*, 113(4):766–786.

Melissa Le Hoa Võ. 2021. The meaning and structure of scenes. *Vision Research*, 181:10–20.

William Webber, Alistair Moffat, and Justin Zobel. 2010. A similarity measure for indefinite rankings. *ACM Transactions on Information Systems (TOIS)*, 28(4):1–38.

Haiyang Wei, Zhixin Li, Feicheng Huang, Canlong Zhang, Huifang Ma, and Zhongzhi Shi. 2021. Integrating scene semantic knowledge into image captioning. *ACM Transactions on Multimedia Computing, Communications, and Applications (TOMM)*, 17(2):1–22.

Chia Chien Wu, Farahnaz Ahmed Wick, and Marc Pomplun. 2014. Guidance of visual attention by semantic information in real-world scenes. *Frontiers in Psychology*, 5.

Peter Young, Alice Lai, Micah Hodosh, and Julia Hockenmaier. 2014. From image descriptions to visual denotations: New similarity metrics for semantic inference over event descriptions. *Transactions of the Association for Computational Linguistics*, 2:67–78.

Rowan Zellers, Yonatan Bisk, Ali Farhadi, and Yejin Choi. 2019. From recognition to cognition: Visual commonsense reasoning. In *Proceedings of the IEEE/CVF Conference on Computer Vision and Pattern Recognition*, pages 6720–6731.

Rowan Zellers, Yonatan Bisk, Roy Schwartz, and Yejin Choi. 2018. SWAG: A large-scale adversarial dataset for grounded commonsense inference. In *Proceedings of the 2018 Conference on Empirical Methods in Natural Language Processing*, pages 93–104, Brussels, Belgium. Association for Computational Linguistics.

Pengchuan Zhang, Xiujun Li, Xiaowei Hu, Jianwei Yang, Lei Zhang, Lijuan Wang, Yejin Choi, and Jianfeng Gao. 2021. Vinvl: Revisiting visual representations in vision-language models. In *Proceedings of the IEEE/CVF Conference on Computer Vision and Pattern Recognition*, pages 5579–5588.

Appendix

A Fine-tuning Details

We fine-tune the VinVL pre-trained base version[6] using the original configuration for 10 epochs on scene descriptions. We refer to it as the *fine-tuned* model. Since the HL-scenes dataset images are included in COCO, we use the pre-computed visual features and labels provided in the original VinVL implementation.

We refer to the *pre-trained* model, as the base model trained on the image captioning task on COCO captions optimized using cross-entropy. All the experiments involving the pre-trained model are performed using the original configuration used in Li et al. (2020b). The fine-tuning is carried out with batch size 32 on a NVIDIA GTX 2080 TI 11 GB.

B Self-attention Details

Attention beyond Layer 1 At higher layers the attention converges on the special token [SEP], used to separate the *text* + *object tags* from the *visual* input, as shown in Figure 10. A similar behaviour has been observed analysing BERT's attention (Clark et al., 2019).

Figure 11 shows how this pattern becomes more pronounced as we move further across the layers, preventing from observing any kind of input interplay. Although the *text*, *object tags* and *visual* sequences can be of different lengths, the [SEP] token sits always in the same position among the inputs, as the padding is always applied to keep the *text* + *object tags* sequence of the same length. We believe that this regularity is used by the model as a sort of pivot among the inputs. This can cause the a high accumulation of attentional resources by the model.

Scene label extraction As described in Section 3, during the data collection, the annotators where asked to answer the direct question: *Where is the picture taken?* As a consequence, the scene-captions often have a regular structure, captured by the following three representative examples:

- the picture has been taken in a *restaurant*
- on a *beach*
- this is in an *airport*

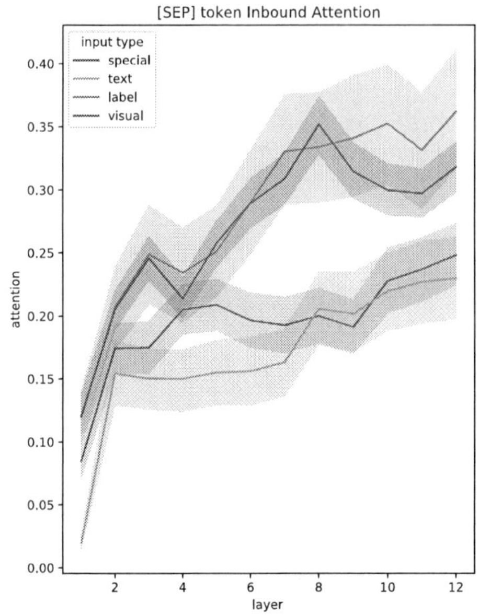

Figure 10: Inbound attention of the [SEP] per input type token across the layers. Special tokens correspond to [CLS], [PAD] and [SEP].

To extract the scene labels, we tokenize the scene-captions and we remove punctuation and stop-words (we add *picture* to the list of the standard stop-words). Among the remaining tokens, we extract all the nouns and we reduce them to lemmas, then we compute the frequencies of the remaining tokens. This allow us to extract the scene-types (*restaurant, beach* and *airport*) from the captions, such as those shown in the examples above. The whole procedure is performed using spaCy. [7]

Rank Biased Overlap RBO (Webber et al., 2010) computes the similarity of two ranked lists, as follows:

$$RBO(S,T,p) = (1-p)\sum p^{d-1}A_d \quad (1)$$

where d is the depth of the ranking being examined, A_d is the agreement between S and T given by the proportion of the size of the overlap up to d, and p determines the contribution of the top d ranks to the final RBO measure. We use the standard value of $p = 1$.

C Ablation Details

As described in Section 6 the ablation is performed by removing the most informative objects from

[6] https://github.com/microsoft/Oscar/blob/master/VinVL_MODEL_ZOO.md#Oscarplus-pretraining

[7] https://pypi.org/project/spacy/

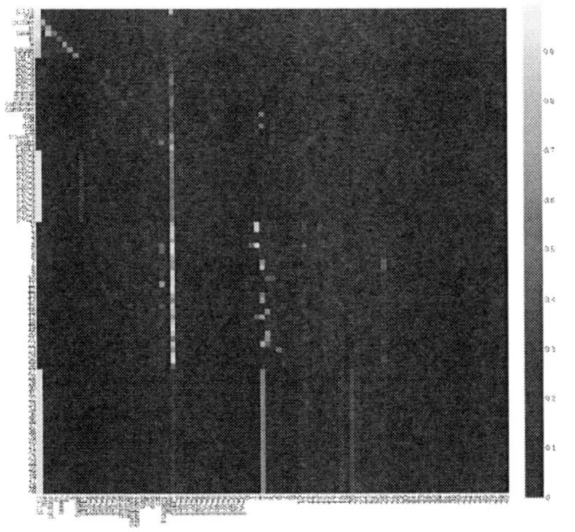

(a) Layer 1

(b) Layer 6

(c) Layer 12

Figure 11: Attention matrices for layers 1, 6 and 12. The attention weights progressively gather on the [SEP] token.

# Ablation	Train-Val	Test
no ablation	13498	1499
1	4269	469
2	2565	274
3	1554	170

Table 5: Sample size of the Train-Val and Test split after ablation of the top 1,2 and 3 most informative objects in the most frequent scenes. The top row corresponds to the original dataset split sizes.

images depicting the most frequent scene types. As a result, an image is included in the ablation study if (i) it belongs to the set of most frequent scenes; and (ii) it contains the objects we want to ablate. This means that the higher the number of objects ablated, the smaller the sample of images matching these constraints. As shown in Table 5, with 3 objects ablated in the test-set we obtain 170 valid images.

We repeat the ablation experiment on both the test and the train-val split. The results obtained on the latter mirror those reported in Section 6 with the test-split only. In Figure 12 we show the comparison of the distributions of the unchanged confidence scores after ablation for the test and train-val split. Moreover, there is no statistically significant difference between the distributions of confidence score shifts of the test set (shown in Figure 7) and the train-val set ($z = 0.13$ with $p = 0.89$ and $\alpha = 0.05$).

D Probing details

Model selection We test two probing models: a multi-layer perceptron and a random forest. We perform hyperparameter tuning of the neural probe by carrying out a random search followed by a probabilistic search. The tuned neural probe is a three-layer feed-forward network with *hidden size* 16, optimized using LBFGS with adaptive learning rate and $\alpha = 1$. Note that no parameter tuning is required for the random forest. As reported in Table 6, the random forest performs better or on a par with the neural probe. Therefore we report the performance of the random forest in the main results in Section 7.

Challenging the probe The probing model performs at ceiling with the more typical 90/10 split, especially when trained on the fine-tuned features (Figure 13). Therefore, we perform multiple experiments for different train/test splits namely, 90/10,

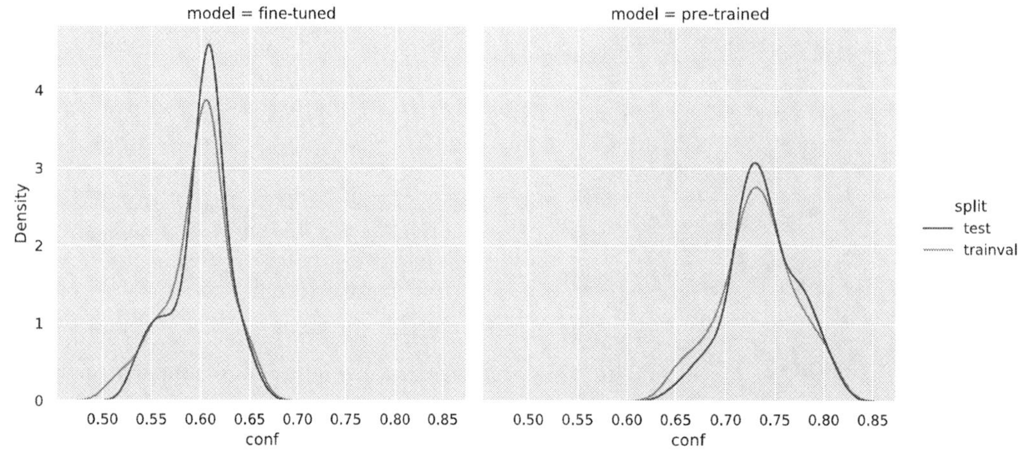

Figure 12: Kernel density estimate of the confidence scores distributions of unchanged captions after ablation for the test (blue) and train-val (orange) split.

Probe	Model	micro-F1	macro-F1	weighted-F1
RB		0.16	0.12	0.16
RF	PRE	0.94	0.67	**0.92**
	FT	**0.99**	**0.96**	**0.99**
	PRE (A)	0.92	0.66	0.90
	FT (A)	0.98	**0.88**	0.97
MLP	PRE	0.94	0.67	0.91
	FT	0.98	0.91	0.98
	PRE (A)	0.92	0.66	0.90
	FT (A)	0.98	0.85	0.97

Table 6: F1-scores of scene classification task in the 50/50 split, for Random Baseline (RB), Random Forest (RF) and Multilayer perception (MLP) trained on encodings extracted from the pre-trained (PRE) and fine-tuned (FT) model without and with ablation (A). In bold the best result for each setting.

70/30 and 50/50. The 50/50 is the most challenging for the probe and it allows us to highlight the performance gap across different settings. Results from all the splits are shown in Table 7.

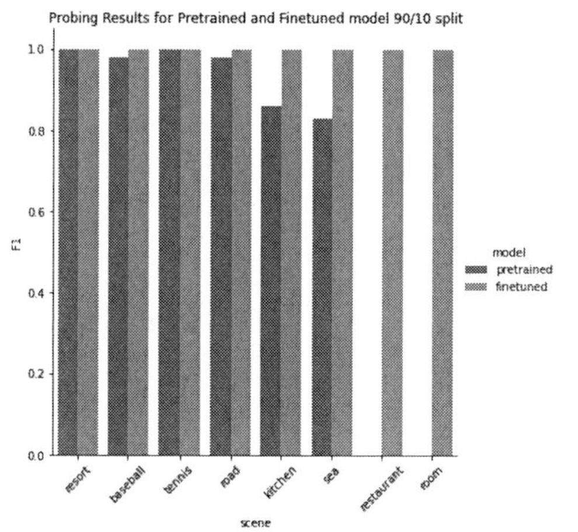

Figure 13: F1-scores of the scene classification task for the pre-trained (blue) and the fine-tuned model (orange) for the 90/10 split.

E HL-Scences examples

Split	Model	micro-F1	macro-F1	weighted-F1
90/10	PRE	0.96	0.71	0.94
	FT	**1.0**	**1.0**	**1.0**
	PRE (A)	0.95	0.69	0.94
	FT (A)	0.99	0.99	0.99
70/30	PRE	0.94	0.67	0.92
	FT	**0.99**	**0.97**	**0.99**
	PRE (A)	0.93	0.66	0.91
	FT (A)	0.98	0.94	0.98
50/50	PRE	0.94	0.67	0.92
	FT	**0.99**	**0.96**	**0.99**
	PRE (A)	0.92	0.66	0.90
	FT (A)	0.98	0.88	0.97

Table 7: F1-scores for scene classification task the random forest in different train/tes splits. The random forest is trained on encodings extracted from the pre-trained (PRE) and fine-tuned (FT) model without and with ablation (A).

Image	Object description (COCO)	Scene description (HL-Scenes)
	a woman and a boy sitting in the snow outside of a cabin.	the picture is shot in a ski resort
	a airplane with a group of people standing next to it.	the picture is shot in an airport
	a man holds his hands up as he stands over a trash can.	the picture is taken in front of a roadside toilet
	a coupe of people that are skateboarding on a ramp	it is at the park.

Table 8: Randomly selected images from the HL-scenes dataset. For both COCO and HL-Scenes we show a randomly picked caption among the the available ones for the image.

DeepParliament: A Legal domain Benchmark & Dataset for Parliament Bills Prediction

Ankit Pal
Open Legal AI
openlegalai@gmail.com

Abstract

This paper introduces DeepParliament, a legal domain Benchmark Dataset that gathers bill documents and metadata and performs various bill status classification tasks. The proposed dataset text covers a broad range of bills from 1986 to the present and contains richer information on parliament bill content. Data collection, detailed statistics and analyses are provided in the paper. Moreover, we experimented with different types of models ranging from RNN to pretrained and reported the results. We are proposing two new benchmarks: Binary and Multi-Class Bill Status classification. Models developed for bill documents and relevant supportive tasks may assist Members of Parliament (MPs), presidents, and other legal practitioners. It will help review or prioritise bills, thus speeding up the billing process, improving the quality of decisions and reducing the time consumption in both houses. Considering that the foundation of the country's democracy is Parliament and state legislatures, we anticipate that our research will be an essential addition to the Legal NLP community. This work will be the first to present a Parliament bill prediction task. In order to improve the accessibility of legal AI resources and promote reproducibility, we have made our code and dataset publicly accessible at github.com/monk1337/DeepParliament

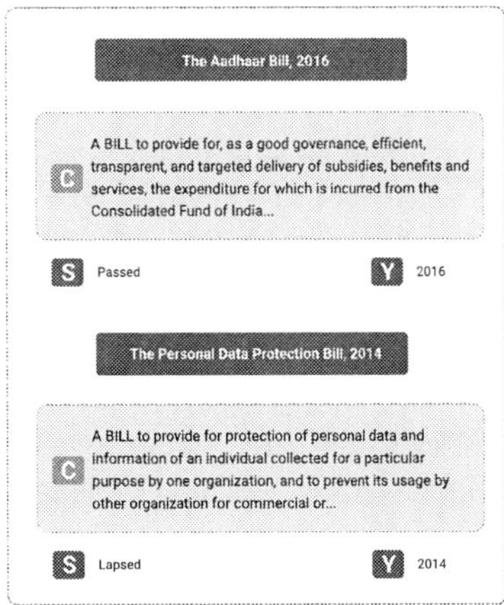

Figure 1: Samples from the DeepParliament dataset. Here C, S, and Y indicate Bill Context, Bill Status, and Bill Year, respectively.

1 Introduction

In recent years, Artificial Intelligence(AI) based methods have been employed in the legal field for several uses and within many sub-areas. In the legal field the majority of resources are available in textual format (e.g., contracts, court decisions, patents, legal articles). Therefore considerable efforts have been made at the intersection of Law and Natural Language Processing research. Efforts can be witnessed in the various projects dealing with NLP applications in the legal domain and recently published scientific papers such as legal judgement prediction (Aletras et al., 2016; Xiao et al., 2018; Chalkidis et al., 2019) legal topic classification (Nallapati and Manning, 2008; Chalkidis et al., 2020), overruling prediction (Zheng et al., 2021). Furthermore, researchers have also explored a variety of Legal AI tasks, including legal question answering (Kien et al., 2020), contract understanding (Hendrycks et al., 2021), court opinion generation (Ye et al., 2018), legal information extraction (Chalkidis et al., 2018), legal entity recognition (Leitner et al., 2019, 2020) and many more. Predictive legal models have the ability to enhance both the effectiveness of decision-making and the provision of services to individuals. Many new datasets have also been proposed in the legal domain to track the recent progress and serve as benchmarks. Recently, there have been initiatives to develop corpora for the India's judicial system.

The foundation of India's democracy is the Parliament and state legislatures. Implementing, amending and removing laws is the primary responsibility of Parliament. The Rajya Sabha (Council of States) and the Lok Sabha (House of the People) are the two houses that constitute India's legislature.

Proceedings of the Workshop on Unimodal and Multimodal Induction of Linguistic Structures (UM-IoS), pages 73 - 81
December 7, 2022

However, the majority of contemporary legal NLP research focuses only on court decisions and cases. This issue, which we refer to and subsequently characterize as "Parliament Bills Prediction", has not been explored. Before qualifying as an act, every bill passes through a long chain of standardized processes, including introduction of the bill, publication in the gazette, first reading, select committee, second reading, and third reading. After the third reading, the bill goes to the other houses, and after the approval of both houses it faces final approval by the president. A significant amount of time and effort is required to pass a bill in either of the Houses of Parliament. Therefore, a lapse of a bill has a negative impact on legislative work.

India's first Lok Sabha (1952–1957) passed 333 bills throughout its five-year existence. The average number of bills approved by Lok Sabhas with terms less than three years is 77. Both houses spent about half their time carrying out legislative business. The lapse count of the bill increases at the end of every Lok Sabha. A total of 22 bills lapsed after the 16th Lok Sabha; three bills have been pending for over 20 years; six have been pending between 10-20 years. Legislative activity accounts for a significant portion of Lok Sabha's working hours. To date, 14 bills are still pending between 5-10 years and 10 bills are pending for under five years. Therefore, time is wasted when bills lapse at the end of the Lok Sabha's tenure, as a new Lok Sabha must start over and consider bills from scratch, taking at least two sessions to reconsider the bills. Thus, in order to improve productivity, it is necessary to re-evaluate the rule governing the lapsing of bills in the House of Representatives. This calls for machine learning strategies to enhance the efficiency of the billing process in Parliament.

To the best of our knowledge, a single dataset does not yet exist, which provides a standard benchmark for parliamentary Bills. To facilitate research on bill documents for text classification, we provide DeepParliament, a legal domain Benchmark & Dataset which gathers bill documents and meta data and performs different status classification tasks. The proposed dataset and benchmark are not meant to replace or compete with the decisions of the Houses of Parliament and the President by any means; instead, the proposed solution offers complementing use cases. Models developed for bill documents and relevant supportive tasks may assist members of the Legislative Assembly (MLA), Members of Parliament (MPs), presidents and other legal practitioners, for example by estimating the likelihood of getting a bill passed, reviewing or prioritizing bills, (thus speeding up the billing process); improving the quality of decisions and finally, reducing the time and energy consumption in both houses. Fig. 1 shows two samples of two parliament bills' context, their corresponding status, and the year from the study dataset.

Applications developed on this dataset, such as automatic summaries, would enable the professionals to decide which documents they should read in detail. Moreover, the model can suggest different sections and acts in need of further exploration by highlighting which areas a new bill falls within. This paper proposes a benchmark and takes initial steps by contributing the dataset and baseline models to the community. Moreover, the plan is to continue to revise and upgrade the DeepParliament dataset in the future.

In brief, the contributions of this study are as follows.

- **New Legal Dataset**. We are proposing a new dataset. To our knowledge, there is no dataset focusing on parliament bills and data. Therefore, this work will be the first to present a parliament bill prediction task having rich information on parliament bills, different acts and laws.

- **Diversity and Difficulty**. The proposed dataset text covers a broad range of bills, including the Government Bill, Private Members Bill, the Money Bill, the Ordinary Bill, the Financial Bill & Constitutional Amendment Bill from 1986 to the present. Moreover, on average, there are 3932.99 tokens per sentence. The documents on the proposed dataset are considerably long. They contain richer information of parliament bill content, testing the reasoning abilities and domain-specific capabilities of language models in the legal domain.

- **Quality** Detailed Statistics, analysis of the dataset, and fine-grained evaluation of different parts of documents are provided. Moreover, we also performed extensive quality experiments to evaluate different types of models ranging from RNN to high-performance pre-trained domain models.

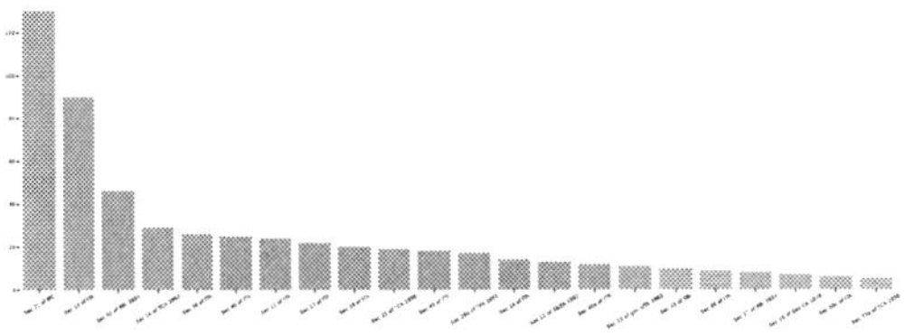

Figure 2: The Distribution of Top India's Act/Law's Section mentioned in the dataset.

- **Reproducible Results** We employ the HuggingFace Transformers library (Wolf et al., 2019) to facilitate our experiments. Furthermore, we pre-process and publish datasets on HuggingFace Datasets (Lhoest et al., 2021) to reproduce the results and experiment with new models in the future.

- **Proposing Two Benchmarks** We are proposing two new benchmarks on the DeepParliament dataset: Binary and Multi-Class Bill Status classification. In addition to the code, we also publish the benchmark on PaperwithCode [1] and Open LegalAI [2] to track the progress.

2 The DeepParliament Dataset

2.1 Task Definition

We model the bill prediction task as a classification problem and design Binary and Multi-Class Classification problem statements on the proposed dataset to evaluate the domain-specific capabilities of language models in the legal domain. For a given collection of labelled bill documents **X**, the objective is to learn a classification function:

$$f : x_i \rightarrow y_i \tag{1}$$

Where x_i is a legal bill document.

2.2 Task 1: Binary Classification

In equation (1) $y_i \in \{0, 1\}$ is target binary label of corresponding status Passed, Failed of classification task.

2.3 Task 2: Multi-Class Classification

Task 2, the coarse-grained classification task, had a total of 5 classes. In equation (1) $y_i \in \{1, ..., K\}$ is the multi-class label of the corresponding status Passed, Negatived, Lapsed, Removed, Withdrawn.

[1]https://paperswithcode.com/dataset/deepparliament
[2]openlegalai.github.io/DeepParliament

2.4 Bill and Lawmaking Procedure

The foundation of India's democracy is the parliament and state legislatures. Making, changing, and removing laws is the primary responsibility of Parliament. The method by which a legislative proposal is turned into an act is referred to as the legislative process or the lawmaking process in relation to Parliament. The procedure of a new act starts with identifying the need for a new law or an amendment to a current part of the legislation. Following the legal requirement, the relevant ministry writes a text for the proposed legislation, known as a Bill. Other relevant ministries are informed about this bill so that they can make any alterations or amendments.

A bill, which is draft legislation, cannot become law until it has been approved by both houses of Parliament and the President of India. Furthermore, the bill is introduced in Parliament after receiving cabinet approval. Prior to becoming an act, every bill passes through several readings in both houses. After both houses have approved a bill of Parliament, it is forwarded to the president for his or her approval. However, the president can request information and an explanation about the bill. The bill may be returned to Parliament for further consideration. The bill is declared an act with the president's assent. Moreover, the bill is then made into law, and the responsible ministry draughts and submits to Parliament the rules and regulations necessary to carry out the Act.

3 Dataset Collection & Preprocessing

We constructed the DeepParliament corpus from raw data collected from the official [3] & open website [4] which put together all the parliament bills from 1986 to the present. In addition to the raw data, additional metadata is also provided, i.e. the title, type of bill such as government or private, source of the bill, pdf URL and status of the bill. We used pdfminer3 [5] to extract bill content from each PDF. Some old pdfs are in image format; we applied an OCR system to convert images to text. The pdf content & metadata were converted into CSV format and combined into a single dataset. Next, we eliminate bill documents with a single token and duplicates. The cleaning pipeline involves removing the special characters, extra spaces etc.

[3]https://loksabhaph.nic.in
[4]https://prsindia.org/billtrack
[5]https://pypi.org/project/pdfminer3

All bill documents in this dataset are specifically in the English language.

4 Dataset statistics

The statistics of our proposed dataset, including the train and the test corpus, are shown in Table 1. Total documents are 5,329, where 4223 are in the train and 1106 are in the test dataset. Each bill document contains many sentences in both cases, and the document's length varies greatly. The performance of the models is influenced by the amount of vocabulary, which is a good indicator of the linguistic and domain complexity associated with a text corpus; Fig 5 shows the distribution of unique tokens of the train & test set. As shown in the table, this dataset has 284103 tokens in total, and the train split contains 243393 tokens where the test vocabulary size is 86616. On average, there are 3932.99 tokens per sentence.

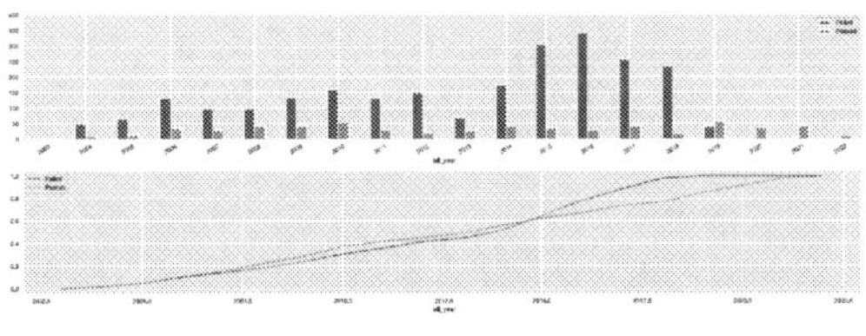

Figure 3: Distribution & Cumulative Frequency Graph of Passed and Failed Bill status in the last 20 years.

5 Dataset Analysis

The documents on the proposed dataset are considerable long and contain richer information on bill content. As described before, the dataset has been categorized into two settings: Binary Classification and Multi-Class classification. The most frequent category status is Lapsed, which occupies 50.6%. Fig 4 shows the percentage of each status type. Lapsed, Passed, and Withdrawal is the dataset's top three common statuses. The proposed dataset text covers a broad range of bills, including Government Bill, Private Member Bill, Money Bill, Ordinary Bill, Financial Bill and Constitutional Amendment Bill. We used word cloud to visualize the top Commonly occurring legal words in the dataset shown in Fig 7.

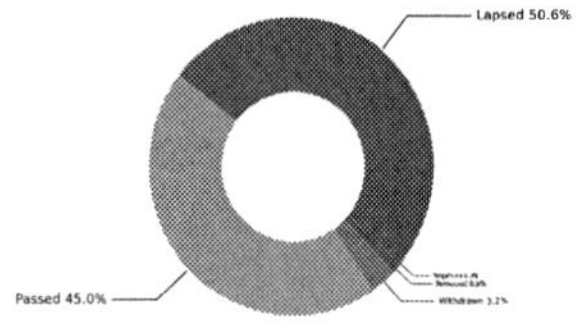

Figure 4: Relative sizes of documents per bill status in Dataset

We visualized the top sections mentioned in the entire dataset. A section is a specific provision of a legal code or body of laws, often laying out a specific legal obligation. Most sections in the dataset come under the Indian panel code and income tax act. Fig. 2 shows the top Indian Act/Law's Section mentioned in the dataset. To understand the dataset better, we also visualize the bill status of the last top 20 years. Fig. 3 shows the visualization. We can see that year 2015 and 2016 has the most significant failure ratio in the last 20 years, while in 2019, most bills were passed compared to other years.

	Train	Test	Total
Documents #	4223	1106	5329
Vocab	243393	86616	284103
Max D tokens	219378	227407	227407
Max T tokens	36	36	36
Avg D tokens	3932.99	4080.97	3963.70
Avg T tokens	11.15	11.48	11.22

Table 1: DeepParliament dataset statistics, where D, T represents the Documents and Title, respectively

6 Methods

Our study considers ten text classification models ranging from long-range RNN and CNN to Transformer-based methods increasing recency and sophistication.

6.1 Sequence & Convolutional models

In this category, we experimented with standard long short-term memory (LSTM) (Hochreiter and Schmidhuber, 1997), Bidirectional LSTM (BiLSTM) and convolutional neural network (CNN) (Kim, 2014) models for bill prediction tasks. We decided to use a shallow CNN model for glove since research has shown that deep CNN models do not consistently outperform other algorithms for text classification tasks. Initially, we utilized Xavier weight initialization (Glorot and Bengio, 2010) for both models' embedding matrices. Later we leverage this by initializing word vectors using pre-trained GloVe embedding (Pennington et al., 2014) of length 300.

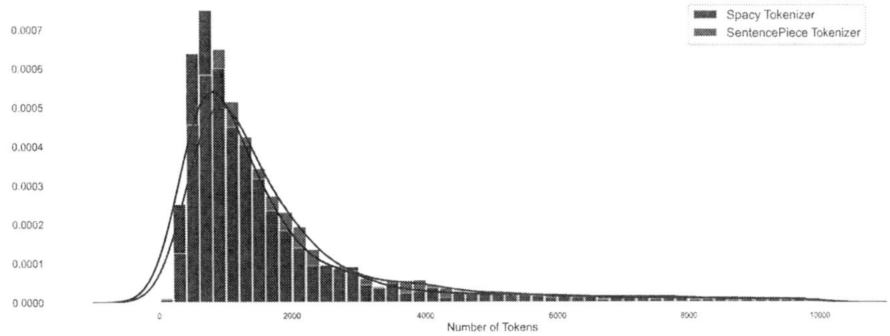

Figure 5: Distribution of the bill document's length in common words (using the spacy tokenizer) and sub-word units (generated by the SentencePiece tokenizer used in BERT)

6.2 General Domain Pre-trained Models

We experiment with Transformer based model BERT (Devlin et al., 2019) and its variants. RoBERTa (Liu et al., 2019) and ALBERT (Lan et al., 2020) are an extension of the standard BERT model. RoBERTa uses a byte-level BPE as a tokenizer and a different pre-training scheme where ALBERT's model has a smaller parameter size than corresponding BERT models.

6.3 Legal Domain Pre-trained Models

Recent research has also demonstrated that language representation models trained on massive corpora and precisely adjusted for a particular domain task perform much better than models trained on task-specific data. This method of transfer learning is beneficial in legal NLP. We thus evaluated three Pre-trained Language models trained from scratch with legal documents, including Legal-BERT (Chalkidis et al., 2020), Legal-RoBERTa and Custom Legal-BERT (Zheng et al., 2021).

7 Experiments

In this section, we evaluate the mentioned models on the proposed Dataset, describe the executed experiments, and examine the results.

7.1 Experimental Settings

In all sequence models, the batch size was set to 64, and the number of epochs was set to 50. At the same time, we iterate through 50 epochs with a batch size of 8 for all Bert-based models.

We used Tensorflow's Keras API (Abadi et al., 2016) to build sequence models. The BERT-based model follows the base configuration, consisting of 12 layers, 786 units, and 12 attention heads. We developed these models using Pytorch (Paszke et al., 2019) and obtained pretrained checkpoints from the HuggingFace library (Wolf et al., 2019).

We evaluate the models in two settings: Binary Classification and Multi-Class Classification. For the first setting, the classification layer consists of a dense layer with 1 unit as output, with sigmoid activation. The loss was calculated using binary cross-entropy.

$$\text{Loss}_{\text{bce}} = -\frac{1}{N}\sum_{n=1}^{N}\left[y_n \log \hat{y}_n + (1-y_n)\log(1-\hat{y}_n)\right] \tag{2}$$

In The Multi-Class setting, we used a dense layer with five units as output, with softmax activation. In this case, categorical cross-entropy was used for loss calculation.

$$\text{Loss}_{\text{cce}} = -\sum_{i=1}^{\text{N}} y_i \cdot \log \hat{y}_i \tag{3}$$

We perform five runs with different seeds for each method and report the average scores. All the experiments were conducted on the Google Colab Pro and used the default GPU Tesla T4 16GB. The proposed dataset & code are available at github.com/monk1337/DeepParliament for reproducibility.

7.2 Evaluation Metrics

We assessed the baseline and other models based on their Macro-averaged F1 scores, accuracy, and recall in multi-class and Binary environments. Before calculating the average across labels, macro-averaging computes the metric inside each label.

8 Results & Discussion

Table 4 & Table 5 shows the performance of all models in Macro-Precision, Macro-Recall and

	Starting Tokens			Middle Tokens			End Tokens		
Model	**Precision**	**Recall**	**F1-score**	**Precision**	**Recall**	**F1-score**	**Precision**	**Recall**	**F1-score**
ALBERT$_{Base}$	92.21	92.54	92.28	90.13	90.38	90.19	89.06	89.31	88.08
Custom Legal-BERT$_{Base}$	92.47	92.83	92.47	89.51	89.80	89.56	89.03	89.31	89.10
RoBERTa$_{Base}$	92.74	93.06	92.83	89.30	89.53	89.36	89.42	89.70	89.47
Legal-RoBERTa$_{Base}$	92.89	93.17	92.92	90.24	90.51	90.32	90.42	90.63	90.45
Bert$_{Base}$	92.92	93.23	93.01	**90.68**	**90.95**	**90.73**	90.02	90.06	90.19
Legal-BERT$_{Base}$	**93.11**	**93.49**	**93.11**	90.62	90.93	90.61	**90.42**	**90.64**	**90.49**

Table 2: Performance of all Transformer based baseline models in Macro-Precision, Macro-Recall and Macro-F1 (%) on Binary test set under different tokens settings.

	Starting Tokens			Middle Tokens			End Tokens		
Model	**Precision**	**Recall**	**F1-score**	**Precision**	**Recall**	**F1-score**	**Precision**	**Recall**	**F1-score**
Custom Legal-BERT$_{Base}$	51.49	49.12	49.42	42.79	39.96	40.58	41.10	41.21	43.25
ALBERT$_{Base}$	56.14	51.55	52.87	52.55	46.28	47.73	50.71	45.05	45.99
RoBERTa$_{Base}$	56.07	54.85	54.89	49.00	47.05	47.60	45.57	45.11	45.03
Legal-RoBERTa$_{Base}$	61.40	54.74	57.44	48.08	44.02	45.53	50.89	46.98	49.06
Bert$_{Base}$	60.55	55.92	57.86	**63.75**	**52.61**	**55.64**	46.13	46.17	46.34
Legal-BERT$_{Base}$	**62.96**	**56.96**	**58.79**	55.47	49.15	49.86	**53.50**	**47.20**	**49.68**

Table 3: Performance of all Transformer based baseline models in Macro-Precision, Macro-Recall and Macro-F1 (%) on Multi-Class test set under different tokens settings.

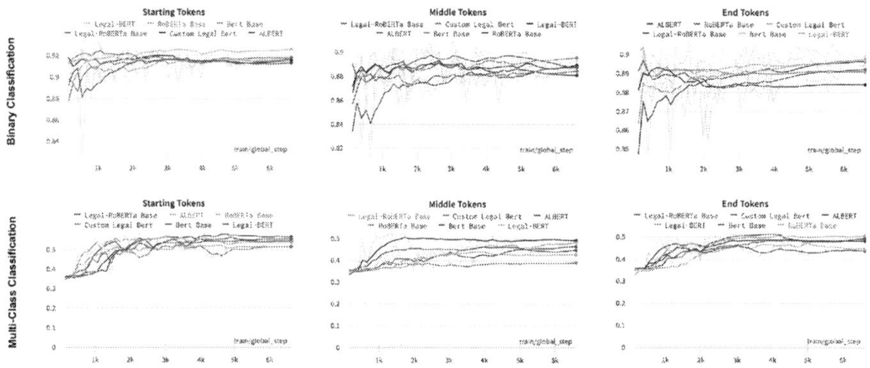

Figure 6: Macro-F1 scores of different Transformer based models on the test dataset.

Macro-F1 on Binary & Multi-Class test set respectively under full token settings. Under the Sequence & Convolutional models category, LSTM performed better than Vanilla CNN in both the Binary and Multi-Class Bill Prediction tasks.

It is observed that there is a significant improvement in the model's performance when Glove embedding is used as word vectors compared to other embeddings results. BiLSTM + Glove performed best in sequential and convolutional models. CNN + glove gave the second-best results in this category. In the General Domain of Pre-trained Models, transformer models outperform sequential & Convolutional models. Bert$_{Base}$ performed best in both Binary and Multi-Class settings while RoBERTa$_{Base}$ and ALBERT$_{Base}$ are a close second with better f1-score of all the models based in Multi-Class and Binary settings, respectively.

Our assumption was that legal domain models would not perform well on the proposed dataset as India's legal systems are completely different. However, our assumption did not hold true. In a few settings, Domain-specific models performed well compared to general domain models; This is likely because most words in the proposed dataset are legal domain-specific. The high frequency of unique, domain-specific terminologies appears in the dataset but not in the vocabulary of the Transformer Models trained on the general domain. It is observed that Bert$_{Base}$ performs best in terms of precision, while In legal domain trained models, the Legal-BERT$_{Base}$ model performs better in recall and f1 score in the Multi-Class classification task. On the other hand, in the Binary classification task, Legal-RoBERTa$_{Base}$ & Custom Legal-BERT$_{Base}$ performs better than other models.

Model	Precision	Recall	F1-score
CNN	72.8	57.8	47.1
LSTM	57.2	57.0	57.0
CNN + Glove	71.6	67.6	64.4
BiLSTM + Glove	66.4	66.0	64.9
ALBERT$_{Base}$	91.7	92.1	91.7
RoBERTa$_{Base}$	92.2	92.5	92.2
Bert$_{Base}$	92.4	92.7	92.5
Legal-BERT$_{Base}$	92.7	93.0	92.7
Custom Legal-BERT$_{Base}$	92.8	93.1	92.7
Legal-RoBERTa$_{Base}$	93.1	93.4	93.1

Table 4: Performance of all baseline models in Macro-Precision, Macro-Recall and Macro-F1 (%) on Binary test set under full tokens setting.

Model	Precision	Recall	F1-score
CNN	26.7	21.3	15.3
LSTM	19.8	19.6	18.3
CNN + Glove	25.2	22.6	18.8
BiLSTM + Glove	27.4	27.3	26.6
RoBERTa$_{Base}$	60.0	43.4	45.3
ALBERT$_{Base}$	52.7	46.3	47.6
Custom Legal-BERT$_{Base}$	54.0	54.5	53.8
Legal-RoBERTa$_{Base}$	58.1	56.8	57.1
Bert$_{Base}$	65.2	54.6	58.0
Legal-BERT$_{Base}$	64.9	59.3	61.4

Table 5: Performance of all baseline models in Macro-Precision, Macro-Recall and Macro-F1 (%) on Multi-Class test set under full tokens setting.

8.1 Which portions of the bill contain the most useful information?

Legal documents are lengthy and include specialist terminology compared to conventional corpora used to train text classification and language models. We did not employ the Longformer (Beltagy et al., 2020) and Reformer (Kitaev et al., 2020) models explicitly designed for lengthy texts due to memory and GPU constraints. We initially experimented with the pre-trained models trained on general-purpose texts. We experimented with various portions of the documents, including Starting tokens, Middle tokens and End tokens, to overcome the restriction on the number of input tokens Bert and other transformer models accept. Table 2 & Table 3 shows the Performance of all Transformer based models in Macro-Precision, Macro-Recall and Macro-F1 on Binary & Multi-Class test set respectively under different token settings.

Among all the combinations of input tokens, we observed that the performance of the prediction algorithm improves when more tokens from the first and middle document sections are being used as input. This leads us to infer that the first and middle portion of the documents contains the most helpful information. The proposed dataset shares the quality of including many domain-specific words relevant to the law. When the dataset is limited, the models depend on prior knowledge utilizing the transfer learning. Legal-BERT$_{Base}$ uncased produced the highest macro-averaged F1 score across first and last token settings under both the Multi-Class & Binary classification categories. Legal-BERT's prior learning is more applicable to the proposed benchmarks.

Moreover, Bert$_{Base}$ performed well in the middle token setting in both classification categories. At the same time, Legal-RoBERTa$_{Base}$ emerged as the second best performing model under the last token

Figure 7: WordCloud of the top words in the dataset

setting. Figure 6 shows the visualization of Macro-F1 scores of different models on the test dataset. We discovered that the best model had a significant advantage over the general domain model since it had been pre-trained in the same language and on data specific to the domain.

9 Conclusion

In this work, DeepParliament, A Legal domain Benchmark Dataset, is presented, which requires a deeper domain and language understanding in the legal field. It covers a broad range of parliament bills from 1986 to the present and tests the reasoning abilities of a model. Based on Extensive quality experiments on different models, It is shown that the dataset is a challenge to the present state-of-the-art methodologies and domain-specific models, with the best baseline obtaining just 59.79% accuracy. This dataset is anticipated to aid future studies in this field.

Limitations

DeepParliament is limited to evaluating English models at this time. In India, bill documents are also available in other local languages. Developing models & datasets for other languages would be an essential road for future research. Besides language, the current version of DeepParliament is also limited by size. However, we will continue to prioritize adding new bill documents from official sources; introduced in either house of Parliament, i.e. the Lok Sabha or the Rajya Sabha. Documents in the dataset are long and unstructured. Current Transformers models are limited by their input size and cannot process full documents at once. Extended sequence models such as Longformer (Beltagy et al., 2020) and BigBird (Zaheer et al., 2020) are not currently evaluated on the dataset. We leave the investigation of those models on the proposed dataset for other groups to experiment with and publish the results.

Despite the limitations as mentioned above, we believe that the dataset will be helpful to many researchers. as it takes the initial steps to establish a well-defined benchmark to evaluate legal domain models in this field. Models developed on this dataset may assist MPs, presidents, and other legal practitioners.

Ethics Statement

This study focuses on proposing the first dataset on Parliament Bill status prediction, adheres to the ethical guidelines outlined in the ACL code of Ethics and examines the ethical implications. DeepParliament gathers its data from two public sources. There is no privacy concern since all bill documents are collected against open-access databases. Moreover, the documents do not include personal or sensitive information, except minor information provided by authorities, such as the names of the presidents, Union Council of Ministers, and other official administrative organisations.

The details of dataset collection and statistics are provided in Sections 3 and 4. The model trained to utilise our dataset is mainly meant to support decision-making during bill analysis, not to replace the human specialists.

References

Martín Abadi, Ashish Agarwal, Paul Barham, Eugene Brevdo, Z. Chen, Craig Citro, Gregory S. Corrado, Andy Davis, Jeffrey Dean, Matthieu Devin, Sanjay Ghemawat, Ian J. Goodfellow, Andrew Harp, Geoffrey Irving, Michael Isard, Yangqing Jia, Rafal Józefowicz, Lukasz Kaiser, Manjunath Kudlur, Josh Levenberg, Dandelion Mané, Rajat Monga, Sherry Moore, Derek Gordon Murray, Christopher Olah, Mike Schuster, Jonathon Shlens, Benoit Steiner, Ilya Sutskever, Kunal Talwar, Paul A. Tucker, Vincent Vanhoucke, Vijay Vasudevan, Fernanda B. Viégas, Oriol Vinyals, Pete Warden, Martin Wattenberg, Martin Wicke, Yuan Yu, and Xiaoqiang Zheng. 2016. Tensorflow: Large-scale machine learning on heterogeneous distributed systems. *ArXiv*, abs/1603.04467.

Nikolaos Aletras, Dimitrios Tsarapatsanis, Daniel Preoţiuc-Pietro, and Vasileios Lampos. 2016. Predicting judicial decisions of the european court of human rights: a natural language processing perspective. *PeerJ Computer Science*, 2:e93.

Iz Beltagy, Matthew E Peters, and Arman Cohan. 2020. Longformer: The long-document transformer. *ArXiv*, abs/2004.05150.

Ilias Chalkidis, Ion Androutsopoulos, and Nikolaos Aletras. 2019. Neural legal judgment prediction in english. *Proceedings of the 57th Annual Meeting of the Association for Computational Linguistics*, pages 4317–4323.

Ilias Chalkidis, Ion Androutsopoulos, and Achilleas Michos. 2018. Obligation and prohibition extraction using hierarchical rnns. *Proceedings of the 56th Annual Meeting of the Association for Computational Linguistics (Volume 2: Short Papers)*, pages 254–259.

Ilias Chalkidis, Manos Fergadiotis, Prodromos Malakasiotis, Nikolaos Aletras, and Ion Androutsopoulos. 2020. Legal-bert: The muppets straight out of law school. *Findings of the Association for Computational Linguistics: EMNLP 2020*, pages 2898–2904.

Jacob Devlin, Ming-Wei Chang, Kenton Lee, and Kristina Toutanova. 2019. Bert: Pre-training of deep bidirectional transformers for language understanding. *Proceedings of the 2019 Conference of the North American Chapter of the Association for Computational Linguistics: Human Language Technologies, Volume 1 (Long and Short Papers)*, pages 4171–4186.

Xavier Glorot and Yoshua Bengio. 2010. Understanding the difficulty of training deep feedforward neural networks. *AISTATS*.

Dan Hendrycks, Collin Burns, Anya Chen, and Spencer Ball. 2021. Cuad: An expert-annotated nlp dataset for legal contract review. *ArXiv*, abs/2103.06268.

Sepp Hochreiter and Jürgen Schmidhuber. 1997. Long short-term memory. *Neural Comput.*, 9:1735–1780.

Phi Manh Kien, Ha-Thanh Nguyen, Ngo Xuan Bach, Vu Tran, Minh Le Nguyen, and Tu Minh Phuong. 2020. Answering legal questions by learning neural attentive text representation. *Proceedings of the 28th International Conference on Computational Linguistics*, pages 988–998.

Yoon Kim. 2014. Convolutional neural networks for sentence classification. *EMNLP*.

Nikita Kitaev, Lukasz Kaiser, and Anselm Levskaya. 2020. Reformer: The efficient transformer. *ArXiv*, abs/2001.04451.

Zhenzhong Lan, Mingda Chen, Sebastian Goodman, Kevin Gimpel, Piyush Sharma, and Radu Soricut. 2020. Albert: A lite bert for self-supervised learning of language representations. *ArXiv*, abs/1909.11942.

Elena Leitner, Georg Rehm, and Julian Moreno-Schneider. 2020. A dataset of german legal documents for named entity recognition. *LREC*.

Elena Leitner, Georg Rehm, and Julián Moreno Schneider. 2019. Fine-grained named entity recognition in legal documents. *SEMANTiCS*.

Quentin Lhoest, Albert Villanova del Moral, Yacine Jernite, Abhishek Thakur, Patrick von Platen, Suraj Patil, Julien Chaumond, Mariama Drame, Julien Plu, Lewis Tunstall, Joe Davison, Mario vSavsko, Gunjan Chhablani, Bhavitvya Malik, Simon Brandeis, Teven Le Scao, Victor Sanh, Canwen Xu, Nicolas Patry, Angelina McMillan-Major, Philipp Schmid, Sylvain Gugger, Clement Delangue, Th'eo Matussiere, Lysandre Debut, Stas Bekman, Pierric Cistac, Thibault Goehringer, Victor Mustar, François Lagunas, Alexander M. Rush, and Thomas Wolf. 2021. Datasets: A community library for natural language processing. *ArXiv*, abs/2109.02846.

Yinhan Liu, Myle Ott, Naman Goyal, Jingfei Du, Mandar Joshi, Danqi Chen, Omer Levy, Mike Lewis, Luke Zettlemoyer, and Veselin Stoyanov. 2019. Roberta: A robustly optimized bert pretraining approach. *ArXiv*, abs/1907.11692.

Ramesh Nallapati and Christopher D Manning. 2008. Legal docket classification: Where machine learning stumbles. *EMNLP*.

Adam Paszke, Sam Gross, Francisco Massa, Adam Lerer, James Bradbury, Gregory Chanan, Trevor Killeen, Zeming Lin, Natalia Gimelshein, Luca Antiga, Alban Desmaison, Andreas Kopf, Edward Yang, Zachary DeVito, Martin Raison, Alykhan Tejani, Sasank Chilamkurthy, Benoit Steiner, Lu Fang, Junjie Bai, and Soumith Chintala. 2019. Pytorch: An imperative style, high-performance deep learning library. In H. Wallach, H. Larochelle, A. Beygelzimer, F. d'Alché-Buc, E. Fox, and R. Garnett, editors, *Advances in Neural Information Processing Systems 32*, pages 8024–8035. Curran Associates, Inc.

Jeffrey Pennington, Richard Socher, and Christopher D Manning. 2014. Glove: Global vectors for word representation. *EMNLP*.

Thomas Wolf, Lysandre Debut, Victor Sanh, Julien Chaumond, Clement Delangue, Anthony Moi, Pierric Cistac, Tim Rault, Rémi Louf, Morgan Funtowicz, and Jamie Brew. 2019. Huggingface's transformers: State-of-the-art natural language processing. *ArXiv*, abs/1910.03771.

Chaojun Xiao, Haoxiang Zhong, Zhipeng Guo, Cunchao Tu, Zhiyuan Liu, Maosong Sun, Yansong Feng, Xianpei Han, Zhen Hu, Heng Wang, and Jianfeng Xu. 2018. Cail2018: A large-scale legal dataset for judgment prediction. *ArXiv*, abs/1807.02478.

Hai Ye, Xin Jiang, Zhunchen Luo, and Wenhan Chao. 2018. Interpretable charge predictions for criminal cases: Learning to generate court views from fact descriptions. *Proceedings of the 2018 Conference of the North American Chapter of the Association for Computational Linguistics: Human Language Technologies, Volume 1 (Long Papers)*, pages 1854–1864.

Manzil Zaheer, Guru Guruganesh, Kumar Avinava Dubey, Joshua Ainslie, Chris Alberti, Santiago Ontanon, Philip Pham, Anirudh Ravula, Qifan Wang, Li Yang, et al. 2020. Big bird: Transformers for longer sequences. *Advances in Neural Information Processing Systems*, 33.

Lucia Zheng, Neel Guha, Brandon R Anderson, Peter Henderson, and Daniel E Ho. 2021. When does pretraining help? assessing self-supervised learning for law and the casehold dataset. *Proceedings of the 18th International Conference on Artificial Intelligence and Law*.

Punctuation and case restoration in code mixed Indian languages

Subhashree Tripathy
Reverie Language Technologies,
Bengaluru
subhashree.tripathy
@reverieinc.com

Ashis Samal
Reverie Language Technologies,
Bengaluru
ashis.samal
@reverieinc.com

Abstract

Automatic Speech Recognition (ASR) systems are taking over in different industries starting from producing video subtitles to interactive digital assistants. ASR output can be used in automatic indexing, categorizing, searching along with normal human readability. Raw transcripts from ASR systems are difficult to interpret since it usually produces text without punctuation and case information (all lower, all upper, camel case etc.), thus limiting the performance of downstream NLP tasks. We proposed an approach to restore the punctuation and case for both English and Hinglish (i.e Hindi vocabulary in Latin script) languages. We have performed a classification task using encoder-based transformers which is a mini BERT consisting of 4 encoder layers for punctuation and case restoration instead of the traditional Seq2Seq model considering the latency constraint in real world use cases. It consists of a total number of 15 distinct classes for the model which includes 5 punctuations i.e Period(.), Comma(,), Single Quote('), Double Quote(") & Question Mark(?) with different combinations of casing. The model is benchmarked on an internal dataset which was based on user conversation with the voice assistant and it achieves a F1(macro) score of 91.52% on the test set.

1 Introduction

Raw transcripts from ASR systems are difficult to interpret and not very user friendly for display purposes.To make the ASR transcripts more readable and interpretable, we need to include appropriate punctuation and segmentation at word and sentence level. We have experimented and pivoted to a unique word level classification approach with certain techniques of model optimizations making it useful in real time.

Punctuation are marks used in printed and written documents to separate sentences and clauses and to help make the meaning of sentences more clear.The standard English punctuation is as follows: period, comma, apostrophe, quotation, question, exclamation, brackets, braces, parenthesis, dash, hyphen, ellipsis, colon, semicolon.

Auto punctuation and capitalization is a way to automatically add punctuation and restore casing to a sentence thereby making it suitable to read for users.

Example 1:
Raw text : lets eat shyam
Converted text : Let's eat, Shyam.

Example 2:
Raw text : shyam khaane chalein
Converted text : Shyam, khaane chalein?

Example 3:
Raw text : hello astor how are you
Converted text : Hello Astor, how are you?

Implementing auto-punctuation and capitalization on ASR output can improve its readability, have better display and help improve several downstream NLP tasks such as,

- ∗ Neural Machine Translation
- ∗ Sentimental Analysis
- ∗ Text summarization
- ∗ Named Entity Recognition

2 Motivation

In recent years, studies on ASR have shown outstanding results but there are still difficulties in standardizing the output of ASR[1] such as capitalization and punctuation restoration for speech transcriptions. The problems restrict readers to understand the ASR output semantically and also cause difficulties for natural language processing models such as NER, POS and semantic parsing. In this paper, we propose a method to restore the punctuation and case for ASR transcription.

Most of the punctuation and case restoration models work in Seq2Seq (Encoder-Decoder) neural

Proceedings of the Workshop on Unimodal and Multimodal Induction of Linguistic Structures (UM-IoS), pages 82 - 86
December 7, 2022

network architectures like T5, BART, GPT etc. Although these models are very good at generating long text sequences based on the task they are trained and fine tuned for, this comes with a challenge of high latency, which is a bottleneck for real time ASR systems. To address this challenge, we have framed the task as a classification problem.

3 Experiment details

We have approached the punctuation and case restoration task as a text classification problem where there are a total of 18 possible combinations of punctuation and casing, out of which we have considered 15 unique classes. Currently, our model supports 5 types of punctuation i.e period (represented as P), comma (C), question mark (?), single quote (SQ) and double quote (DQ) & 3 types of casing i.e lower cased (represented as OTHERS), upper cased (ALL_CAP) and sentence cased (CAP_INIT).
We have given a few examples of each category as mentioned in Table 1.

4 Model Architecture

Our base model is a pre-trained bert-mini model which has 4 bert encoder layers. We have wired two linear layers on top of it as a classification head for the word level text classification. This could process a maximum 256 tokens in one sequence of text[2].
The main purpose of using BERT-encoder is, it is faster in comparison to any Seq2Seq model and the context of words is learnt better which helps us understand the patterns of the language. A glimpse of how BERT[3] works is shown in Figure 1.

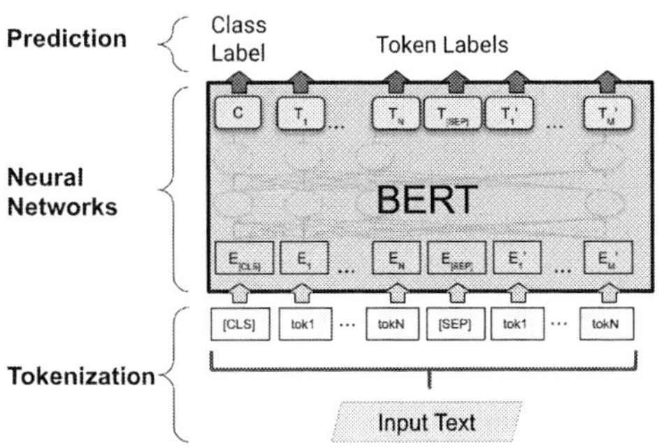

Figure 1: Bert architecture

The training of the task is done in two phases : -

1. **Pre-training :** The original sentence is usually passed to BERT and then tokenized using the word piece encoder, which generates contextual - embeddings i.e the embeddings depend on the context . Transformer reads the entire sequence of words based on its surroundings from both directions simultaneously instead on left to right/ right to left[4].

2. **Fine-tuning :** In order to fine tune the pretrained BERT, we added a few layers at the end as well where the model learns to perform downstream tasks. The proposed methodology to our problem statement is a token classification approach where it predicts the punctuation mark associated with the given word. just as shown below.

   E.g : For the sentence, "i have a pen do you", the corresponding punctuation labels for it is predicted as, "CAP_INIT, OTHERS, OTHERS, P, CAP_INIT, Q" respectively.

5 Training Details

For model training purposes, textual data from publicly available NCERT textbooks along with prepared in-house data was used. Approximately 500000 sentences were used as training data which were cleaned and formatted to get rid of noisy data and make it suitable for a machine learning model. It consists of 15 unique labels i.e 'ALL_CAP', 'ALL_CAP_C', 'ALL_CAP_P', 'ALL_CAP_Q', 'ALL_CAP_SQ', 'C', 'CAP_INIT', 'CAP_INIT_C', 'CAP_INIT_P', 'CAP_INIT_Q', 'CAP_INIT_SQ', 'OTHERS', 'P', 'Q' & 'SQ'.
Since we are using a supervised learning technique, input data (lower case with removed punctuation) and their corresponding labeled data were fed to the model. We have performed the complete experiment in one Tesla V100 GPU system, which got 16 GB of memory.
Some of the hyper-parameters used in the training are as follows:

- Epochs : 15
- Warmup_steps : 500
- Train_batch_size: 128
- Learning_rate: 0.0001

It took around 4 hours of time to complete the training process. The accuracy of the model improves significantly with consistent training. Class wise distribution of different labels is in the Figure 2

Category	Example	Category	Example
CAP_INIT	Dial, What, Hey	DQ	“he, “said”
OTHERS	possible, there, hot	Q	person?
ALL_CAP	IPL, SBI, FM	C	here,
P	done., here.	ALL_CAP_P	JIO.
SQ	teacher's/ 'teacher	ALL_CAP_SQ	CSK's/ 'CSK
ALL_CAP_DQ	“JIO / ”JIO”	CAP_INIT_SQ	Jio's/ 'Jio
ALL_CAP_Q	JIO?, ICICI?	CAP_INIT_DQ	“Jio
ALL_CAP_C	JIO,	CAP_INIT_Q	Jio?
CAP_INIT_P	Hello., Fine.	CAP_INIT_C	Jio,

Table 1: Labels with their examples

below. The y and x axis represent the labels and count of the labels respectively. The objective is

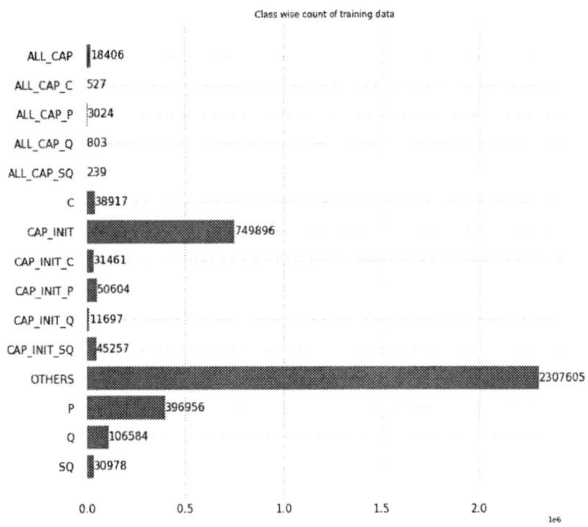

Figure 2: Class wise count of training data

to make the model output be as close as possible to the desired output or ground truth values. During model training, the model weights are adjusted iteratively to minimize the loss.

Cross entropy loss is popularly used in classification tasks both in machine learning and deep learning[5]. Cross-entropy is defined in Figure 3.

$$L_{\mathrm{CE}} = -\sum_{i=1}^{n} t_i \log(p_i), \quad \text{for n classes,}$$

where t_i is the truth label and p_i is the Softmax probability for the ith class.

Figure 3: Cross entropy loss function

6 Model optimization

Model optimization helps us in achieving below objectives.

- **Smaller storage size :** Smaller models occupy less storage space on the deployed devices
- **Less memory usage :** Smaller models use less memory when they are running during inference
- **Latency reduction :** Latency is the time it takes to run a single inference with a given model. Some forms of optimization can reduce the amount of computation required to run inference using a model, resulting in lower latency. Latency can also have an impact on power consumption. Latency reduction is a major concern for us since we are integrating this with STT (Speech-To-Text) output and the overall result should not add more than 50ms latency to speech transcriptions. We have leveraged PyTorch JIT Compiler[6], which performs run-time optimization on model's computation. TorchScript is the recommended model format for doing scaled inference with PyTorch models. We use torch.jit.trace and provide model and sample input as arguments. The input will be fed through the model as in regular inference and the executed operations will be traced and recorded into TorchScript.

7 Results

We prepared an internal testing dataset with 2050 data which was based on user conversation with the voice assistant. It consists of 15 different classes with macro-averaged F1- score[7] achieved is 91.527%.
Class wise precision score, recall score and F1-score is illustrated below in Table 2.
The class level confusion matrix from the test set

Class	Precision	Recall	F1-Score
ALL_CAP	0.996	0.963	0.979
ALL_CAP_C	1	1	1
ALL_CAP_P	0.857	0.909	0.882
ALL_CAP_Q	0.947	0.947	0.947
ALL_CAP_SQ	1	1	1
C	0.181	0.5	0.27
CAP_INIT	0.966	0.992	0.979
CAP_INIT_C	0.571	0.727	0.64
CAP_INIT_P	0.857	0.947	0.9
CAP_INIT_Q	0.883	0.892	0.887
CAP_INIT_SQ	0.987	1	0.993
OTHERS	0.996	0.983	0.990
P	0.944	0.978	0.961
Q	0.984	0.964	0.974
SQ	1	0.947	0.972

Table 2: Class level evaluation

performance is shown in Figure 4 below. The x-axis represents different classes of punctuation and the y-axis represents the predicted labels by the classifier. The blue diagonal denotes the percentage of true positives, i.e accurately detected classes which have a mean of 93.9%. The remaining yellow cells in the confusion matrix are false positives with respect to the predicted labels.

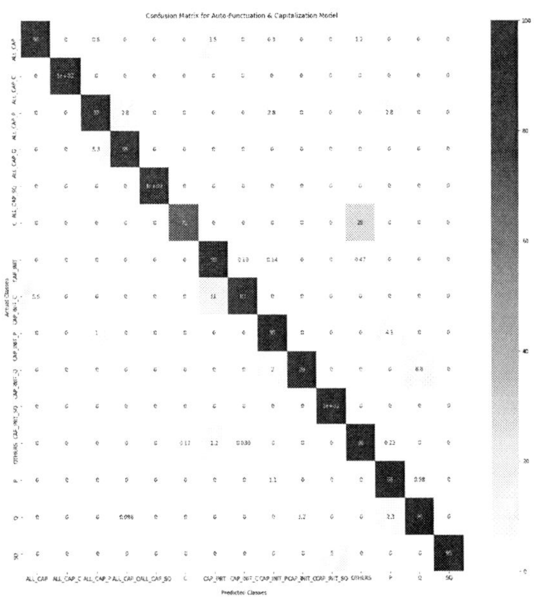

Figure 4: Class level confusion matrix of testing dataset

On a sentence level evaluation, the performance of our model on the test set is shown in Table 3. In the table, the correctly predicted sentences is referred as True and the incorrectly predicted sentences is referred as False which has an accuracy score of 82%.

Sentences	True	False
2034	1664	370

Table 3: Sentence level count

8 Observations

Since our problem statement is framed as a classification task we have only used the encoders. We were able to reduce the computational power to half and reduce the latency significantly. Considering our model is trained on both English and romanized Hindi, there are some words which are spelled the same but mean completely different in different sentences which could cause ambiguity. Here's an example below.

Sentence 1 : Do you know me?

Sentence 2 : Do apple chahiye.

Although both sentences start with "Do", sentence 1 should end with a question mark ('?') while sentence 2 should end with a period('.'). We have trained the model with sentences using maximum possible ambiguous words in different contexts to handle these challenges due to the code mix. After benchmarking our test dataset, we observed that out of all the labels used, 'C' seems to be difficult to predict and place in the right position which could be due to less training data with commas. We could revisit the data preparation phase and include more sentences with "," in different positions and evaluate the model.

9 Limitation

There are a few limitations to our model. First being, not able to evaluate our model on any public dataset due to lack of resources in Hinglish data for auto-punctuation domain. Due to lack of hardware resources, our current model is limited to 32 tokens which is approximately 25 words in Hindi.

10 Future work

We would improve our existing model through the following steps.

- For better accuracy, we would add quality and diverse data to our training and validate our model on a public domain dataset and release our Hinglish testset for more research and collaboration.

- We would optimize our model by further reducing the latency.
- We would include more punctuation types like exclamation marks, brackets (braces, parenthesis, square), dash, hyphen, ellipsis, colon, semicolon in further training.
- We would extend our language domain as well by including native and romanized versions of different Indian languages.
- In future, we plan to overcome the token count limitation so we can extend our model for longer sentences as well.

11 Conclusion

We present an approach to restore punctuation and case of the raw output obtained from the ASR system with significantly reduced latency. Currently our model is trained on English and Hinglish (i.e Hindi vocabulary in English script) data and achieves expected performance under different conditions.

Acknowledgements

Our research would not have been possible without the exceptional support from our colleagues from Speech team who helped us with suitable in-house resources to train and test on auto-punctuation and capitalization. Their valuable insights assited our research significantly and is highly appreciated.

References

[1]Attila Nagy, Bence Bial, Judit Ács, Automatic punctuation restoration with BERT-models, January 2021, URL: https://www.researchgate.net/publication/348618580_Automatic_punctuation_restoration_with_BERT_models

[2]Hugging Face : Bert-mini. https://huggingface.co/prajjwal1/bert-mini

[3]Google AI Blog : A Fast WordPiece Tokenization System https://ai.googleblog.com/2021/12/a-fast-wordpiece-tokenization-system.html

[4]Jacob Devlin, Ming-Wei Chang, Kenton Lee, Kristina Toutanova, BERT: Pre-training of Deep Bidirectional Transformers for Language Understanding, October 2018, URL: https://arxiv.org/abs/1810.04805

[5]Machinelearningmastery : A Gentle Introduction to Cross-Entropy for Machine Learning https://machinelearningmastery.com/cross-entropy-for-machine-learning/

[6]PyTorch Tutorial : TORCHSCRIPT FOR DEPLOYMENT https://pytorch.org/tutorials/recipes/torchscript_inference.html

[7]Towardsdatascience : Multi-Class Metrics Made Simple, Part II: the F1-score https://towardsdatascience.com/multi-class-metrics-made-simple-part-ii-the-

Probing Script Knowledge from Pre-Trained Models

Zijia Jin[¶], Xingyu Zhang[♮], Mo Yu[♣], Lifu Huang[♠]
[¶]New York University, [♮]Xi'an Jiaotong University, [♣]WeChat AI, [♠]Virginia Tech
[¶]zj2076@nyu.edu, [♮]xy.zhang@stu.xjtu.edu.cn,
[♣]moyumyu@tencent.com, [♠]lifuh@vt.edu

Abstract

Script knowledge is critical for humans to understand the broad daily tasks and routine activities in the world. Recently researchers have explored the large-scale pre-trained language models (PLMs) to perform various script related tasks, such as story generation, temporal ordering of event, future event prediction and so on. However, it's still not well studied in terms of how well the PLMs capture the script knowledge. To answer this question, we design three probing tasks: *inclusive sub-event selection*, *starting sub-event selection* and *temporal ordering* to investigate the capabilities of PLMs with and without fine-tuning. The three probing tasks can be further used to automatically induce a script for each main event given all the possible sub-events. Taking BERT as a case study, by analyzing its performance on script induction as well as each individual probing task, we conclude that the stereotypical temporal knowledge among the sub-events is well captured in BERT, however the inclusive or starting sub-event knowledge is barely encoded.

1 Introduction

A script is a structure that describes a stereotyped sequence of events that happen in a particular scenario (Schank and Abelson, 1975, 2013). It allows human to keep track of the states and procedures that are necessary to complete various tasks from daily lives to scientific processes. Taking the task of *Eating in a Restaurant* as an example. A classic example script for this task may consist of a chain of subevents, such as *Enter→Order→Eat→Pay (and Tip)→Leave*. The script knowledge has shown benefit to many downstream applications, such as story generation (Li et al., 2013, 2018; Guan et al., 2019; Zhai et al., 2019; Lin et al., 2022), machine reading comprehension (Tian et al., 2020; Ostermann et al., 2018; Sugawara et al., 2018), commonsense reasoning (Ding et al., 2019; Huang et al., 2019; Bauer and Bansal, 2021) and so on.

Recent large-scale pre-trained language models (PLMs) (Devlin et al., 2019; Liu et al., 2019; Radford et al., 2019; Raffel et al., 2019) have shown competitive performance on many natural language processing tasks. Abundant studies have demonstrated that these models either directly capture certain types of syntactic (Goldberg, 2019; Clark et al., 2019; Htut et al., 2019; Rosa and Mareček, 2019), factual (Petroni et al., 2019a, 2020; Bouraoui et al., 2020; Wang et al., 2020) and commonsense knowledge (Zhou et al., 2020; Rajani et al., 2019; Lin et al., 2020) during the pre-training or acquire inductive capability to more efficiently induce such knowledge from natural language text (Pandit and Hou, 2021; Bosselut et al., 2019). However, as another important type of cognitive and schematic knowledge describing human routine activities, scripts are not yet well probed in the language models by prior studies.

To investigate how well the pre-trained language models have captured the script knowledge, in this work, we design three probing tasks and language model prompting methods to probe the script knowledge from PLMs, and further leverage the language model prompting methods to induce the scripts given the main events. Specifically, we aim to answer the following two research questions:

Whether and what script knowledge is captured by the pre-trained language models. To answer this question, we design three sub-tasks to probe the script knowledge, including **inclusive sub-event selection** (i.e., whether a sub-event is included or excluded in a main event or task), **starting sub-event selection** (i.e., which sub-event is the start of the script for a particular main event), and **sub-event temporal ordering** (i.e., predicting a temporal before or after relation between two sub-events). On these sub-tasks, we explore both template-based and soft prompting methods to query the knowledge from pre-trained language models. By investigating their performance gaps to

Proceedings of the Workshop on Unimodal and Multimodal Induction of Linguistic Structures (UM-IoS), pages 87 - 93
December 7, 2022 ©2022 Association for Computational Linguistics

the fine-tuning results, we find that both the inclusive and starting sub-event selection sub-tasks have relatively poorer performance than that of temporal ordering, which is likely due to the lack of relevant objectives to encourage the models to capture such knowledge during pre-training, and further suggests future research directions to enhance the PLMs to better capture the script knowledge.

How to better generate the scripts from these pre-trained models. With the language model prompting methods, we can select the inclusive sub-events of a particular script, the starting sub-event and subsequent events by predicting the temporal order among all the inclusive sub-events, which can ultimately generate a sequence of events as the script of a main event. Thus, we further design a benchmark dataset to fine-tune the models for the three sub-tasks and evaluate their performance on generating the whole scripts for various main events from diverse domains and topics.

The contributions of this work can be summarized as follows:

- We are the first to formulate the sub-tasks and set up benchmark datasets to probe the script knowledge from pre-trained language models.
- We are the first to research on the generation and evaluation of the whole scripts from pre-trained language models.

2 Related Work

Script Knowledge The definition of Script Knowledge was first proposed in 1981 (Feigenbaum et al., 1981), which aims to detect the relation between two events. Chambers and Jurafsky (2008) created the first unsupervised data-driven method based on point-wise mutual information (PMI) to automatically extract narrative event chains. Recently, researchers explored deep neural networks, especially large-scale pre-train language models to predict the temporal relation between two events (Pustejovsky et al., 2003; Chambers, 2013; Ferraro and Durme, 2016; Reimers et al., 2016) or generate the future event (Pichotta and Mooney, 2014; Jans et al., 2012; Zhang et al., 2020). Comparing with these studies, our work focuses more on investigating how well the PLMs encode or capture the script knowledge from pre-training and their bottleneck, suggesting possible directions for future research.

Language Model Probing Probing is a popular way to detect what knowledge is encoded in PLMs. At first, probing method is designed for detect morphology knowledge(Belinkov et al., 2017) ,syntactic knowledge (Peters et al., 2018) and semantic knowledge(Tenney et al., 2019). Then researchers began to pay more attention to more complex knowledge like commonsense knowledge. The two main standard approaches in probing commonsense knowledge is building classifiers(Hewitt and Liang, 2019) or filling text in the gap(Petroni et al., 2019b). In our study, we extend the accuracy based methods and designed a series of downstream tasks specific to Scripts Knowledge.

3 Method

3.1 Script Knowledge Probing

Our first goal is to probe the script knowledge from pre-trained language models. To do so, we divide the script knowledge into three categories: the *Inclusive* and *starting* relation between each sub-event and main event, indicating whether the sub-event should be included in or the start of the script of a particular main event, and the *temporal* relation (i.e., *Before* or *After*) among the sub-events. To probe these knowledge from PLMs, we design the following tasks.

Task 1: Inclusive Sub-event Selection As Figure 1 shows, given a main event, e.g., *"Clean laundry"*, and a candidate sub-event, e.g., *"Gather dirty clothes."*, we aim to have the language model to determine whether the sub-event belongs to the script of the target main event. To do so, we use `[MASK]` to connect them into a whole sequence and use a PLM to encode the sequence into contextual representations. In order to predict the *Inclusive* relation, we apply a linear function (i.e., a MLM head) to project the `[MASK]` into a probability distribution over the whole vocabulary of the PLM. By exploring many candidate tokens from the target vocabulary to represent each relation, we finally select "include" to denote the *Inclusive* relation and "except" for *Exclusive*.

Task 2: Starting Sub-event Selection Given a main event and a set of sub-events that are predicted to belong to the script of the main event, we aim to select the most probable sub-event as the start of the script. We formulate it as a sequence classification problem. We concatenate the main event and each sub-event candidate with a prompt "*start with*", e.g., *Taking bus start with finding bus stop*, and use a MLP layer to predict a score indicating how likely

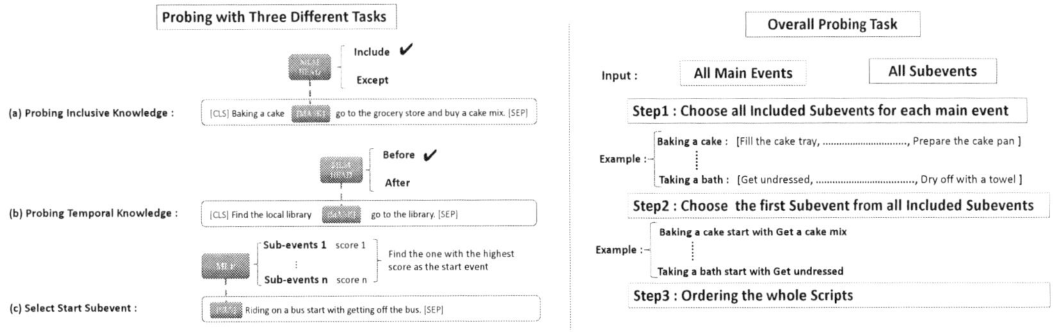

Figure 1: Overview of the probing approaches for (1) Inclusive Sub-event Selection, (2) Starting Sub-event Selection, and (3) Sub-event Temporal Ordering. And an overall evaluation stage for generating scripts with main events and subevents as input.

the sub-event is the start of the script of the main event, based on the contextual representation of the [CLS]. As a result, we use the sub-event with the highest score as the first sub-event. We design a margin based loss function to encourage the score of the positive start sub-event to be higher than others.

$$L(s^*, s_i) = \sum_{\tilde{s}_i \in \tilde{S}} max(score(\tilde{s}_i) + m - score(s^*), 0)$$

where s^* represents the positive start sub-event of a particular script and $\tilde{S}$ denotes the set of other sub-events from the same script. The margin m is a hyper-parameter, which is set as 1.0 in our experiment. During inference, given a set of candidate sub-events, we compare their scores and select the one with the highest score as the starting sub-event.

Task 3: Sub-event Temporal Ordering This probing task is to show the capability of the PLMs on correctly organizing the sub-events into a temporally ordered event sequence. To do so, we design a new language model probing approach following (Petroni et al., 2019c). As shown in Figure 1, given two subevents, e.g., *"put clothes in dryer."* and *"turn on dryer."* , we use [MASK] to connect them into a sequence and use a PLM to encode it. The temporal relation is predicted by comparing the probability of tokens "*before*" and "*after*" based on the contextual representation of [MASK].

3.2 Script Induction with PLMs

The second goal in this work is to design a simple yet effective approach to automatically induce scripts based on PLMs. Given a particular main event and a set of candidate sub-events, to induce the script for the target main event, we design a pipeline approach consisting of three steps: (1) selecting a subset of inclusive sub-events from all the candidates; (2) determining the starting sub-event; and (3) ordering all the inclusive sub-events by predicting the temporal relation between each pair of them. These three steps correspond to the three approaches designed for script knowledge probing.

4 Experiment Setup

We take BERT-base-uncased (Devlin et al., 2019) as the target PLM to investigate how well it encodes the script language via the three probing tasks. We combine three script datasets, including DeScript (Wanzare et al., 2016), OMICS (Gupta and Kochenderfer, 2004) and Stories (Trinh and Le, 2018), where each main event is annotated with 7 to 122 scripts written by different crowd-sourcing workers. We sample 60 main events as the evaluation set, 39 main events as the development set and use the remaining 98 main events for training. For the main events in training and development sets, we keep all the scripts, while for each main event in the evaluation set, we only keep the longest script as the target. Table 1 shows the statistics of each dataset.

Datasets	# Main Events	# Scripts
Training	98	4,685
Development	39	1,791
Test	60	60

Table 1: Data statistics for training, development and evaluation Sets.

To create the training samples for the *inclusive sub-event selection* task, for each script, we use all the ground truth subevents as positive samples and randomly choose 100 times of negative samples from other main events' scripts. For evaluation, as the inclusive sub-event selection requires a pool of all the possible candidate events, we combine the sub-events of all scripts in the evaluation dataset. To create the training samples for the *start sub-event selection* task, we use the first sub-event of each script as the positive sample and all the remaining sub-events from the same script as the negative samples. During the inference, we select the starting sub-event from the inclusive sub-events predicted by the inclusive sub-event selection approach. We use accuracy as the evaluation metric. Finally, for the temporal ordering task, we create each training sample based on each sub-event together with one of its following sub-events. We randomly shuffle the order of each pair of sub-events and create its corresponding label: *"before"* or *"after"*. To evaluate the quality of the temporal ordering among all the sub-events, we first generate a script based on the predicted temporal order and then use ROUGE-L to evaluate the longest common subsequence between the generated script and the gold script.

We compare the following approaches for each probing task as well as the script induction:

BERT Pre-trained: Directly use the pre-trained BERT model to make the predictions on the evaluation set.

BERT Fine-tuning: Fine-tune BERT with task-specific training data and evaluate those fine-tuned models on the evaluation set.

BERT Ptuning: Following the Ptuning framework (Liu et al., 2021), fine-tune the parameters of both BERT model and prompt tokens.

BERT Ptuning Freeze: Only fine-tune the prompt tokens while freezing the parameters of BERT model.

5 Results and Analysis

5.1 Overall Script Induction

We first show the results of end-to-end script induction given each main event and the pool of all candidate sub-events. As Table 2 shows, without any fine-tuning, BERT-Pretrained can barely induce any reasonable scripts. The high precision and low recall indicates that the bottleneck is likely in correctly selecting the inclusive sub-events for each main event. However, with fine-tuning either on the whole BERT parameters or a few prompt parameters, the script induction performance can be improved significant, demonstrating that the pre-trained BERT actually captures certain level of script knowledge but requires external probes to induce such knowledge from it. Finally, by analyzing of the performance of fine-tuning approaches, we notice a more significant improvement on recall. We conjecture that with fine-tuning, the inclusive sub-event selection is more likely to be improved.

Method	Rouge-L		
	Rec	Prec	F-score
BERT-Pretrained	3.25	22.60	4.81
BERT-Finetuning	37.19	28.07	28.73
BERT-Ptuning	48.70	28.78	32.52
BERT-Ptuning-Freeze	85.16	0.41	0.80

Table 2: Performance of script induction

5.2 Probing on Individual Tasks

We further analyze the capability of BERT on encoding each type of script knowledge based on the three probing tasks. To avoid error propagation, for both starting sub-event selection and temporal ordering, we use the gold inclusive sub-events of each main input as input.

As Table 3 shows, for inclusive sub-event selection, without fine-tuning, both BERT-Pretrained and BERT-Ptuning-Freeze cannot correctly select any inclusive sub-events. This is likely due to the discrepancy between the pre-training objectives of BERT (i.e., MASK language modeling and next sentence prediction) with the objective of inclusive sub-event selection. With fine-tuning, the performance of both BERT-Finetuning and BERT-Ptuning is improved significantly, which is aligned with our assumption in Section 5.1. Starting sub-event selection is hard to all the approaches, which is likely due to two reasons: one is the limited training samples, and the other is that though we formulate each sub-task as mask prediction to better induce the knowledge from BERT, the pattern "*Main_Event starts with Sub_Event*" is less likely to appear in the unlabeled corpus than other patterns, such as "*Main_Event includes Sub_Event*" and "*Event_A before/after Event_B*". Finally, all the approaches show consistently descent performance on temporal ordering, no matter whether BERT is fine-tuned or not, demonstrating that BERT has well captured the relations among the events with stereotypical temporal orders, possibly

Method	Inclusive Subevent Selection			Starting Subevent Selection	Temporal Ordering
	Rec	Prec	F-score	Accuracy	Rouge-L F1
BERT-Pretrained	7.44	0.64	1.17	18.33	63.79
BERT-Finetuning	33.83	44.71	38.51	21.66	62.87
BERT-Ptuning	31.16	56.24	40.10	20.00	63.62
BERT-Ptuning-Freeze	98.69	0.52	1.03	28.33	66.02

Table 3: Performance on each individual task.

due to the next sentence prediction objective during pre-training.

6 Conclusion

In this work, we investigate the capability of large-scale pre-trained language models (PLMs) on capturing three aspects of script knowledge: *inclusive sub-event knowledge*, *starting sub-event knowledge* and *temporal knowledge* among the sub-events from the same script. These three types of knowledge can be further leveraged to automatically induce a script for each main event given all the possible sub-events. We use BERT as a target PLM. By analyzing its performance on script induction as well as each individual probing task, we achieve the conclusions that the stereotypical temporal knowledge among the sub-events is well captured in BERT, however the inclusive and starting sub-event knowledge are not well encoded.

7 Limitations

In this paper, we design a three-stages method to evaluate PLMs' performance in Scripts Knowledge. Although we design those three tasks with pre-prepared candidates as inputs, a more practical condition in real life needs the PLMs to generate scripts from scratch. We plan to use generate models like GPT in the next paper to solve open-domain scripts generation tasks. Moreover, the datasets we used in this paper mostly focused on daily life which not include much scrips knowledge in other domains.

References

Lisa Bauer and Mohit Bansal. 2021. Identify, align, and integrate: Matching knowledge graphs to commonsense reasoning tasks. *arXiv preprint arXiv:2104.10193*.

Yonatan Belinkov, Nadir Durrani, Fahim Dalvi, Hassan Sajjad, and James Glass. 2017. What do neural machine translation models learn about morphology? In *Proceedings of the 55th Annual Meeting of the Association for Computational Linguistics (Volume 1: Long Papers)*, pages 861–872, Vancouver, Canada. Association for Computational Linguistics.

Antoine Bosselut, Hannah Rashkin, Maarten Sap, Chaitanya Malaviya, Asli Celikyilmaz, and Yejin Choi. 2019. Comet: Commonsense transformers for automatic knowledge graph construction. *arXiv preprint arXiv:1906.05317*.

Zied Bouraoui, Jose Camacho-Collados, and Steven Schockaert. 2020. Inducing relational knowledge from bert. In *Proceedings of the AAAI Conference on Artificial Intelligence*, volume 34, pages 7456–7463.

Nathanael Chambers. 2013. Event schema induction with a probabilistic entity-driven model. In *Proceedings of the 2013 Conference on Empirical Methods in Natural Language Processing, EMNLP 2013, 18-21 October 2013, Grand Hyatt Seattle, Seattle, Washington, USA, A meeting of SIGDAT, a Special Interest Group of the ACL*, pages 1797–1807. ACL.

Nathanael Chambers and Daniel Jurafsky. 2008. Unsupervised learning of narrative event chains. In *ACL 2008, Proceedings of the 46th Annual Meeting of the Association for Computational Linguistics, June 15-20, 2008, Columbus, Ohio, USA*, pages 789–797. The Association for Computer Linguistics.

Kevin Clark, Urvashi Khandelwal, Omer Levy, and Christopher D Manning. 2019. What does bert look at? an analysis of bert's attention. *arXiv preprint arXiv:1906.04341*.

Jacob Devlin, Ming-Wei Chang, Kenton Lee, and Kristina Toutanova. 2019. Bert: Pre-training of deep bidirectional transformers for language understanding. In *Proceedings of the 2019 Conference of the North American Chapter of the Association for Computational Linguistics: Human Language Technologies, Volume 1 (Long and Short Papers)*, pages 4171–4186.

Xiao Ding, Kuo Liao, Ting Liu, Zhongyang Li, and Junwen Duan. 2019. Event representation learning enhanced with external commonsense knowledge. *arXiv preprint arXiv:1909.05190*.

Edward A Feigenbaum, Avron Barr, and Paul R Cohen. 1981. The handbook of artificial intelligence.

Francis Ferraro and Benjamin Van Durme. 2016. A unified bayesian model of scripts, frames and language. In *Proceedings of the Thirtieth AAAI Conference on Artificial Intelligence, February 12-17, 2016,*

Phoenix, Arizona, USA, pages 2601–2607. AAAI Press.

Yoav Goldberg. 2019. Assessing bert's syntactic abilities. *arXiv preprint arXiv:1901.05287*.

Jian Guan, Yansen Wang, and Minlie Huang. 2019. Story ending generation with incremental encoding and commonsense knowledge. In *Proceedings of the AAAI Conference on Artificial Intelligence*, volume 33, pages 6473–6480.

Rakesh Gupta and Mykel J. Kochenderfer. 2004. Common sense data acquisition for indoor mobile robots. In *Proceedings of the Nineteenth National Conference on Artificial Intelligence, Sixteenth Conference on Innovative Applications of Artificial Intelligence, July 25-29, 2004, San Jose, California, USA*, pages 605–610. AAAI Press / The MIT Press.

John Hewitt and Percy Liang. 2019. Designing and interpreting probes with control tasks. In *Proceedings of the 2019 Conference on Empirical Methods in Natural Language Processing and the 9th International Joint Conference on Natural Language Processing, EMNLP-IJCNLP 2019, Hong Kong, China, November 3-7, 2019*, pages 2733–2743. Association for Computational Linguistics.

Phu Mon Htut, Jason Phang, Shikha Bordia, and Samuel R Bowman. 2019. Do attention heads in bert track syntactic dependencies? *arXiv preprint arXiv:1911.12246*.

Lifu Huang, Ronan Le Bras, Chandra Bhagavatula, and Yejin Choi. 2019. Cosmos qa: Machine reading comprehension with contextual commonsense reasoning. *arXiv preprint arXiv:1909.00277*.

Bram Jans, Steven Bethard, Ivan Vulic, and Marie-Francine Moens. 2012. Skip n-grams and ranking functions for predicting script events. In *EACL 2012, 13th Conference of the European Chapter of the Association for Computational Linguistics, Avignon, France, April 23-27, 2012*, pages 336–344. The Association for Computer Linguistics.

Boyang Li, Stephen Lee-Urban, George Johnston, and Mark Riedl. 2013. Story generation with crowdsourced plot graphs. In *Proceedings of the AAAI Conference on Artificial Intelligence*, volume 27.

Zhongyang Li, Xiao Ding, and Ting Liu. 2018. Constructing narrative event evolutionary graph for script event prediction. *arXiv preprint arXiv:1805.05081*.

Bill Yuchen Lin, Seyeon Lee, Rahul Khanna, and Xiang Ren. 2020. Birds have four legs?! numersense: Probing numerical commonsense knowledge of pre-trained language models. *arXiv preprint arXiv:2005.00683*.

Li Lin, Yixin Cao, Lifu Huang, Shuang Li, Xuming Hu, Lijie Wen, and Jianmin Wang. 2022. Inferring commonsense explanations as prompts for future event generation. *arXiv preprint arXiv:2201.07099*.

Xiao Liu, Yanan Zheng, Zhengxiao Du, Ming Ding, Yujie Qian, Zhilin Yang, and Jie Tang. 2021. Gpt understands, too. *arXiv preprint arXiv:2103.10385*.

Yinhan Liu, Myle Ott, Naman Goyal, Jingfei Du, Mandar Joshi, Danqi Chen, Omer Levy, Mike Lewis, Luke Zettlemoyer, and Veselin Stoyanov. 2019. Roberta: A robustly optimized bert pretraining approach. *arXiv preprint arXiv:1907.11692*.

Simon Ostermann, Ashutosh Modi, Michael Roth, Stefan Thater, and Manfred Pinkal. 2018. Mcscript: A novel dataset for assessing machine comprehension using script knowledge. *arXiv preprint arXiv:1803.05223*.

Onkar Pandit and Yufang Hou. 2021. Probing for bridging inference in transformer language models. *arXiv preprint arXiv:2104.09400*.

Matthew E. Peters, Mark Neumann, Mohit Iyyer, Matt Gardner, Christopher Clark, Kenton Lee, and Luke Zettlemoyer. 2018. Deep contextualized word representations. In *Proceedings of the 2018 Conference of the North American Chapter of the Association for Computational Linguistics: Human Language Technologies, Volume 1 (Long Papers)*, pages 2227–2237, New Orleans, Louisiana. Association for Computational Linguistics.

Fabio Petroni, Patrick Lewis, Aleksandra Piktus, Tim Rocktäschel, Yuxiang Wu, Alexander H Miller, and Sebastian Riedel. 2020. How context affects language models' factual predictions. *arXiv preprint arXiv:2005.04611*.

Fabio Petroni, Tim Rocktäschel, Patrick Lewis, Anton Bakhtin, Yuxiang Wu, Alexander H Miller, and Sebastian Riedel. 2019a. Language models as knowledge bases? *arXiv preprint arXiv:1909.01066*.

Fabio Petroni, Tim Rocktäschel, Sebastian Riedel, Patrick Lewis, Anton Bakhtin, Yuxiang Wu, and Alexander Miller. 2019b. Language models as knowledge bases? In *Proceedings of the 2019 Conference on Empirical Methods in Natural Language Processing and the 9th International Joint Conference on Natural Language Processing (EMNLP-IJCNLP)*, pages 2463–2473, Hong Kong, China. Association for Computational Linguistics.

Fabio Petroni, Tim Rocktäschel, Sebastian Riedel, Patrick S. H. Lewis, Anton Bakhtin, Yuxiang Wu, and Alexander H. Miller. 2019c. Language models as knowledge bases? In *Proceedings of the 2019 Conference on Empirical Methods in Natural Language Processing and the 9th International Joint Conference on Natural Language Processing, EMNLP-IJCNLP 2019, Hong Kong, China, November 3-7, 2019*, pages 2463–2473. Association for Computational Linguistics.

Karl Pichotta and Raymond J. Mooney. 2014. Statistical script learning with multi-argument events. In *Proceedings of the 14th Conference of the European*

Chapter of the Association for Computational Linguistics, EACL 2014, April 26-30, 2014, Gothenburg, Sweden, pages 220–229. The Association for Computer Linguistics.

James Pustejovsky, Patrick Hanks, Roser Sauri, Andrew See, Robert Gaizauskas, Andrea Setzer, Dragomir Radev, Beth Sundheim, David Day, Lisa Ferro, et al. 2003. The timebank corpus. In *Corpus linguistics*, volume 2003, page 40. Lancaster, UK.

Alec Radford, Jeffrey Wu, Rewon Child, David Luan, Dario Amodei, Ilya Sutskever, et al. 2019. Language models are unsupervised multitask learners. *OpenAI blog*, 1(8):9.

Colin Raffel, Noam Shazeer, Adam Roberts, Katherine Lee, Sharan Narang, Michael Matena, Yanqi Zhou, Wei Li, and Peter J Liu. 2019. Exploring the limits of transfer learning with a unified text-to-text transformer. *arXiv preprint arXiv:1910.10683*.

Nazneen Fatema Rajani, Bryan McCann, Caiming Xiong, and Richard Socher. 2019. Explain yourself! leveraging language models for commonsense reasoning. *arXiv preprint arXiv:1906.02361*.

Nils Reimers, Nazanin Dehghani, and Iryna Gurevych. 2016. Temporal anchoring of events for the timebank corpus. In *Proceedings of the 54th Annual Meeting of the Association for Computational Linguistics, ACL 2016, August 7-12, 2016, Berlin, Germany, Volume 1: Long Papers*. The Association for Computer Linguistics.

Rudolf Rosa and David Mareček. 2019. Inducing syntactic trees from bert representations. *arXiv preprint arXiv:1906.11511*.

Roger C Schank and Robert P Abelson. 1975. Scripts, plans, and knowledge. In *IJCAI*, volume 75, pages 151–157.

Roger C Schank and Robert P Abelson. 2013. *Scripts, plans, goals, and understanding: An inquiry into human knowledge structures*. Psychology Press.

Saku Sugawara, Kentaro Inui, Satoshi Sekine, and Akiko Aizawa. 2018. What makes reading comprehension questions easier? *arXiv preprint arXiv:1808.09384*.

Ian Tenney, Patrick Xia, Berlin Chen, Alex Wang, Adam Poliak, R. Thomas McCoy, Najoung Kim, Benjamin Van Durme, Samuel R. Bowman, Dipanjan Das, and Ellie Pavlick. 2019. What do you learn from context? probing for sentence structure in contextualized word representations. In *7th International Conference on Learning Representations, ICLR 2019, New Orleans, LA, USA, May 6-9, 2019*. OpenReview.net.

Zhixing Tian, Yuanzhe Zhang, Kang Liu, Jun Zhao, Yantao Jia, and Zhicheng Sheng. 2020. Scene restoring for narrative machine reading comprehension. In *Proceedings of the 2020 Conference on Empirical Methods in Natural Language Processing (EMNLP)*, pages 3063–3073.

Trieu H. Trinh and Quoc V. Le. 2018. A simple method for commonsense reasoning. *CoRR*, abs/1806.02847.

Chenguang Wang, Xiao Liu, and Dawn Song. 2020. Language models are open knowledge graphs. *arXiv preprint arXiv:2010.11967*.

Lilian D. A. Wanzare, Alessandra Zarcone, Stefan Thater, and Manfred Pinkal. 2016. A crowdsourced database of event sequence descriptions for the acquisition of high-quality script knowledge. In *Proceedings of the Tenth International Conference on Language Resources and Evaluation LREC 2016, Portorož, Slovenia, May 23-28, 2016*. European Language Resources Association (ELRA).

Fangzhou Zhai, Vera Demberg, Pavel Shkadzko, Wei Shi, and Asad Sayeed. 2019. A hybrid model for globally coherent story generation. In *Proceedings of the Second Workshop on Storytelling*, pages 34–45.

Li Zhang, Qing Lyu, and Chris Callison-Burch. 2020. Reasoning about goals, steps, and temporal ordering with wikihow. In *Proceedings of the 2020 Conference on Empirical Methods in Natural Language Processing, EMNLP 2020, Online, November 16-20, 2020*, pages 4630–4639. Association for Computational Linguistics.

Xuhui Zhou, Yue Zhang, Leyang Cui, and Dandan Huang. 2020. Evaluating commonsense in pre-trained language models. In *Proceedings of the AAAI Conference on Artificial Intelligence*, volume 34, pages 9733–9740.

A Appendix

A.1 Examples of Errors

In this section, we'd like to use a couple of examples of errors to show that what kind of information are usually being missed by PLMs. We choose 2 scripts as inputs and test BERT's(Without Finetuning) ability to choose the right candidates and order them.

Author Index

Association for Computational Linguistics
209 N. Eighth Street
Stroudsburg, Pennsylvania 18360

CURRAN ASSOCIATES INC.
proceedings.com

ISBN 978-1-7138-9151-2
9 781713 891512

4th Workshop on Technologies for MT of Low Resource Languages (LoResMT 2021)

Held at MT Summit 2021

Online
16 – 20 August 2021